*St Antony's Series*

General Editor: **Richard Clogg** (1999–), Fellow of St Antony's College, Oxford

*Recent titles include*:

Tiffany A. Troxel
PARLIAMENTARY POWER IN RUSSIA, 1994–2001
President vs Parliament

Elvira María Restrepo
THE COLOMBIAN JUDICIARY IN CRISIS
Fear and Distrust

Julie M. Newton
RUSSIA, FRANCE AND THE IDEA OF EUROPE

Ilaria Favretto
THE LONG SEARCH FOR A THIRD WAY
The British Labour Party and the Italian Left Since 1945

Lawrence Tal
POLITICS, THE MILITARY, AND NATIONAL SECURITY IN JORDAN,
1955–1967

Louise Haagh and Camilla Helgø (*editors*)
SOCIAL POLICY REFORM AND MARKET GOVERNANCE IN LATIN AMERICA

Gayil Talshir
THE POLITICAL IDEOLOGY OF GREEN PARTIES
From the Politics of Nature to Redefining the Nature of Politics

E. K. Dosmukhamedov
FOREIGN DIRECT INVESTMENT IN KAZAKHSTAN
Politico-Legal Aspects of Post-Communist Transition

Felix Patrikeeff
RUSSIAN POLITICS IN EXILE
The Northeast Asian Balance of Power, 1924–1931

He Ping
CHINA'S SEARCH FOR MODERNITY
Cultural Discourse in the Late 20th Century

Mariana Llanos
PRIVATIZATION AND DEMOCRACY IN ARGENTINA
An Analysis of President–Congress Relations

Michael Addison
VIOLENT POLITICS
Strategies of Internal Conflict

Geoffrey Wiseman
CONCEPTS OF NON-PROVOCATIVE DEFENCE
Ideas and Practices in International Security

Pilar Ortuño Anaya
EUROPEAN SOCIALISTS AND SPAIN
The Transition to Democracy, 1959–77

Renato Baumann (*editor*)
BRAZIL IN THE 1990s
An Economy in Transition

Israel Getzler
NIKOLAI SUKHANOV
Chronicler of the Russian Revolution

Arturo J. Cruz, Jr
NICARAGUA'S CONSERVATIVE REPUBLIC, 1858–93

Pamela Lubell
THE CHINESE COMMUNIST PARTY AND THE CULTURAL REVOLUTION
The Case of the Sixty-One Renegades

Mikael af Malmborg
NEUTRALITY AND STATE-BUILDING IN SWEDEN

Klaus Gallo
GREAT BRITAIN AND ARGENTINA
From Invasion to Recognition, 1806–26

David Faure and Tao Tao Liu
TOWN AND COUNTRY IN CHINA
Identity and Perception

Peter Mangold
SUCCESS AND FAILURE IN BRITISH FOREIGN POLICY
Evaluating the Record, 1900–2000

Mohamad Tavakoli-Targhi
REFASHIONING IRAN
Orientalism, Occidentalism and Historiography

Louise Haagh
CITIZENSHIP, LABOUR MARKETS AND DEMOCRATIZATION
Chile and the Modern Sequence

**St Antony's Series**
**Series Standing Order ISBN 0–333–71109–2**
(*outside North America only*)

You can receive future titles in this series as they are published by placing a standing order. Please contact your bookseller or, in case of difficulty, write to us at the address below with your name and address, the title of the series and the ISBN quoted above.

Customer Services Department, Macmillan Distribution Ltd, Houndmills, Basingstoke, Hampshire RG21 6XS, England

# Parliamentary Power in Russia, 1994–2001

## President vs Parliament

Tiffany A. Troxel

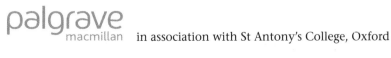

palgrave
macmillan    in association with St Antony's College, Oxford

First published 2003 by
PALGRAVE MACMILLAN
Houndmills, Basingstoke, Hampshire RG21 6XS and
175 Fifth Avenue, New York, N.Y. 10010
Companies and representatives throughout the world

PALGRAVE MACMILLAN is the global academic imprint of the Palgrave
Macmillan division of St. Martin's Press, LLC and of Palgrave Macmillan Ltd.
Macmillan® is a registered trademark in the United States, United Kingdom
and other countries. Palgrave is a registered trademark in the European
Union and other countries.

ISBN 0–333–99283–0

This book is printed on paper suitable for recycling and made from fully
managed and sustained forest sources.

A catalogue record for this book is available from the British Library.

Library of Congress Cataloging-in-Publication Data
Troxel, Tiffany A., 1975–
    Parliamentary power in Russia, 1994–2001: president vs parliament/
Tiffany A. Troxel.
      p. cm. – (St. Antony's series)
    Includes bibliographical references and index.
      ISBN 0–333–99283–0 (cloth)
      1. Russia (Federation). Federal§'oe Sobranie. Gosudarstvennaëi
Duma. 2. Legislative bodies – Russia (Federation). 3. Representative
government and representation – Russia (Federation). 4. Russia
(Federation) – Politics and government – 1991– I. Title. II. St Antony's
series (Palgrave Macmillan (Firm))

JN6697.8 .T76 2002
328.47—dc21                               2002028746

10   9   8   7   6   5   4   3   2   1
12  11  10  09  08  07  06  05  04  03

Printed and bound in Great Britain by
Antony Rowe Ltd, Chippenham and Eastbourne

*To my parents,*
*Richard Earl and Kathy Ann Troxel*

# Contents

# List of Tables

# List of Figures

# Preface

*Parliamentary Power in Russia 1994–2001: President vs Parliament* is the first in-depth study of the power of the Russian Parliament in the policy process from 1994 to 2001 within the context of executive–legislative relations. It challenges the widely held view that between 1994 and 2001 *Russia had a presidential system with a strong, authoritarian leader who ruled by decree and a weak Parliament which did not have much power.* The main questions addressed are the following: What powers were granted to Russia's Parliament and President in the 1993 Constitution? How much power did Russia's Parliament actually exercise relative to the President and Government? Why and to what extent did these powers increase or decrease after 1994? What type of political system existed in Russia from 1994 to 2001, and what effect did this have on democratic transition, consolidation, and stability in Russia? Empirical data, interviews, transcripts of parliamentary debates and negotiations, roll-call analysis, case studies on the use of constitutional powers, and secondary sources are employed to answer these questions.

Given that the main part of this book is based on my PhD dissertation completed in 1999 at St Antony's College, Oxford University, a postscript has been added to discuss the events from 1999 to 2001, although these events are treated less fully than the preceding period.

I am grateful to a number of people who contributed to this work and supported me while researching and writing this book. Most importantly, I would like to thank my PhD supervisor, Professor Archie Brown. I am grateful for his continued enthusiasm over the three years of my doctoral studies and the subsequent months of transforming the dissertation into a book and updating it. He encouraged me to pursue a subject in which I could combine my interests in law, legislatures, and politics with the study of Russia. I am also grateful for his comments and suggestions on all drafts of my work.

I also wish to thank Dr Stephen Whitefield, Professor Alfred Stepan, Dr Alex Pravda, and Professor Stephen White for their comments and critiques of draft chapters.

I would also like to acknowledge Professor Ronald Suny for inspiring my initial interest in Russian history and politics, and Professor William Zimmerman and Professor Ronald Inglehart for encouraging me to pursue a PhD in Russian politics.

I appreciate the generous amount of time offered by State Duma Deputies, Members of the Council of the Federation, people in the executive branch, and academics at research institutes for the interviews and materials.

While in Moscow, I received gracious assistance from the librarians of the State Duma's Library. I have benefited greatly from documents provided by Anatoliy Eliseev and his colleagues in the Records Department of the State Duma. Valeriy Fadeev, State Duma Consultant, was invaluable in helping to arrange interviews and access to Duma Deputies.

I also wish to thank the librarians of the Bodleian Library, Social Studies Faculty Library, Nuffield College Library, St Antony's College Library, and St Antony's College Russian and East European Centre Library in Oxford. Also the librarians at the Institute of State and Law of the Russian Academy of Sciences in Moscow and SSEES at the University of London generously provided access to resources.

My research trips to Russia were generously funded by the Oxford University Committee for Graduate Studies grants, St Antony's College Russian and East European Centre's Elliott Fund, St Antony's College Carr and Stahl Funds, Cyril Foster Funds, and the BASEES Fund.

I appreciate the generous hospitality of Colonel Roy Giles, William Fleming, Dr Alexander Lukin, Eugene Mazo, and others who contributed to my visits to Moscow by helping to arrange interviews and showing me what life in Moscow is like.

I am grateful to Dr Jonathan Lewis, who encouraged me both to work hard and to enjoy life during my doctoral studies.

From August 1999 to June 2001 I was affiliated with the John F. Kennedy School of Government at Harvard University. During this time I updated this book to include 1999–2001. I am grateful to Professor David King who supervised the writing of the postscript and provided feedback. Benjamin Bolger motivated me to explore the implications for politics of this work. The librarians at Harvard University's libraries, especially at the JFK School of Government, provided access to relevant sources. I appreciate the encouragement Nishith Shah offered while revising my manuscript.

Finally, I am extremely thankful to my parents, Richard and Kathy Troxel, who generously funded my studies. Without my family's continued support and encouragement this book would not have been possible. The dedication of this book to them is only a small gesture for all they have done.

TIFFANY A. TROXEL

# 1

# Introduction: Theoretical Models of Neo-Institutionalism and the Problem of the Russian Case

> It may be too great a temptation to human frailty apt to grasp at Power, for the same Persons who have the Power of making Laws, to have also in their hands the power to execute them, whereby they may exempt themselves from Obedience to the Laws they make, and suit the Law, both in its making and execution, to their own private advantage, and thereby come to have a distinct interest from the rest of the community, contrary to the end of Society and Government.
>
> John Locke, *Two Treatises of Government*

On 21 September 1993 President Boris Yel'tsin[1] *unconstitutionally*[2] dissolved the Russian Congress of People's Deputies (CPD) and the Supreme Soviet (the legislative branch) by issuing Decree 1400[3] and called for a new legislature, the Federal Assembly, to assume power. Some Deputies from the CPD and Supreme Soviet, fearing that this meant political destruction, were reluctant to relinquish their positions and remained in the White House from 21 September to 4 October 1993. In an attempt to fight back, the Deputies appointed Vice-President Aleksandr Rutskoy acting President of Russia, in place of Yel'tsin. Parliament refused to be subordinate to Yel'tsin and Yel'tsin fought for greater control over Parliament. Largely due to the – at first reluctant – support of the military, Yel'tsin was able to force the Deputies out of the White House. On 12 December 1993, the Russian electorate voted on a new Russian Constitution and new parliamentary elections were held that day.[4] The stand-off between Yel'tsin and Parliament was a struggle to determine whether the President, Parliament, or both would have ultimate decision-making power in Russia. Though structurally it culminated with the 1993 Russian Constitution, which redistributed legislative and executive powers, I shall argue that the struggle for power between the Russian Parliament and President still continues.[5]

Since the 1993 Russian Constitution grants more powers to the President than to Parliament, many academics believe that *Russia has a presidential system with a strong, authoritarian leader who rules by decree and a weak Parliament which does not have much power.*[6] There has yet to be an in-depth study of Parliament's power and regime type in Russia from 1994 to 2001 to prove (or disprove) this, mainly because the time period is so recent and most of the research on executive–legislative relations focuses on the executive, not the legislature.[7] The type of political system in a democratic country is also important because several scholars have proved that a correlation exists between regime type and democratic stability.[8] In this chapter, I will apply the existing models for evaluating regime type to Russia and argue that a revised model is needed. Without an accurate method for determining regime type in a given country, conclusions about democratic success/failure, based on regime type, can be flawed. I maintain that the definitions of political systems in the existing literature tend to be based on the constitutional powers of presidents and parliaments. I argue that one cannot accurately define political systems solely on the basis of constitutional and structural powers[9] because, as the case of Russia particularly illustrates, regime type should also be defined by the extent to which a president or parliament actually use their constitutional powers. A president can have considerable constitutional powers, such as the power to issue decrees at will, dissolve the parliament and government, and veto legislation without being overridden by parliament, but if he/she rarely exercised these powers, the entire nature of the political system and relations between branches would change. Constitutional, structural, and actual powers of the Russian President and Parliament will be examined in this study to understand their roles in the policy process, the type of political system in Russia, and how and why the Russian Parliament is becoming more powerful.

Moreover, because the State Duma (lower chamber of the Russian Parliament) elected on 12 December 1993 was the *only* parliament in the history of Russia to survive past its first term, hold regular sessions, and come to power in open elections with competing political parties,[10] its survival is of particular importance to democracy in Russia and warrants extensive study. Democracy in Russia, though, is still in a relatively fragile state and it is unclear whether it will withstand the political changes in the coming years. Since laws enacted by parliament are much more conducive to democracy than a leader ruling by decree, the powers of parliament *vis-à-vis* the executive branch constitute an essential issue for determining the likelihood of democratic stability in Russia, the success of which remains an open but highly important question.

## Research questions and hypotheses

This book is a study of executive–legislative relations in Russia from 1994 to 2001, with an emphasis on the Parliament. The main questions addressed are the following: What powers were granted to Russia's Parliament and President in the 1993 Constitution? How much power does Russia's Parliament *actually* exercise relative to the President? Why and to what extent have these powers increased or decreased since 1994? What type of political regime exists in Russia and what effect does this have on democratic transition, consolidation, and stability in Russia? Other questions to be examined include: How does the internal power structure (or structural powers) of the Russian presidency and Parliament affect their overall powers? How do struggles between the President and Parliament affect the balance of power? This book seeks to determine whether the above statement (that Russia's Parliament is 'weak' and the President is 'strong,' in terms of power) is correct. It does so by using empirical data, interviews, parliamentary debates and negotiations, roll-call analysis, case studies of specific constitutional powers, and several secondary sources.

This study hopes to contribute to the current literature on neo-institutionalism and the comparative literature on executive–legislative relations by (1) establishing a method for evaluating regime type which surmounts the problems with existing models; (2) examining the powers of the Russian President and Parliament from 1994 to 2001 in detail; and, (3) determining Russia's regime type, level of democratic transition/ consolidation and likelihood for democratic success.

I argue that, based on the actual and written powers of the Russian President and Parliament, Russia has a semi-presidential (president-parliamentary) system. I also hypothesize that the powers of the legislature are *gradually* increasing and thus, democratic transition is occurring, at least in the political sphere. The nature of relations between the executive and legislative, I argue, is shifting from confrontational to cooperative. The sources and nature of this crucial trend in executive–legislative relations from 1994 to 1999 seem to be evident as a result of: (a) the political composition of the State Duma; (b) the nomination and approval of Prime Minister Yevgeniy Primakov in September 1998; (c) the internal structure of the Council of the Federation and State Duma with reference to committee strength, electoral cycles, length of sessions, round-table discussions between the President and party leaders, and the President's and Prime Minister's attendance at parliamentary sessions; (d) changes in the actual powers of the President and Parliament, such as the former's use of decree and veto power; and (e) the state of President Yel'tsin's health. This book attempts an in-depth analysis of these factors.

Parliament's ability to form oppositionist coalitions which can defeat the President's vetoes and challenge the President on the ratification of treaties and the approval of Prime Ministers means that Parliament has greater bargaining power in the policy process and the President cannot as easily dictate his will on the legislature. Moreover, when Primakov became Prime Minister, he worked continually to improve relations between the executive and legislature by holding regular meetings with top party elite, attending parliamentary sessions, and negotiating on more bills. In addition, the internal structures of the two chambers of Parliament need consideration for several reasons. Election cycles are important because a legislature whose members are elected in regular, scheduled elections that are fair and competitive strengthens the legitimacy and power of parliament.[11] The Duma that was elected in the December 1993 elections lasted for only two years because the 1993 Constitution stated that it would only have a short 'trial' period. If the Duma can endure for successive elections and pass important laws that are enforced, it will gain greater legitimacy and increase in power. Moreover, the change in the structure of the Council of the Federation in 1995 from Members being appointed by Yel'tsin to membership comprised of elected Governors and legislative heads from Russia's 89 regions means that it is no longer just an extension of the executive branch or a rubber-stamp body.

The internal structure of the Duma has also changed in two main ways: it is becoming more effective and compact (because it now has a working majority and has seven factions with at least 35 members instead of 11 factions as in the previous Duma) and it is trying to pass more laws to constrain the executive (by attempting to regulate the Government, Presidential Administration and the Security Council, and bargaining for the power to approve the nomination and dismissal of Deputy Prime Ministers and other Government officials).[12] In addition, Yel'tsin cooperated with the legislature more and more, partly because of his poor health. For example, from Spring 1997 to Spring 1998, Yel'tsin held regular meetings with party leaders and heads of the Duma's and Council of the Federation's committees. This shows, depending on the timing of the meeting, that he was making an effort to work with the Duma instead of working against it and that he had less power than in 1994 when he issued decrees at will, without consulting Parliament. He established a committee comprised of the speakers of the Duma and Council of the Federation, the Prime Minister, and himself which met regularly to discuss issues. Yel'tsin's acceptance of the Duma's suggestion of Primakov for Prime Minister in September 1998, after the Duma rejected his candidate twice, meant that he found it necessary to work with the Duma to avoid further political crises. Also, the President exercised his decree and veto power less frequently in 1998, though this will be explored further in Chapters 4 and 5.

## Theoretical importance

Neo-institutionalism will be used for the initial theoretical discussions of this study.[13] I follow March and Olsen in their characterization of the main theories of politics since the 1950s as

(a) *contextual*, inclined to see politics as an integral part of society, less inclined to differentiate the polity from the rest of society; (b) *reductionist*, inclined to see political phenomena as the aggregate consequences of individual behavior, less inclined to ascribe the outcomes of politics to organizational structures and rules of appropriate behavior; (c) *utilitarian*, inclined to see action as the product of calculated self-interest, less inclined to see political actors as responding to obligations and duties; (d) *functionalist*, inclined to see history as an efficient mechanism for reaching uniquely appropriate equilibria, less concerned with the possibilities for maladaptation and non-uniqueness in historical development; and (e) *instrumentalist*, inclined to define decision making and the allocation of resources as the central concerns of political life, less attentive to the ways in which political life is organized around the development of meaning through symbols, rituals, and ceremonies.[14]

These theories define decision-making as influenced by society, individual behavior, calculated self-interest, or history, respectively. To these five theories, March and Olsen add 'new' institutionalism, which suggests that institutions are not only affected by the aforementioned influences but also affect them.[15] While I agree with the instrumentalist approach that decision-making is a central concern of political life, neo-institutionalism was chosen for this study because institutions are political actors which affect decision-making.

## Neo-institutionalism

The theory of 'new' institutionalism has attracted a growing number of political scientists in the past two decades. It stresses the importance of using *political* variables to explain political outcomes.[16] Because this study considers the comparative weight of two institutions, the presidency and the parliament, in order to determine their powers and roles in the decision-making process, the 'neo'-institutionalist approach is adopted. James March and Johan Olsen reconstituted the current debate on institutionalism, hence 'neo'-institutionalism, and defined it as the following:

> new institutionalism insists on a more autonomous role for political institutions. The state is not only affected by society but also affects it. Political democracy depends not only on economic and social conditions but also on the design of political institutions. The bureaucratic agency, the legislative committee, and the appellate court are arenas for contending social forces, but they are also collections of standard operating procedures and structures that define and defend interests. They are political actors in their own right ... Political outcomes [are] a function of three primary factors: the distribution of preferences (interests) among political actors, the distribution of resources (powers), and the constraints imposed by the rules of the game (constitutions).[17]

Though much of this is not new to 'old institutionalists,'[18] new institutionalism is not identical to old institutionalism. It is best described as 'blending elements of an old institutionalism into the non-institutionalist styles of recent theories of politics.'[19]

'Neo-institutionalism' was also chosen because in the literature on institutions and democracy, the concepts of power, neo-institutionalism, and democratic transition and consolidation are treated as interrelated issues and will be considered as such for this study. Within the neo-institutionalist framework,[20] the powers of a president and parliament are used as a basis for determining regime types and then, conclusions are made about which regime type is best suited for democratic consolidation. For example, Matthew Shugart and John Carey in *Presidents and Assemblies: Constitutional Design and Electoral Dynamics* develop a system of scoring the powers of a president using constitutions and then determining the regime type for each nation under consideration.[21] I accept this approach for analyzing constitutional powers, but also suggest revisions to their model.

## Problems with the neo-institutionalist literature

In the existing literature on neo-institutionalism several models can be used to determine the type of political system in a given country. The problem, which is particularly evident in the case of Russia, is that these models consider different factors from a country's constitution to judge regime type. This makes it possible to arrive at drastically different conclusions about a country's regime type depending on what model one uses. One model might classify country A as semi-presidential while another might characterize country A as presidential. This is especially problematic because regime type is used as a basis for making conclusions about democratic stability and consolidation. If the method for classifying regime type is not appropriate, conclusions drawn about democracy may also be flawed. The Russian case clearly illustrates this point, that regime classifications can differ based on the model chosen. Later a revised model will be presented which takes account of problems with existing models.

When the main models in the neo-institutionalist literature for evaluating regime type and parliamentary/presidential power are applied to Russia we arrive at four completely different results. None of the models would classify Russia as parliamentary between 1994 and 2001 though they leave it unclear whether it is a super-presidential (non-democratic), presidential, or semi-presidential (that is, president-parliamentary) regime.

Matthew Shugart and John Carey in their seminal book, *Presidents and Assemblies: Constitutional Design and Electoral Dynamics*, use constitutional powers of presidents to determine regime type.[22] They define presidentialism as

> a regime type based on the ideal of maximum separation of powers and full and exclusive responsibility of the cabinet to the president. We define premier-presidentialism as a type in which the president has certain significant powers, but the cabinet is responsible only to the assembly. The third type is president-parliamentary, a common type with shared – or confused – responsibility over cabinets between president and assembly.[23]

Both premier-presidentialism and president-parliamentarism are often referred to as semi-presidentialism in the literature, but Shugart and Carey distinguish between the two sub-types. For this study, when semi-presidentialism is used it refers to Shugart and Carey's definition of president-parliamentarism, while semi-parliamentarism (a term which does not exist in the current literature but is necessary for a better conceptualization of regime types, as illustrated in Figure 1.1) relates to their definition of premier-presidentialism. Parliamentarism is not examined in the Shugart and Carey study. Similarly, it is not considered here for two reasons: the regime in Russia is not parliamentary on the basis of both the powers ascribed to each branch in the 1993 Constitution and the *actual* powers they use.[24]

In Shugart and Carey's study they score ten legislative and non-legislative poweis of presidents and on this basis, make conclusions about regime type. Legislative powers of the president include the ability to propose referenda, exclusively introduce legislation, prepare the budget, and issue partial or package vetoes and decrees. Non-legislative powers are cabinet formation, cabinet dismissal, dissolution of the assembly, and censure. A scale of 0 to 4 for each factor is used, with 4 meaning that the president has significant powers and 0 for very little or no power.

Applying Shugart and Carey's model to the powers of the Russian President based on the 1993 Constitution, we find the results given in Tables 1.1 and 1.2. Shugart and Carey's model is a useful way of scoring

*Table 1.1*  Legislative powers of the Russian President based on the 1993 Constitution

|  | Package veto | Partial veto | Decree | Exclusive intro. | Budgetary power | Proposal of referenda | Total |
|---|---|---|---|---|---|---|---|
| Russia | 2 | 0 | 3 | 0 | 1 | 2 | 8 |

*Table 1.2*  Non-legislative powers of the Russian President based on the 1993 Constitution

|  | Cabinet formation | Cabinet dismissal | Censure | Dissolution | Total |
|---|---|---|---|---|---|
| Russia | 2 | 4 | 2 | 3 | 11 |

Tables 1.1 and 1.2 are the author's own calculations when the 1993 Russian Constitution is applied to the Shugart and Carey model from Matthew Shugart and John Carey, *Presidents and Assemblies: Constitutional Design and Electoral Dynamics* (Cambridge: Cambridge University Press, 1992), 150, table 8.1.

* Even though Shugart and Carey do not provide a score of 3 for decree powers or 2 for cabinet formation, they occasionally use such intermediary numbers when the ones in Table 1.1 do not apply. This was the case for cabinet formation and decree powers of the Russian President (see Chapter 2 for further discussion of the use of intermediary numbers).

the constitutional powers of presidents but it needs to be modified for the reasons given in the next chapter.

Shugart and Carey chart these powers with legislative power on the y-axis and non-legislative power on the x-axis. The resulting clusters of countries are divided into regions. Regions I and VI are presidential, while Regions II, III, IV, and V are semi-presidential (meaning in Shugart and Carey's terms, premier-presidential or president-parliamentary), and those regimes with presidents scoring 0 for both legislative and non-legislative powers are parliamentary. When the powers of the Russian President, calculated from the above model, are applied to Shugart and Carey's chart on regime types, we find that on the basis of written powers, Russia's system is presidential. According to Shugart and Carey's chart on the frequency of democratic failure in each region, Russia is in the region (Region I) with the most breakdowns. Indeed, in 50 percent of the systems in this region democracy has failed.[25] The regions where democracy was most successful are Regions II, III and IV, which are semi-presidential and parliamentary according to Shugart and Carey's classification. In Regions V and VI, presidential and semi-presidential systems, 25 percent of the democratic systems collapsed.[26] Thus, it seems that presidential systems are the most susceptible to breaking down.

Matthew Shugart applied three of the above factors (the president's power to dissolve the assembly and to form and dismiss the cabinet) and added one additional factor (impeachment) to analyze executive–legislative relations in post-communist countries in an article written four years after Shugart and Carey's model of presidential powers was published.[27] Some problems with the numerical codings of presidential powers in the Shugart and Carey model were realized and partially rectified in this updated article. Using the revised numerical codes for the four factors, Shugart applies them to the 1993 Russian Constitution and finds that Russia is a president-parliamentary system. It is not even close to the region of presidential systems based on his model. Obviously, then, depending on what coding one uses and the factors one considers, regime type can vary greatly, as proven by applying two charts by the same person to Russia which result in two very different outcomes.

Maurice Duverger further utilizes presidential and ministerial powers to define semi-presidentialism. In his article, 'A New Political System Model: Semi-presidential Government', Duverger claims that

> a political regime is considered as semi-presidential if the constitution which established it combines three elements: (1) the president of the republic is elected by universal suffrage; (2) he possesses quite

considerable powers; (3) he has opposite him, however, a prime minister and ministers who possess executive and governmental power and can stay in office only if the parliament does not show its opposition to them.[28]

He does not differentiate between systems within a semi-presidential government, as Shugart and Carey do, but his model would lead to a characterization of the political system in Russia as semi-presidential. Like Shugart and Carey, Duverger's definition is based on constitutional powers ascribed to each branch, but he also stresses the importance of both *de jure* and *de facto* powers, which makes it particularly relevant to this study. According to Duverger,

> in actual fact, the interpretation of a constitution cannot be separated from the interrelationship of political forces to which it is applied. If the interrelationship varies, the structure and functioning of the form of government established by the constitution vary at the same time … Constitutions which lay down semi-presidential governments are relatively homogeneous. It will be seen that they show considerable differences with regard to the powers of the Head of State. These differences, however, remain secondary in relation to the general physiognomy of the system. They are far less important than the variety of political practices … similarity of rules, diversity of games.[29]

This study follows from Duverger's in that it considers both written and actual powers to determine the regime type and the level of democratic transition/consolidation. Duverger's model of a president's constitutional and actual powers clearly illustrates that there is a considerable difference between actual and written powers in most of the countries he considers, especially France and Iceland. Duverger's conclusion is that

> although the constitution plays a certain part in the application of presidential powers, this role remains secondary compared to that of the other parameters; the cases of France and Iceland show this in an undeniable way. In both cases, the constitutions are not violated, despite the fairly great differences which separate what is written in the constitutions and actual practices.[30]

The difference between the powers granted to a president and parliament in a constitution and the powers they actually exercise is of crucial importance to any classification.

As Duverger's study demonstrated, the constitution is an important basis from which parliament and president draw their power but they may or may not choose to use some of their constitutional powers. Constitutional powers of the Russian President and Parliament will be discussed in Chapter 2 but the main focus of this study is an analysis of their actual powers.

Arend Lijphart's model in *Parliamentary Versus Presidential Government* classifies Russia as presidential.[31] Lijphart, using some of Douglas Verney's eleven 'propositions' concerning parliamentary and presidential regimes,[32] classifies systems based on how the executive is selected (by the voters or by the legislature) and whether there is a collegial or one-person executive (who is dependent or not dependent on legislative confidence). Using this typology, a parliamentary system has a collegial executive which is dependent on legislative confidence and an executive which is selected by the legislature. A presidential system has a one-person executive, who is not dependent on legislative confidence but was selected by voters. Russia and the French Fifth Republic, then, would be a presidential system because the President is one person who is directly elected by voters and whose position does not depend on legislative confidence. Other combinations represent 'mixed' (or semi-presidential) systems, according to Lijphart. *The difficulty with the current literature on regime types is that there is no consensus as to what factors should be used to determine regime types.*

Classifications described thus far use systematic models to assess regime type, but there are also several important and widely used definitions which must be considered. One such definition is of superpresidentialism which Stephen Holmes believes describes the Russian case.[33] A system is classified as superpresidentialism if it has 'swollen' presidential powers. This is an undemocratic regime where the president has veto power, can dissolve the assembly, legislate by decree, ignore the assembly and cohabitation is not permitted. Because of this Holmes argues that 'law-making and law-executing powers are fused, since the president can legislate by *ukazi* (decrees). Moreover, checks and balances work solely for the president.'[34] Based on these powers granted to the President in the Constitution, Russia can be called superpresidential. It must be noted that Holmes wrote this article in early 1994 when the Russian legislature was just beginning to be formed, but the term has been referred to since to describe Russia.

Two further definitions are found in Juan Linz's chapter in *The Failure of Presidential Democracy* and Alfred Stepan and Cindy Skach's article 'Constitutional Frameworks and Democratic

Consolidation: Parliamentarism and Presidentialism'.[35] Linz classifies presidential systems as ones where

> (1) both the president, who controls the executive and is elected by the people (or an electoral college elected by the people for that sole purpose), and an elected legislature (unicameral or bicameral) enjoy democratic legitimacy ... and, (2) both the president and congress are elected for a fixed term, the president's tenure in office is independent of the legislature, and the survival of the legislature is independent of the president ... [Mixed systems are defined as having] a president who is elected by the people either directly or indirectly, rather than nominated by the parliament, and a prime minister who needs the confidence of parliament. Other characteristics not always found but often associated with dual executive systems are: the president appoints the prime minister, although he needs the support of the parliament, and the president can dissolve the parliament.[36]

Although some of the features of Linz's definition of a presidential system apply to Russia, except that the president's survival is not independent of the parliament and vice versa, all of his conditions for a 'mixed' system are met in the case of Russia. Thus, Russia's political system is semi-presidential according to Linz's definition. Using similar factors of electoral mandate and legitimacy, Stepan and Skach define political systems as follows:

> (a) a pure-parliamentary regime in a democracy is a system of mutual dependence: the chief executive power must be supported by a majority in the legislature and can fall if it receives a vote of no confidence [and] the executive power (normally in conjunction with the head of state) has the capacity to dissolve the legislature and call for elections; (b) a pure presidential regime in a democracy is a system of mutual independence: the legislative power has a fixed electoral mandate that is its own source of legitimacy [and] the chief executive power has a fixed electoral mandate that is its own source of legitimacy [and, (c) a semi-presidential system has] a directly elected president and a prime minister who must have a majority in the legislature.[37]

With Stepan's and Skach's definition it is difficult to deduce which type of political system exists in Russia as some of the features of both the presidential and semi-presidential systems can be found there. Even though there is a directly elected President in Russia, the Prime Minister does not need to have a majority in the legislature. For example, Viktor Chernomyrdin, Prime Minister from January 1994 to March 1998, was never approved by the State Duma elected in December 1993 and a vote of confidence in his Government was not held until 1995.[38] This will be examined in greater detail in Chapter 6. Stepan's and Skach's definition of presidentialism relates more to Russia than their description of semi-presidentialism because the Russian Parliament and President both have an electoral mandate, although the President can dissolve Parliament and Parliament can impeach the President. Still, neither definition of presidentialism or semi-presidentialism completely applies in this case. It must be noted that the second condition for parliamentary regimes, that the president 'has the capacity to dissolve the legislature and call for elections', is also met in Russia.

A sufficient number of studies have now been described and applied to Russia to prove that the factors one uses to evaluate regime type can greatly influence how a political system is classified. The Russian case makes this point particularly clear since, as noted above, Russia has been characterized as (1) superpresidential by Holmes; (2) semi-presidential by Duverger and Linz and president-parliamentary by Shugart; (3) presidential by Lijphart, Stepan and Skach, and Shugart and Carey's quantitative model. One or some of these models/definitions must be, at least partially, accurate since the above results fit into every possible category except parliamentarism, which was shown not to be a plausible description of Russia's political system from 1994 to 2001. But, why are there vast differences in the classification of Russia's regime type? How can we design a model which accurately determines regime type?

Based on the literature for using constitutional powers to ascertain the type of political system, it is unclear what type of regime really exists in Russia. Indeed, as we have seen, a case can be made for all three types. My explanation for this inconsistency is that using only written powers to determine a regime type can lead to flawed conclusions because it does not account for the actual powers which a parliament or president exercises. While constitutions are important, they do not explain changes in power over time, so neo-institutionalism can only take us so far in this analysis. That is, based on the powers granted to the Russian President and Parliament in the 1993 Constitution one might, for example, classify Russia as presidential. But, what if the President chooses not to use all of his powers or uses them only temporarily if a crisis or event necessitates it? Or, what if in actuality the Parliament and/or President exercise more power than is granted to them in the Constitution? Since the Constitution is a document which is seldom amended, to base an analysis of parliamentary/presidential power solely on this document would be to overlook the intense struggles for power which occur in Russia. Moreover, Duverger proved that written powers can be vastly different from actual powers.[39] Only by considering the actual powers of a president and parliament within the framework of their constitutional powers can we truly understand how much power Parliament has to influence decision-making in Russia and the extent to which the President rules by decree. This author believes, like Duverger, that the only way to solve this problem is to consider both written and actual powers.

## Regime type defined

Because there is some confusion in the existing literature as to the precise meaning and factors for classification of regime type, I conceptualize the democratic regime types as the following:

This classification is only meant as a starting point for analysis as the next chapters will examine the specific criteria for each regime type. I argue that an analysis of the constitutional, structural, and actual powers of a president and parliament must be considered before conclusions can be made about regime type and then, democratic transition or consolidation. In Figure 1.1, the concept of semi-presidentialism referred to is one in between presidentialism and a system of dual powers, where the president has slightly more power than parliament. Premier-presidentialism is better understood as a system of semi-parliamentarism and not as a sub-category within semi-presidentialism because it is defined (by Shugart and Carey) as a system where parliament has more power over the executive (the cabinet) than the president. Figure 1.1 allows one to talk, with greater clarity, about 'mixed' systems because

| Non-democratic | Democratic | | | | | Non-democratic |
|---|---|---|---|---|---|---|
| Super-Presidentialism | Presidentialism | Semi-Presidentialism (president-parliamentary) | Dual Powers | Semi-Parliamentarism (premier-presidential) | Parliamentarism | Super-Parliamentarism |
| Super-strong president, very weak or non-existent parliament | Strong president, president is much more powerful than parliament | President is slightly more powerful than parliament | President and parliament both have supreme or little power | Parliament is slightly more powerful than the president | Strong parliament, parliament is much more powerful than the president | Super-strong parliament, very weak or non-existent president |

*Figure 1.1*   Model for regime type based on written and actual powers of the President and Parliament.

Strength and power are used interchangeably. This figure is elaborated in later chapters, where power is defined in constitutional, structural and actual terms.

often in the literature, the above classifications of semi-presidentialism, dual powers, and semi-parliamentarism are combined into one system referred to as 'semi-presidentialism', 'mixed', or 'confused'. By separating them into three sub-categories a more exact reference to these 'mixed' systems can be made. Moreover, since Stephen Holmes defines systems where the president has 'swollen' powers as superpresidential, there should also be a category (which is absent in the literature) for when parliament has 'swollen' powers over the executive. This system is termed superparliamentarism and it is undemocratic. This study seeks to determine which system exists in Russia.

## Structure of legislative and executive institutions in Russia

The Federal Assembly, according to Article 94 of the 1993 Russian Constitution, is the Parliament of the Russian Federation which functions as a representative and legislative body. It is comprised of two chambers: the State Duma, the lower house, and the Council of the Federation, the upper house. Figure 1.2 shows the structure of the legislative branch as dictated by the 1993 Constitution. The Federation Council is comprised of two Members from each of Russia's 89 regions, while the State Duma has 450 Deputies, 225 are from electoral districts (one Deputy from each single-member constituency) and 225 are from electoral blocs (political parties and public organizations). On 5 December, 1995, the Duma adopted a federal law 'On the Formation of the Council of the Federation,' because Article 96 of the Constitution states that 'the

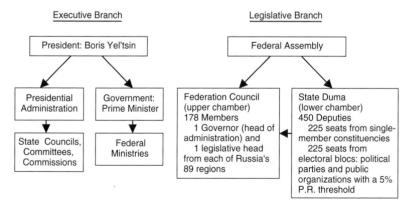

*Figure 1.2* Executive and legislative branches in Russia after the December 1993 Constitution.

procedures for forming the Council of the Federation and the procedures for electing Deputies to the State Duma are established by federal laws'.[40] As a result of this law, the Council of the Federation was comprised of one Governor (head of the administration) and one legislative head from each of the 89 subjects in Russia. The total number of Members in the Council of Federation remained the same, but now regional leaders control it. Later in this study I will analyze what effects, if any, this change has had on executive–legislative relations and on Parliament's power. The powers granted to the President and Parliament in the 1993 Constitution will be discussed in greater detail in Chapter 2.

## Methodology: analytical models

As shown, there are problems with the existing models for evaluating a president's and parliament's powers and regime type. Because an improved model is needed, an analytical model is presented in the following chapters to assess constitutional powers of a president and parliament which takes account of the problems with current models. An analytical model is useful as a basis for determining and comparing constitutional powers of presidents and parliaments. This model is explained and then applied to Russia. Based on the constitutional powers considered in the model, those powers that are also in the 1993 Russian Constitution are examined to determine the extent to which they are exercised by the Russian President and Parliament. The model thus sets the framework for the chapters on actual powers. Because the only four constitutional powers in the analytical model that apply to Russia are decree power, veto/veto override power, budgetary power, and cabinet formation/dismissal, a study of the use of each of these constitutes a separate chapter. Structural powers also place constraints on the president's and parliament's ability to realize their constitutional powers so a separate chapter is devoted to an analysis of this. Both quantitative and qualitative analysis is used in this model. To evaluate a president's and parliament's powers using this model, first, use the Troxel–Skach model in Chapter 2 to determine constitutional powers. Applying these results to Figure 2.2 results in a regime type based solely on constitutional powers. Since actual and structural are also deemed to be important, the next step is to calculate structural powers. As discussed in Chapter 3, this involves several factors. After analyzing these factors in a given country, conclusions can be drawn about regime type. Structural powers provide a more descriptive, qualitative conclusion about regime type, but the methods for reaching these conclusions are highly quantitative. Then, to assess actual powers, the factors from the Troxel–Skach model which the president and parliament actually exercise should constitute a separate study. It is essential to examine to what extent a president and parliament use their constitutional powers. Conclusions are then drawn about regime type based on actual powers. If all three conclusions are the same (for example, all three are presidential) then that is the regime type for the system. If two of the three types of powers (constitutional, structural and actual) lead to one regime type then that is the regime type. But, if there is a large deviance between the resulting regime types, such as presidentialism, semi-presidentialism, and dual powers, then the conclusion is that the system is semi-presidential. Conclusions can then be drawn about the effect of regime type on democratic transition and consolidation, as discussed in Chapter 8.

## Chapter outline

Following this theoretical and methodological introduction, a chapter on constitutional powers analyzes the prerogatives granted to the Russian President and Parliament in the 1993 Constitution and amendments to it. Although constitutional powers of issuing decrees/laws and vetoes/veto overrides, dissolving the assembly/impeaching the President, cabinet formation/dismissal in Russia have been analyzed before by Shugart and Carey, Holmes, Remington and Smith, and Orttung and Parrish, these powers have not been compared and weighed. Is the ability to issue decrees a sign of a more powerful president than the ability to propose referenda? What impact does weighing constitutional powers have on our understanding of regime type in Russia? I will present a revised version of Shugart and Carey's model which will correct some of the problems with their original model. The model will be applied to Russia to quantify written powers of the President and Parliament.

Structural powers of the Presidency and Parliament are evaluated in Chapter 3. Empirical data on the Russian Parliament's committee structure and size, length of sessions, political parties, electoral cycles, and the composition of Parliament are compared with data on the executive branch's structure, President's length of term and political party association (if any), and how the President is elected. On the basis of documentation and interviews, conclusions are drawn about the structural constraints on the Russian President's and Parliament's constitutional powers.

Chapters 4 to 7 consider the actual powers of the Russian President and Parliament. In Chapter 4, the President's frequency and use of decree power is assessed using empirical data on: the number of decrees each year/month, policy areas of the decrees, decrees outside the main policy areas (for example, appointments/dismissals), and the number of decrees that amend previous decrees. Any trends are highlighted. The issuance of decrees is compared with the number of parliamentary laws passed every month/year, and the policy areas of each are also analyzed. Laws passed by parliament are more powerful than decrees because decrees cannot contradict parliamentary laws, but parliamentary laws can contradict, and thus override decrees. The number of times that this actually happened is considered. The constraints on using these powers, an examination of the influence of the electorate, and the President's and Parliament's incentives to use these powers are discussed.

The frequency and use of the President's veto power and Parliament's power to override vetoes are the focus of Chapter 5. Empirical data on the number of presidential vetoes each year/month, the policy areas in which vetoes are issued, and vetoes of legislation related to who introduced the bill are compared with the same issues for Parliament's veto overrides. Again, an in-depth analysis of these powers is provided because the empirical data cannot tell us why vetoes/veto overrides were issued. By understanding the incentives of the President and Parliament to employ their veto powers, their ability to command majorities to vote in favor or against veto overrides, and the influence of the electorate, we can further understand why the President uses his veto power and the Parliament overrides vetoes in certain cases and not in others.

Chapter 6 covers the non-legislative powers of the President and Parliament, with specific reference to cabinet formation and dismissal. Empirical data on the President's use of his power to appoint and dismiss Ministers, including the number of ministerial appointments/ dismissals since 1994, the classification of Ministers' status before dismissal, and general reasons for dismissal are compared with the State Duma's votes of no-confidence in the Government, including the number of successful and unsuccessful attempts, the reasons for the vote, and the party which initiated the vote. Case studies, on the dissolution of the entire Government in April and August 1998, provide detailed analysis of these issues. The questions examined include: to what extent was the Duma able to exert power in these events?; how, if at all, did the executive and legislature cooperate or confront each other during the approval of the Prime Minister?; and, does the timing of votes of no-confidence coincide with the President's dismissal of Ministers or issuing decrees/vetoes?

Chapter 7 considers the use of budgetary powers by the President and Parliament. Even though this is a legislative power, this chapter follows the discussion of the composition of the Government because the Duma and President often threaten to vote no-confidence or dismiss the Government, respectively, when there are significant problems with the budget. It would be difficult to consider each body's incentives in such situations without first studying this power. Moreover, the budget determines which laws, decrees, and resolutions are funded, and thus, implemented. A legislative act might pass through the Duma and Council of the Federation and be signed by the President, but if there is no money to execute it, it can become meaningless. Parliament's most important task each year is to approve a federal budget. Although the Government submits a draft budget to Parliament and the President must sign the final version, the Duma's and Council of the Federation's approval are also required. The 1997 Budget law particularly illustrates both the cooperative and confrontational nature of budget negotiations between the executive and legislature. I examine issues of which branch wields more power in budget negotiations, when they have incentives to negotiate, and whether budget negotiations are generally cooperative or confrontational. Roll-call analysis of budget votes, interviews with those directly involved in the budget process, and stenographic records of proceedings are the main sources of evidence.

The eighth chapter draws upon the above analysis of powers to determine the extent of democratic transition or consolidation in Russia. Conclusions are made about parliamentary power in Russia from 1994 to 1999 by considering trends in executive–legislative relations and the results from previous chapters on the constitutional, actual and structural powers of the Russian Parliament and President. This chapter includes answers to the following questions: Has Parliament's power increased or decreased since the 1993 conflict, and to what extent? Are there any discernible trends in Parliament's attempts to gain power or in Yel'tsin's attempts to reduce Parliament's power? How do the executive and legislature interact? In addition to answering these questions, I return to the hypothesis that Parliament's power has increased since 1994 and consider whether it has been validated. Does Parliament now have more decision-making power and has it become a more influential decision-making body?

A postscript has been added as Chapter 9 to update this study since the book was originally written. The postscript considers all of the factors for assessing the actual and structural powers of Russia's Parliament and President from 1999 to 2001.

# 2
# Constitutional Powers of the Russian Presidency and Parliament: the 1993 Russian Constitution

Constitutions provide the framework within which the president and parliament can legally function. Chapter 1 found that it is not possible to conclusively determine what type of political system exists in Russia using existing models. Depending on the factors that one chooses to employ and the time period in a given country to which they are applied, one can have up to four different outcomes to classify the system in Russia (superpresidentialism, presidentialism, semi-presidentialism, president-parliamentary). Although Maurice Duverger was not alone in showing that constitutional powers differ from actual practice, he especially clearly illustrated that while the constitution is an important basis from which parliament and president draw their power, they may or may not choose to exercise some of these powers.[1] While it is important to consider the executive and legislature's constitutional powers, they do not completely explain what powers are exercised in reality. Only by considering *both* written and actual powers can one determine which type of political system exists in a given country, in this case, Russia. This chapter will analyze the written powers of the Russian President and Parliament from the 1993 Constitution and compare the results with other countries. Later chapters will examine the extent to which these powers are actually utilized.

## Evaluating constitutional powers: theoretical review

In Matthew Shugart and John Carey's[2] seminal work on presidents and assemblies a system was devised whereby the powers of popularly elected presidents could be assessed on the basis of the constitution. It is the only model to date which scores a president's constitutional powers to evaluate his/her power and then, on this basis, determines the type of political system in that country. Shugart and Carey's model is useful because of its comparative value for cross-country analysis of legislative and non-legislative presidential powers, which can then be charted to judge both regime type and the likelihood of democratic success or failure in a given regime.

As Shugart and Carey, themselves, admit, 'this is not a perfect model'.[3] There are several improvements which should be made to their model, enough to warrant a new, revised version. One problem with Shugart and Carey's model is that for some factors, they do not have a ranking which can be applied to Russia (or, for that matter, to many of the other countries of the former Soviet Union). To apply their model to Russia in Chapter 1, I used intermediary numbers or the one that seemed closest when no ranking corresponded to the Russian Constitution, making the process of choosing a number in the Shugart and Carey model, at times, a matter of judgment. For example, the Russian President has significant decree powers, which allow him to make unlimited decrees that can only be overridden by a parliamentary law (and then *only* if the President does not veto the law) and that cannot contradict an existing parliamentary law. This was coded as 3, an intermediate number, when I applied Shugart and Carey's model to Russia in Chapter 1 because they only code 2 as 'president has temporary decree authority with few restrictions' and 4 as 'reserved powers, no rescission'. Neither of these applies to the Russian case where the President has more than temporary decree power but decrees can be rescinded, which places the decree authority of the Russian President in between Shugart and Carey's scores of 2 and 4. Shugart and Carey also occasionally chose intermediate numbers when the scores do not apply or a president's powers fall in between two scores. For example, for Cuba (1940), Shugart and Carey code the powers of censure as 3 when only scores of 2 and 4 are given.[4] The problem, though, is that this leaves the interpretation to the reader. I might score Cuba (1940) as 3.5 instead of Shugart and Carey's intermediate score of 3. Shugart and Carey, then, plot the president's powers on a graph and divide it into regime types. If a regime is on the border, the difference between one's *choice* to code a power as 3 instead of 4, when no intermediary scores are given, could possibly change the resulting regime type from presidential to president-parliamentary, for example. This particularly applies to Russia as Russia is on the border between presidentialism and semi-presidentialism and a one-point difference could alter the assigned regime type.[5] Moreover, with the example of Cuba (1940), the difference between coding censure powers as 3

(Shugart and Carey) and 3.5, 2 or 4 would completely change the resulting regime classification. Shugart and Carey classify Cuba (1940) as presidential, but it is only half a point away from being semi-presidential. If I thought Cuba's (1940) censure powers were 3.5 or 4, since an applicable score is not available in their chart, this could make Cuba (1940) semi-presidential. The inapplicability of scores to some countries and the gaps between numbers (from 2 to 4) makes the codings less objective and it can lead to inaccurate conclusions about the regime type.

Another criticism is that Shugart and Carey do not weigh the factors. For example, the Russian President does not have the exclusive right to introduce legislation, even in reserved policy areas. Although he is one of several people and organizations that can introduce legislation, the fact that he can decree whatever law he wants (as long as it does not contradict the Constitution or a law passed by Parliament) surely outweighs merely having the power to introduce legislation in certain areas. For the exclusive right to introduce legislation factor, the Russian President's power is coded as 0, even though his power to legislate by decree far outweighs his power to introduce legislation. Their model does not account for this.

Moreover, the factors chosen are slightly limited. Since constitutional powers are the sole basis for this model, the power to amend the constitution (thereby, the ability to possibly change the balance of power) should be considered as an important factor. Also, emergency powers are not factored into the Shugart and Carey model. These are particularly important in countries, such as the French Fifth Republic, where the emergency powers of the president can temporarily make a 'weak' president into a 'strong' leader with significant legislative powers.

A model is not presented for assessing the powers of the legislature, which would be a great asset to the existing literature. (It should be noted that Shugart and Carey also consider electoral cycles and the number of political parties in their analysis, but these factors are the subject of the next chapter.) For example, even though the president has the power to dissolve the assembly, what if the assembly has significant powers to impeach the president? Shugart and Carey's model can show that there is a strong president, but it does not show whether parliament is strong or weak. If parliament is also strong in similar or other areas, then the system could be semi-presidential, semi-parliamentary or one of dual powers. By *solely* quantifying presidential powers we cannot necessarily determine which of these regime types exist in a given country.

Even with these criticisms, Shugart and Carey's model is still useful as a starting point for evaluating the powers of a president for lack of a better comparative model on powers and regime types. In a paper co-authored with Cindy Skach, I revise and build on Shugart and Carey's model for assessing the powers of presidents. The Troxel and Skach approach, Figure 2.1, takes into account the important aspects of Shugart and Carey's model while avoiding many of the problems associated it.

**Legislative Powers**

**Package Veto/Override**
4-Veto with no override
3-Veto with override requiring a vote greater than 2/3 of the total MPs
2-Veto with override requiring 2/3
1-Veto with override requiring majority of assembly or resubmission by president
0-No veto powers
0-No veto override
1-Veto override requires a vote greater than 2/3 of the total MPs
2-Veto override requires 2/3
3-Veto override requires absolute majority of assembly or president can resubmit it
4-No package veto

**Partial Veto (line-item)/Override**
4-No override
3-Override by extraordinary majority
2-Override by absolute majority of total membership
1-Override by simple majority of quorum, or only a resubmission by president
0-No partial veto
0-No override
1-Override by extraordinary majority
2-Override by absolute majority of total Membership
3-Override by simple majority of quorum, or president can only resubmit it
4-No partial veto

**Budgetary Power**
4-President prepares budget, no amending
2-President must approve the final version of the budget
1-Assembly may amend president's proposed budget, but not draft a new budget     President
0-No budgetary power
0-No budgetary power
1-President can amend the assembly's proposed budget, but not draft a new Budget     Parliament
2-Assembly must approve the final version of the budget, or the assembly can override a veto by the president
4-Assembly prepares budget, no amending

**Exclusive Introduction of Legislation**
4-No amendment possible by assembly
2-Restricted amendment by assembly
1-Unrestricted amendment by assembly
0-No exclusive powers
0-No exclusive powers
1-Unrestricted amendment by president
2-Restricted amendment by president
4-No amendment possible by president

**Proposal of Referenda**
4-Unrestricted for president
2-Restricted
0-No authority
0-No authority
2-Restricted
4-Unrestricted for parliament

**Amending the Constitution**
4-No restrictions
3-Countersignature needed
2-Assembly's approval needed or a referendum
0-No power
0-No power
2-Majority vote greater than 2/3 needed or countersignature of PM or Pres. or a referendum
3-Two-thirds vote needed
4-No restrictions or simple majority

**Decree Power**
6-Unrestricted decree power
4-Temporary decree power with few restrictions     President
2-Limited decree power
0-No decree power
0-Unrestricted decree power
2-Temporary decree power     Parliament
4-Limited decree power
6-No decree power

**Non-legislative Powers**

**Dissolve the Assembly or Impeach the President**
4-Unrestricted
3-Restricted by frequency or point within term, or needs confirmation by another
2-Requires new presidential election
1-Restricted: only as response to censures
0-No provision
0-No provision
1-Restricted: only in response to attempts to dissolve the Assembly
2-Requires new parliamentary elections
3-Restricted by frequency or point within term, or needs confirmation by another
4-Unrestricted

**Emergency Powers**
5-No limits, no countersign
4-Temporary emergency power with no countersignature
2-Temporary and limited emergency powers with assembly's approval
0-No emergency powers
0-No limits on president's emerg. powers
2-Assembly's approval needed for limited and temporary emergency powers
5-No emergency power

**Cabinet Formation**
5-President names cabinet and PM, no confirmation by assembly needed
4-President names cabinet, subject to confirmation by assembly
3-President names PM, subject to confirmation, who then names cabinet
2-President names PM, but cabinet is chosen by assembly
1-Assembly names pres., who then names ministers and/or PM
0-President cannot name PM
0-Assembly cannot name PM/cabinet
1-Assembly confirms president's choice of cabinet/PM
2-Assembly confirms president's choice of PM, who then names cabinet
3-Assembly names cabinet, but PM is chosen by president
4-Assembly names president, who then names ministers and/or PM
5-Parliament names PM and cabinet

**Cabinet Dismissal**
4-Unlimited dismissal power
3-Dismissal limited
2-President may only dismiss if assembly approves replacement minister     President
1-President may only dismiss if assembly suggests it
0-President cannot dismiss ministers
0-Parliament cannot dismiss/remove Cabinet
1-Parliament can suggest to the president that cabinet be dismissed
2-Assembly may dismiss if president approves a replacement minister     Parliament
3-Limited dismissal power, needs 2/3 support of all MPs
4-Unlimited dismissal power, needs simple majority vote

*Figure 2.1* Constitutional powers of democratically elected presidents and parliaments assessed.
*Source*: Tiffany Troxel and Cindy Skach, working paper, 'Comparing the Constitutions of the CIS and Eastern Europe', 2000.

## A model for evaluating the constitutional powers of presidents and parliaments

A model on the written powers of the president and parliament must therefore include both the president's and parliament's legislative powers of package veto or override, partial veto or override, issuing decrees or passing laws which rescind decrees, proposing referenda, budget preparation, exclusive introduction of legislation, and amending the constitution. Non-legislative powers of the president and parliament considered in the model are cabinet formation, cabinet dismissal, impeaching the president or dissolving the assembly, and emergency powers. The first six factors of the legislative and first three of the non-legislative presidential powers are from both Shugart and Carey's model and Shugart's follow-up article, but the last factor in both the legislative and non-legislative categories and all those relating to parliamentary power are from the Troxel and Skach model.[6] Each factor can be scored using a given country's constitution to produce an overall assessment of presidential and parliamentary power.

Scores, partially from Shugart and Carey's model but mostly from a working paper co-authored with Cindy Skach, are assigned to each factor in Figure 2.1. Only a few of the numerical values correspond with Shugart and Carey's model and Shugart's later article. There are four main advantages to this revised model: (1) the factors are weighed, for example, unlimited decree power is coded as 6 (instead of Shugart and Carey's top score of 4) because the power to issue decrees at will is a sign of a much stronger president than, for example, the power to propose referenda; (2) the codings are more applicable to post-communist countries (as noted, Shugart in his recent article changed the codings of three factors from the original model to account for differences in post-communist countries); (3) both the president's and parliament's constitutional powers are evaluated, with the president's powers listed first and the parliament's second; (4) and, two additional important factors are included which were absent from the Shugart and Carey model.

### Legislative powers

#### Decree power

Arguably, the most important power any president can wield, the power to decree laws in any policy area without restrictions, can greatly reduce the importance of parliamentary institutions, so it is scored as 6. This is especially the case if presidential decrees can supersede laws passed by parliament, though this is not common. For decree power we consider the power of the president to issue decrees, without the approval of other bodies, which are laws and not regulations. The score of 6, instead of Shugart and Carey's top score of 4, is justifiable as the power to 'rule by decree' is much greater than, for example, the power to veto parliamentary legislation which can be overridden anyway by parliament. The countries of the CIS and Central and Eastern Europe are unique in that several of the democratically elected presidents have unrestricted power to issue decrees. The only exception to this is Brazil, where the President can issue and re-decrees which last for 30 days though the National Congress can overrule them.[7] In Russia, Belarus and Romania, the President can issue decrees in any policy area, which last for the President's term in office.[8] Article 99 of Romania's Constitution states that 'in the exercise of his powers, the President of Romania shall issue decrees which shall be published in the *Official Gazette of Romania*. Absence of publicity entails the non-existence of a decree'.[9] The Belarus and Russian Constitutions are also very similar in wording, with the Belarus Constitution declaring that 'the President shall, within the limits of his powers, issue edicts and orders and organize and monitor their implementation' and the Russian Constitution stating that 'the President of the Russian Federation issues edicts and decrees'.[10] A president with temporary decree power, but with few other restrictions, is scored a 4 because even though it is limited to a set time period, the president still has great powers to decree the laws he chooses. Even further limits on a president's power to issue decrees, such as only in specific policy areas, is scored a 2.

Even though parliaments do not have decree-making authority as parliamentary laws are usually more binding than decrees, the lack of a president's ability to issue decrees means that there is more reliance on parliamentary laws. If a president has unrestricted decree powers, then the 'law of the land' is most likely a combination of presidential decrees and parliamentary laws. When this power is restricted, then parliament has even greater responsibility and ability to determine the laws. Taking account of this, parliament's power is scored based on the degree of the president's power, as an inverse relationship, with a 6 if the president has no decree power, 4 for limited decree power, and 2 if he/she has temporary decree power. With unrestricted decree power the president can legislate by decree to fill in the gaps of legislation with his/her own policy agenda, so in this case, parliament's power is coded as 0.

## Exclusive introduction of legislation

If the president or parliament has the exclusive right to introduce legislation, even in only reserved policy areas, this is an important power, scored as 4, because he/it can set the agendas for the policy issues discussed. With unrestricted power, if the president or parliament does not want a bill to even be considered, it will not be. In some cases, Chile (1969) or Uruguay,[11] parliament has unrestricted power to amend the president's proposed bill. When parliament or the president has exclusive powers to introduce legislation but the other branch has unrestricted or restricted powers to amend the bill, this is coded as 1 and 2, respectively. In most countries, however, the parliament or president is one of several bodies that can introduce legislation so a score of 0 is the most common. This is even true in the countries of the former Soviet Union where, during the Soviet period and until the late 1980s, Parliament 'assembled only long enough each session to give unanimous approval to policies and laws advanced by Party and Government',[12] but now several different subjects in each of the former USSR countries can propose legislation.

### Amending the Constitution

The power to amend the Constitution is one of the most important factors a president and/or parliament can have because it means that they can change the structure of rules that govern a country and increase or restrict the powers of any body/branch. Although it is unusual for a president or parliament to be given the sole power to amend the Constitution, it has happened before, in Russia for example, and is scored a 4 for that body (the Congress of People's Deputies could amend the constitution). It can be a great source of power and tension when one branch wants more power over another and has power to amend the constitution to get that power, so it is given the highest score of 4 in this area. When the president needs the countersignature of the prime minister or another person/institution or when the parliament must have a two-thirds vote in favor of amending the constitution, their power to act is slightly restricted, so this is assigned a score of 3. Moreover, if the president or parliament requires the approval of the other branch to amend the constitution, this is scored a 2 because they have less power to act independently.

### Package veto/veto override

Besides the power to introduce legislation and issue decrees, a president's power in the law-making process is dependent on his/her power to veto bills. A president who can veto entire pieces of legislation without being overridden by parliament has significant powers over the legislature. This is scored a 4 for the president and 0 for parliament. Similar to the exclusive power of introducing legislation, with ultimate veto power the president has significant agenda-setting capabilities in that he/she can ensure that only the bills he/she supports are passed. This is very rare, however, and most often a veto can be overridden by parliament. Depending on the president's ability to command a majority in parliament, he/she will be more or less able to convince parliamentarians not to override the veto. As a result, if a vote of more than two-thirds of parliamentarians is required to override the veto, it is less likely that it will be overridden, so this is scored a 3 for the president and 1 for parliament, as parliament still has at least some chance to override it. Similarly, a veto override needing a two-thirds vote in favor of the override by the total number of MPs is coded as 2 for both the president and parliament. Since it is much easier to override a veto with a simple or absolute majority vote, this has a score of 1 for the president and 3 for parliament. In some countries, such as Poland,[13] the president can resubmit the entire bill for reconsideration by parliament, which is coded as 1 for the president and 3 for parliament, because the president can force parliament to hold a new vote but parliament has the ultimate power to decide on the legislation.

**Partial veto/veto override**

Similar to the package veto, the partial or line-item veto gives a president the ability to veto parts of legislation instead of the entire bill. This can be particularly important if he supports the bill but disagrees with only a few parts. In many countries, such as the United States, where pork-barreling by congresspeople often ensures that amendments will be added to a bill in the interest of a few delegates or the opponents of the bill, the president can veto the parts he chooses. This is especially useful if he proposed the bill, so he can use a partial veto to pass legislation closer to his own policy objectives. Because of this, the president's power to issue partial vetoes that cannot be overridden is given a 4, but if the president does not have partial veto power parliament has more power to legislate without the disapproval of the president so this is scored a 4 for parliament. There is a similar division among the codings as those for pocket veto and veto override powers, with an override by an extraordinary majority coded as 3 for the president and 1 for parliament, override by an absolute majority of parliamentarians is 2 for both the president and parliament, and override by a simple majority is 1 for the president and 3 for parliament. In addition to the last score, a 1 is given to the president and 3 for parliament when the president can only ask parliament to reconsider parts of the bill.

## Budgetary power

Preparing a federal budget with no amendments by another branch is a considerable power as it is the source of funding for most policy objectives. Without sufficient funds allocated for a given policy area or bill, the bill might not pass or be implemented. If the president or parliament is solely responsible for drafting and approving the budget, this is scored a 4 for that body. Hungary is one of a few countries where parliament prepares and adopts the budget, without confirmation from another body.[14] Most often, the branch that drafts it must also seek another branch's approval either in part or for the entire bill. When the president or parliament approve the final version of the budget law, this is coded as 2 for that branch. In instances where one branch can amend the other branch's proposed budget but not draft a new one, this is scored as 1 because although they can change the draft budget, it must still be within the constraints of the original version.

## Proposal of referenda

The proposal of referenda can be used to pass legislation rejected by the assembly, adopt a new constitution, or as a measure of or to gain public confidence. Belarus's and Hungary's Constitutions grant both the President and Parliament unrestricted powers to propose referenda, so each are given a 4.[15] In such cases, the wording of the referenda is decided by the proposer(s). Countries which restrict the president's and/or parliament's power to propose referenda are coded as 2. In Latvia, both the President and Parliament have restricted powers to initiate referenda because one-tenth of voters must confirm that a national referendum should be called.[16] Even though the President has no power to propose referenda in Macedonia, Parliament has some powers to do so but these are restricted by the policy areas of the referenda.[17] Restrictions can also be placed on the wording of the referenda, requiring consent from another body or limiting the areas which are binding. In the French Fifth Republic, the approval of another body is needed, and referenda are limited only to amendments to the Constitution, Government bills in certain policy areas, and approval for the ratification of treaties.[18] According to Article 11 of the French Fifth

Republic's Constitution:

> on a proposal from the Government during the sessions of Parliament, or on a joint motion of its two Houses published in the *Official Journal*, the President of the Republic may put to a referendum any Government bill dealing with the organization of the public authorities, entailing approval of a Community agreement, or providing for authorization to ratify a treaty which, while not contrary to the Constitution, would affect the functioning of its institutions.[19]

Any such restrictions placed on the proposal of referenda are coded as 2, while 0 is applied to presidents or parliaments which do not have the authority to propose referenda.

## Non-legislative powers

### Cabinet formation

In several countries the president or parliament has the sole power to name the prime minister and cabinet without confirmation needed from another body; this is coded as 5. A score of 5 is given in this instance, instead of a high score of 4, because the power to form the cabinet and appoint the prime minister means that you can choose the government. This is a greater power than the power to veto legislation or propose referenda, for example, because the government is usually responsible for implementing laws. If a government appointed by the president works against parliament, regardless of the parliamentary laws passed, it can affect the implementation of those laws. When parliament and the president work together to form the cabinet by the president nominating its members subject to confirmation by parliament, this is coded as a 4 for the president and 1 for parliament. If parliament appoints the president who then appoints the ministers and/or prime minister, this is scored a 4 for parliament and a 1 for the president. Other possibilities are that the president names the prime minister, who must be confirmed by parliament, and then the prime minister chooses his/her cabinet (scored a 3 for the president and 2 for parliament). In instances where the president appoints the prime minister but the cabinet is chosen by parliament, this is given a 2 for presidential powers and 3 for parliament. A score of 0 is used when the president or parliament is legally prohibited from having any role in the formation of the cabinet.

## Cabinet dismissal

When the president or parliament have unlimited power to dismiss the cabinet this is scored as 4. It is not given a 5, as in cabinet formation, because the power to choose appointments to certain posts is slightly more significant than being able to dismiss these people. Occasionally, dismissal power is limited by a point within a term, the number of times it can be used, or a pre-set time frame, making this a 3 for president or parliament. If one branch dismisses a cabinet minister but the other branch must approve a replacement, this is coded as 2 for that branch. In some regimes, the president or parliament can only suggest to the other body that the cabinet should be dismissed and this is scored 1. This is still some power, though, as the branch is responsible for initiating the dismissal process. 0 is restricted for cases where a president or parliament cannot dismiss the prime minister and/or cabinet.

## Emergency powers

Emergency powers must also be considered because they often allow a president to suspend civil liberties, rule by decree without recessions, and take direct command of state affairs. For this reason but also because emergency powers are limited to, at most, the duration of the state of emergency, having unlimited emergency powers with no countersignature is scored a 5 instead of the highest score of 6 given to unrestricted decree power. The importance of emergency powers to classifications of regime type is well known, as in the case of the French Fifth Republic. The French Fifth Republic is classified as semi-presidential since Article 16 of the French Constitution grants periods of cohabitation, with the President and Prime Minister, and gives substantial emergency powers to the President,

> when the institutions of the Republic, the independence of the nation, the integrity of its territory or the fulfillment of its international commitments come under serious and immediate threat and the proper functioning of the constitutional public authorities is impaired.[20]

If a president's emergency powers are limited in time during the state of emergency but no countersignature is needed this would be scored a 4. While time limits on emergency powers restrict the duration of these powers, the president still has considerable power in such cases, so it is coded as 4, only one point less than unlimited power (5). A score of 2 is used for both a president's and parliament's powers when the assembly must approve the president's limited and temporary emergency powers. Even though the president has emergency powers, this requires him/her to be dependent on parliament's decision of when and to what extent these powers can be exercised. In countries where the president does not have emergency powers, parliament usually assumes responsibility or procedures follow the normal routines during states of emergency, so parliamentary power is coded as 5.

### Dissolution or impeachment

The unrestricted power of the president to dissolve parliament or of parliament to impeach the president allows the one to have considerable power over the other because its existence is partially dependent on the other branch's desire not to have a new person or people replace them (which is a 4). For parliament, the unrestricted power to impeach the president means that only a simple majority vote is needed but no confirmation is required from another body. When this power is restricted by frequency or a point within the term or must be confirmed by another body, this is scored 3 for parliament and the president. If new elections must be called for the branch that dissolved the other branch, this reduces the advantages of dissolution as one risks one's own position and power, so this is coded as 2. The power to disband the assembly or impeach the president can be limited to a response to censures or attempts to dissolve the assembly, respectively (which is a 1).

### Powers of the president and parliament and regime type

Figure 2.2 compares the powers of presidents and parliaments on the basis of the codings in Figure 2.1. Regime type is defined from the powers which are outlined in this section. Since superpresidentialism and superparliamentarism are undemocratic regimes where the president or parliament, respectively, have considerable power to usurp the other branch(es), these systems are located in the bottom right corner and top left corner of the chart. Russia, from September to December 1993, was superpresidential and undemocratic because Yel'tsin disbanded Parliament and ruled by decree. This is an extreme case and it is located at the lower right corner of Figure 2.2. All of the other systems listed are democratic. Parliamentarism exists when a parliament has significantly more powers than the president and, thus, it is in the upper left region.

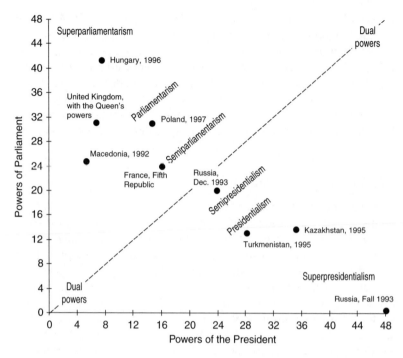

*Figure 2.2*   Powers of presidents and parliaments in democratic and undemocratic regimes.

\* The year given above refers to the year the constitution for that country came into force.

*Table 2.1*   Powers of the Russian President and Parliament based on the 1993 Constitution

| Russia (December 1993) | Exclusive introduction of legislation | Dissolve the assembly or impeach the President | Emergency powers | Package veto/ override | Partial veto (line-item) |
|---|---|---|---|---|---|
| President | 0 | 3 | 2 | 2 | 0 |
| Parliament | 0 | 3 | 2 | 2 | 4 |

| | Proposal of referenda | Budgetary power | Decree power | Cabinet formation | Cabinet dismissal | Amending the Constitution | Total (48) |
|---|---|---|---|---|---|---|---|
| President | 2 | 2 | 6 | 3 | 4 | 0 | 24 |
| Parliament | 2 | 2 | 0 | 2 | 1 | 2 | 20 |

Hungary (1996), the United Kingdom, Poland (1997), and Macedonia (1992) are all parliamentary regimes. Semi-parliamentarism, defined in the first chapter as a regime where parliament's powers are slightly greater than the president's, is located in the region under parliamentarism and along the diagonal line. The French Fifth Republic falls into this category. While the French Fifth Republic is usually referred to as semi-presidential or a 'mixed' regime, semi-parliamentarism is very similar to semi-presidentialism and is, indeed, a 'mixed' form. The slight difference between the classifications of semi-presidentialism and semi-parliamentarism is that the president has slightly more power than parliament in the former and the reverse is true for the latter. A regime is one of dual powers when both the president and parliament have a great deal of power (upper right corner) or very little power (lower left corner). Semi-presidentialism, which is the area just below the diagonal, describes a regime where the president has slightly greater powers than parliament. Russia, from 1994 to 1999 based on the 1993 Constitution, is semi-presidential. Since Russia is the focus of this study, the scores for Russia are listed in Table 2.1. The other countries in Figure 2.2 are given only for comparison.[21]

Presidentialism, found in the lower right area of the chart, defines a regime where the president has significantly more powers than parliament. Kazakhstan (1995) and Turkmenistan (1995) have presidential systems, with Kazakhstan verging on superpresidentialism. It should be noted that the Constitutions of Kazakhstan and Turkmenistan have been amended since these countries were scored in Figure 2.2 to give the presidents even more power. When the powers of the Russian Parliament and President are compared in Figure 2.2, it appears that even though the President exercises greater powers than Parliament, Russia still has a semi-presidential system. An examination of the powers of the Russian Parliament and President follows.

## The model of constitutional powers applied to Russia

### Constitution by a public vote

On 21 September, 1993 President Boris Yel'tsin issued Decree 1400 which called for a 'single agreed draft' of the Russian Constitution.[22] Another decree on 15 October 1993 stated that the Constitution would be put to a vote of the people, which was held on 12 December.[23] The Russian people were asked: 'Do you approve of the Constitution of the Russian Federation?' A simple 'yes' or 'no' answer to this very general question

would determine the institutional framework for the legislative and executive branches. For the December 1993 Constitution to be adopted half of
the electorate must vote and the majority of those voters must vote in
favor of the Constitution.[24] According to official statistics, 54.8 percent of
the electorate voted; 58.4 percent of those voting (or 31 percent of the total
electorate) supported the Constitution, while 41.6 percent (or 22.1 percent
of the electorate) voted against it.[25] So, the Constitution was approved.[26]

As a result of the 'struggle for constitutional supremacy' between the
President and Parliament from 1990 to 1993, which culminated in
Yel'tsin forcibly dissolving Parliament and the following stand-off in the
White House from 21 September to 4 October 1993, Yel'tsin was deter-
mined to create a strong executive in the new Constitution. Thomas
Remington, a leading scholar on executive–legislative relations in Russia
since 1991, suggested that from 1990 to 1993

> neither group [side – the President or Parliament] was strong enough
> to impose its will on the other and each defended a different model of
> rule. Yel'tsin demanded a presidential republic with strong executive
> power; his preferred system, now enacted in a new constitution,
> resembles the French Fifth Republic. The forces opposing him [in
> Parliament] generally sought a system of parliamentary supremacy,
> with a weak presidency.[27]

After Yel'tsin disbanded Parliament on 21 September 1993, a federal legislative body did not exist to assist in drafting the new Constitution.
According to Anatoliy Sobchak, former Mayor of St Petersburg and a member of Yel'tsin's committee for drafting the new Constitution, the 1993
Constitution was produced by a committee overseen by Yel'tsin and was tai-
lored to his desire to create a system with a powerful President and a much
weaker legislature.[28] Indeed, Yel'tsin himself acknowledged this in an
interview with *Izvestiya*. He stated that the powers of the Russian President
in the new Constitution were 'indeed considerable ... but what can you
expect in a country accustomed to Tsars and leaders with extraordinarily
weak executive discipline and steeped in legal nihilism?'[29] To determine
the powers granted to the Russian President and Parliament in the 1993
Constitution, the Constitution must be examined in greater detail.

## Constitutional powers of the Russian President

According to the 1993 Russian Constitution, the President is the Head of
State, guarantor of the Constitution, and has the power to set the basic

guidelines for domestic and foreign policy.[30] He can nominate the Prime Minister (Chairman of the Government), who must then be approved by the State Duma, and can dismiss the entire Government or individuals in the Government. The Prime Minister nominates Deputy Prime Ministers and Federal Ministers, but the President officially appoints and dismisses them. Though the Government, which is a part of the executive branch, can issue resolutions and directives, the President can annul them if they contradict his decrees, federal laws, or the Constitution.[31] The President nominates judges, who must be approved by the Council of the Federation, to the Supreme Court, Higher Court of Arbitration, and Constitutional Court, which makes important decisions about the constitutionality of laws and decrees and other violations of the Constitution.[32] He also chooses his presidential staff.[33]

Moreover, he has vast powers relating to the military and foreign affairs. Not only does the Constitution designate him as the leader of foreign affairs, but he also signs international treaties, though they must be ratified by the Duma.[34] As President, he is the Supreme Commander-in-Chief of the Armed Forces and appoints and dismisses the Supreme Command of the Armed Forces. He forms and heads the Security Council. When deemed necessary, the President can introduce martial law or a state of emergency, in accordance with the procedures outlined in a federal constitutional law.[35] Quite a few of the procedures for how the President exercises his powers are stipulated by federal constitutional law, which must be passed by the legislature.[36]

Procedures for impeaching the President and transferring powers in his absence are vaguely worded in the Constitution, which made Parliament appeal to the Constitutional Court for clarification. The President can be removed from office in three ways: with an accusation from the Federation Council that he committed high treason or another serious crime, a decision by the Constitutional Court, or an allegation made by the State Duma and confirmed by the Supreme Court that the President committed criminal acts. The Constitution does not specify the conditions under which the President must resign. It is unclear what constitutes high treason or being totally unable to exercise his powers for reasons of health. Impeachment charges must be initiated by at least one-third of the Duma Deputies and decided upon by two-thirds of the total number of Duma Deputies and Council Members, following a finding by a special Duma commission. Council Members have three months to approve the Duma's decision to impeach the President, thereafter it is considered void.[37] If the President cannot exercise his powers for reasons of health, early resignation, or impeachment, the Prime Minister temporarily performs his duties. A presidential election must be held no later than three months after the termination of the President's powers.[38]

His powers relating to the Federal Assembly and the legislative process include the ability to submit draft laws, veto laws (but not a line-item veto), and sign and promulgate federal laws. Scheduling elections to the State Duma and dissolving the State Duma are further powers he wields over the lower house of Parliament. For the President to dissolve the Duma constitutionally (though he has also unconstitutionally disbanded the Duma, in 1993), the Duma must have expressed two votes of no-confidence in the Government within three months, voted no-confidence in the Government after the question was raised by the Prime Minister, or rejected the President's third nomination for Prime Minister.[39] In order to encourage some cooperation between the Duma and President, the President cannot dissolve the Duma during its first year in session, within six months of presidential elections, when martial law or a state of emergency is imposed, or when the Duma has brought an accusation against the President.[40] He can schedule referendums, but the procedure for doing this was established by a federal constitutional law and not stipulated in the Constitution.[41] Some academics claim that the Russian President is very powerful because he has unlimited decree power, though decrees cannot contradict federal laws or the Constitution.[42] Decrees are binding and are treated as law, but they expire when a new president is elected. Parliament can only 'override' them by passing a law that contradicts them. With these vast powers it is difficult to deny that the Russian President is constitutionally very powerful – exactly how powerful the President is relative to the Parliament will now be examined.

## Constitutional powers of Russia's Parliament

Even though the Federal Assembly, Russia's Parliament, is comprised of two chambers, the State Duma (lower) and Council of the Federation (upper), the State Duma is the main decision-making body as the Constitution states that the Council only functions on a part-time basis.[43] This does not mean that the Council of the Federation is powerless by any means, but only that its power in the policy process is much more limited than the Duma's by the infrequency of sessions and in the policy areas of laws it can approve. The introductory chapter to this study showed that many academics believe that Parliament is a very weak institution in Russia which does not have much power to influence substantial policy decisions. The accuracy of this statement will now be analyzed based on the constitutional powers of the Parliament and in later chapters by the actual powers it exercises.

State Duma Deputies are elected for four-year terms, but two federal constitutional laws passed in 1995 determined the procedure for electing Deputies and forming the Council of the Federation. Indeed, adopting these two constitutional laws was among the most important accomplishments of Parliament in its first provisional, two-year term of office. Since electoral laws and the structure of the legislative branch are part of the focus of the next chapter, they will be discussed in greater detail then, but it is worth noting them now as areas where Parliament had power to affect the policy process.

Both the Duma and Council are in charge of their own affairs and decide on their own rules and routine activities. They each elect their own Chairman and Vice-Chairmen to conduct the meetings. Occasionally, both chambers form joint and standing committees and hold parliamentary hearings on questions that fall under their jurisdiction.[44] Normally, though, they hold separate meetings.

The State Duma is the primary legislative body in Russia. All federal laws must first be submitted to the Duma and then adopted, with a majority vote, before they can pass to the Council and President for consideration. In addition to the President, the Government, legislative bodies in the 89 federal subjects, and the Constitutional and Supreme Courts, the State Duma (as a whole or individual Deputies) can also introduce draft laws for consideration.[45] Figure 2.3 illustrates the stages of the legislative process in Russia in greater detail.

Moreover, the Duma has important non-legislative powers according to the Constitution. It can appoint and dismiss the Chairman of the Central Bank of Russia, a Human Rights Commissioner, and the Chairman of the Accounting Office and half its auditors. Approving the President's nomination for Prime Minister is another important responsibility, but if the Duma rejects the President's choice three times, the President can dissolve the Duma and schedule new elections.[46] The State Duma also has the power to impeach the President, the procedure for which is outlined earlier in this chapter. Questions of no-confidence in the Government can be raised by the Duma with a majority vote of the total number of Deputies. After the Duma expresses a vote of no-confidence, the President can either disagree with it or dismiss the Government. But, if the Duma issues two votes of no-confidence in the Government within a three-month period, the President can either dismiss the Government or dissolve the Duma. The Prime Minister can also ask the Duma to vote on its confidence in the Government. If the majority of Deputies

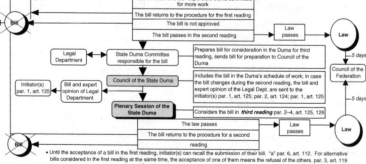

Legal subject (person or body) of the legislative initiative (initiator(s)) art. 103

Bill and complete documents par. 1–3, art. 105, 106

Department responsible for providing documentation — Registers documents and passes them to the Chairman of the State Duma   par. 1, art. 107

Associations (parties/factions) of deputies in the State Duma

Chairman of the State Duma — Sends documents to associations of deputies in the Duma and to the Duma committee responsible for issues discussed in the bill   par. 1, art. 107

Legal department

Committee of the State Duma — Determines if the bill corresponds to (actual) needs art. 104 of the Constitution of the Russian Federation and art. 105 of State Duma's Regulations;   par. 1, art. 107

— 14 days

Council of the State Duma — Returns the bill to its initiator(s) or appoints a committee responsible for the bill, includes the bill in the Duma's planned work, sends it to committees, commissions, deputies' associations and initiator(s), sets the date for presentation of opinions, suggestions, and remarks on the bill and date of the bill's preparation for the first reading; can send the bill with an expert's opinion to Government RF; organizes joint consideration of alternative bills.   par. 4, art. 105, art. 108, 109;   par. 2–4, art. 110

Initiator(s) art. 109 — Bill

Council of the Duma sets the time period

Opinions, suggestions and remarks

Legal Dept.

State Duma Committee responsible for the bill — Prepares the bill for consideration by the Duma in the first reading; sends bill to Council of the Duma, art. 111–114

Complete Documents art. 114

— for 14 days until submitting the bill for consideration in the State Duma

For 3 days until the Plenary session

Council of the State Duma — Introduces the bill for the State Duma's consideration; sends the bill to initiator(s) par. 1, art. 114; 'zh' par. 1, art. 114 and par. 1, art. 117

Initiator(s) par. 1, art. 117

Plenary Session of the State Duma — Considers the bill in the *first reading*   art. 118–119

The bill is not approved

Initiator(s) par. 7, art. 119 — Bill

The bill passes in the first reading — Law passes — Law

— 5 days

Bill is brought into discussion nationwide

Council of the Federation

Amendments art. 120

State Duma Committee responsible for the bill — Prepares bill for consideration in the Duma for the second reading, sends the documents for consideration of the bill to the Council of the State Duma art. 121; par. 1, art. 122

Legal Dept.

Complete Documents par. 1, art. 122

For 15 days until plenary session

Council of the State Duma — Includes the bill in the calendar for the consideration of questions by the State Duma, sends the bill to the initiator(s)   par. 2

Initiator(s) par. 3, art. 122

Plenary Session of the State Duma — Considers the bill in the *second reading*   art. 123

The bill returns to the responsible Duma committee for more work

The bill returns to the procedure for the first reading

The bill is not approved

The bill passes in the second reading — Law passes — Law

— 5 days

Council of the Federation

Legal Department

State Duma Committee responsible for the bill — Prepares bill for consideration in the Duma for third reading, sends bill for preparation to Council of the Duma

Council of the State Duma — Includes the bill in the Duma's schedule of work; in case the bill changes during the second reading, the bill and expert opinion of the Legal Dept. are sent to the initiator(s) par. 1, art. 125; par. 2, art. 124; par. 1, art. 125

Initiator(s) par. 1, art. 125

Bill and expert opinion of Legal Department

Plenary Session of the State Duma — Considers the bill in *third reading* par. 2–4, art. 125, 126

— 5 days

The law passes — Law passes — Law

The bill returns to the procedure for a second reading

• Until the acceptance of a bill in the first reading, initiator(s) can recall the submission of their bill. "a" par. 6, art. 112. For alternative bills considered in the first reading at the same time, the acceptance of one of them means the refusal of the others. par. 3, art. 119

Council of the Federation

Law is vetoed

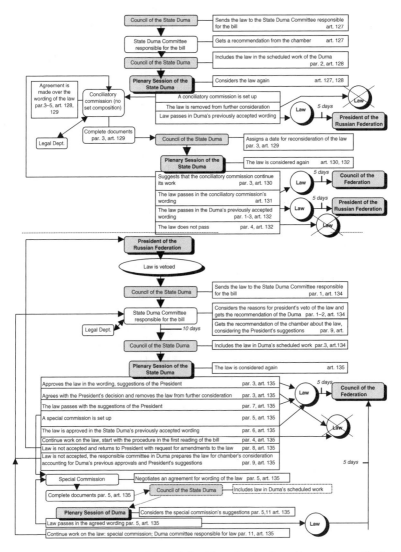

*Figure 2.3*   Passage and veto of draft federal laws by the State Duma, Council of the Federation and President (except bills about ratification, discontinuation, and suspension of Russia's active international treaties and bills of the federal budget).

- Cited articles above are from *Reglament: Gosudarstvennoy Dumy Federal'nogo Sobraniya Rossiyskoy Federatsi* (Moskva, Gosudarstvennoy Dumy, 1998).
- Author's translation of official document, 'Diagram of the Passage and Veto of Draft Federal Laws in the State Duma', Department for Analysis of the Legislative Process, State Duma, Russia. Author granted permission to use from Records Department, State Duma.

vote no-confidence, then the President must again choose to dissolve the Duma or Government within seven days, unless impeachment proceedings have started against the president or for any of the other reasons given above.[47] Decrees and resolutions can be adopted with a majority vote of the State Duma on questions within its jurisdiction.

Because the upper chamber, constitutionally, is a part-time body that meets, on average, less than twice a month (from 1996 to 1999),[48] its legislative responsibilities and powers are slightly less than the Duma's. The Council of the Federation or any of its Members can submit a draft law to the Duma for consideration. After the Duma approves a law, it is sent to the Council of the Federation which has 14 days to consider it. Half of the total number of Council Members must vote in favor of it for it to pass, but if it is not considered within 14 days, it is also considered to be approved. If the Council rejects the law, then a reconciliation commission is established to negotiate differences. The Duma can override the Council's veto of a law if at least two-thirds of the Deputies vote to override it.[49] As explained in the next chapter, Duma Deputies do not need to be present to vote. They can phone in their vote and a representative from their party will vote for them. This reduces the likelihood of the vote not passing because of the difficulty of two-thirds of the Deputies being present.

When the Duma and Council pass a law, the President has 14 days to sign or veto it. If he vetoes a law, the Duma and Council can override his veto with a two-thirds vote in favor of the law by the total number of Deputies and Council Members.[50] Again, Duma Deputies and Council Members do not need to be present to vote as long as they phone in their position on the matter. The President must then sign the law within seven days.

The Council has significant powers on non-legislative matters that are of importance. It has the ability to confirm the President's decrees on the introduction of martial law and state of emergency, schedule presidential elections, decide when to use the Armed Forces outside Russia, impeach the President, confirm border changes within Russia, and appoint judges to the Constitutional Court, Supreme Court, and Higher Court of Arbitration. For these matters under the Council's jurisdiction, it can issue resolutions, which are adopted by a majority vote.[51]

## Constitutional provisions for amending the Russian Constitution

Amending the 1993 Constitution is much more difficult than it was under the 1977 Soviet Constitution, which could be amended by a vote of at least two-thirds of the total number of Deputies in each of the Supreme Soviet's chambers.[52] The relative ease in amending the Constitution created problems between 1991 and 1993 when Parliament frequently amended the Constitution which increased tensions between the executive and legislative branches. To amend the 1993 Constitution, a proposal must be submitted by the President, Council of the Federation, State Duma, Government, legislative bodies of Russia's subjects, or a group of at least one-fifth of State Duma Deputies or Council of Federation Members.[53]

Based on the amendment procedures, it is much easier to amend Chapters 3 through 8 (on federal structure and the powers of the President, Parliament, Government, judicial branch, and local self-government, respectively) than Chapters 1 (fundamental rights), 2 (human rights), and 9 (amendment procedures). Amendments to Chapters 3 through 8 are made based on the procedure for adopting federal constitutional laws, which are laws that are adopted on issues stipulated in the Constitution and are superior to the other federal laws.[54] A federal constitutional law is adopted if three-fourths of the total number of Council of the Federation members and two-thirds of State Duma Deputies vote in favor of it. Before 1995, the President's signature was required, within 14 days, for it to be adopted.[55] In 1995, the Constitutional Court ruled that amendments cannot be vetoed by the President, making his signature unimportant.[56] In addition, amendments to Chapters 3 to 8 must be approved by at least two-thirds of the legislative bodies of Russia's 89 federal subjects,[57] each subject being able to determine its own voting procedures (the result of a ruling by the Constitutional Court).[58]

Amending Chapters 1, 2 and 9 is more difficult because they cannot be revised by the Federal Assembly, only by a decision of a Constitutional Assembly. Three-fifths of the total number of State Duma Deputies and Federation Council Members must first support the proposed amendment. Then, either the Constitutional Assembly adopts the amendment with a two-thirds vote of the total number of its members or it submits the amendment to a nationwide vote, where half of the electorate must participate and half of those voting must vote in favor of it for it to pass.[59] These procedures make it challenging to amend the present Constitution. Vil'yam Smirnov, a prominent scholar on executive power in Russia, explains that 'it is very difficult to change the Constitution, just as it is [difficult] to dismiss the President…There is almost no opportunity to change something in the Constitution even though there are still contradictions in the Constitution.'[60] Significant gaps and contradictions in the Constitution combined with the arduous process of amending it have 'triggered political struggles over whether or not, or how much, to amend the document'.[61] Attempts to adopt constitutional laws and amendments will be discussed in Chapter 4.

## Summary

The purpose of this chapter has been to present a model for assessing constitutional powers and then to determine the constitutional powers of the President and Parliament in Russia, using the 1993 Russian Constitution. The Troxel and Skach model suggests that Russia indeed has a semi-presidential system on the basis of the written powers of the President and Parliament. It remains to compare this finding with the analysis in the following chapters on the structural and actual powers of Russia's Parliament and President.

# 3
# Powers Inherent in the Structural Design of the Russian Presidency and Parliament

In Chapter 2, the constitutional powers of the Russian President and Parliament provided an initial framework for determining the executive and legislature's spheres of influence in the policy process and the type of political system in Russia. The political structure in a given country defines how and the extent to which a president and parliament can exercise their constitutional powers. Structural factors, such as the procedure for selecting the president and parliament, the composition and strength of political parties and committees and the length of sessions and autonomy of agenda-setting in the chamber, are examined in this chapter to further analyze the power of the President and Parliament in Russia.

The structural design of the presidency and parliament can hinder or enhance the use of constitutional powers. David Olson and Philip Norton maintain that:

> the extent to which a legislature is well organized and well equipped can affect its ability to participate in the policy process ... if it has some latitude for independent thought and action, its ability to take advantage of those opportunities is affected by the extent to which it is internally organized. The main means by which legislatures are internally organized are political parties and committees. Parties in democratic legislatures are usually few in number, large in size, and relatively 'strong', while committees tend to be more numerous, smaller in size and 'weak'.[1]

Both the ability of political parties to command a majority and form effective coalitions and the mandated size of parliamentary committees show the extent of parliament's power, on a structural level, to compete in the policy process. Empirical data on the Russian Parliament's committee structure and size, the frequency and duration of sessions, the number, size and strength of political parties, the timing of elections and the composition of Parliament will be compared with data on the executive branch's cabinet structure, the President's length of term and political association (if any) and the process of electing the President. The main aim of this chapter, then, is to evaluate how the internal power structure of the Russian Presidency and Parliament affects their overall powers.

## Definitions of political regimes based on structural factors

Political regimes cannot be classified or described accurately without considering structural factors. Structural factors employed to characterize systems vary between studies in the existing literature. In the introductory chapter leading definitions, such as Arend Lijphart's,[2] which apply structural criteria to definitions of regime type, were discussed. There are three apparent structural factors for creating a typology of political regimes: how the executive and legislature are selected (by voters or by another body),[3] whether the executive (either collegial or one-person) or legislature has a fixed electoral mandate or is dependent on the confidence of another body,[4] and whether the president and parliament heads the government.[5] The first two factors are the most widely accepted in the literature for classifying political systems on a structural basis. Amalgamating these theories, a presidential system, then, is one where the president is elected by voters, he/she is one-person who has a fixed mandate and is not dependent on legislative confidence, and he/she directs the government. In contrast, a parliamentary system has a collegial executive which is selected by the legislature and dependent on legislative confidence, and parliament heads the government. Systems with other combinations of these factors are considered to be 'mixed' or semi-presidential forms. On the basis of these factors alone, Russia would be considered presidential because the President controls the Government, is elected by the public, and has a fixed mandate, even though Parliament is also selected by voters and has a fixed mandate. Olson and Norton and Shugart and Carey extend their analysis of structural powers past mere definitions by examining the actual structure in which the legislature and executive function.[6] This approach is more comprehensive and accurate as the definitions one chooses to apply can affect the resulting regime type, as shown in Chapter 1. Only by examining the exact nature of structural powers, in addition to constitutional and actual powers, in a given country can we truly understand what type of political regime exists and how much power the executive and legislature have to influence the policy process.

I follow Olson and Norton in their assessment that structural powers can, along with constitutional and actual powers (or, what they define as attributes of policy), demonstrate 'the ability of legislatures to function actively and autonomously in the policy formation process of their respective democratic political system'.[7] But it is important to extend this analysis to the structural powers of the president. After all, parliamentary power is, in many respects, relative to other branches of power. It seems incomplete to consider it without explaining the president's structural powers. That is, if the president has little opposition in parliament, he/she is better able to ensure that his/her policy agendas are passed. Conversely, if parliament has a political party or coalition, with a majority of votes, which opposes the president, it is more likely that it will function as an independent body. Depending on the power of the president, it will negotiate with the president in some instances and adamantly uphold its own position in other circumstances. Only by considering the powers of both bodies can we truly understand the structural powers of the legislative branch in Russia.

Olson and Norton define parliament's structural powers (or what they refer to as internal characteristics) as a combination of the following three *principal* factors: (a) parliamentary parties: party system in the legislature; internal organization and decision-making; factionalism; relations among parties; (b) the chamber: length of sessions; autonomy of agenda setting; resources for chamber, parties, committees and members; (c) committees: number and size; permanence of jurisdiction and membership; relations to administrative agencies; and autonomy.[8] But they maintain that 'the main means by which legislatures are internally organized are political parties and committees'.[9] In this chapter, I will focus on political parties, committees and the chamber in relation to the Russian Presidency and Parliament to examine the structural powers of both bodies.

## Political parties in Russia

### The party system

The party system is influenced by a number of institutional factors.[10] One of the most important of these is the type of electoral system in a given country. As Reina Taagepera and Matthew Shugart note, 'an electoral system can make a difference in which party wins and how decisively it wins. It can also influence which losing parties can stay around to compete again and which are eliminated for good'.[11] The electoral system, because it can affect the strength of opposition parties and the political composition of parliament and the presidency, can, thereby, determine relations between the executive and legislature and the extent to which the presidency and parliament function effectively. Maurice Duverger found that electoral rules affect the party system. Duverger's law is that plurality systems tend to reduce the number of parties to two, while proportional representation (PR) systems tend to be associated with more parties.[12] More recently, Matthew Shugart and John Carey observed that '*two* variables are critical in shaping the nature of the party system: electoral rules and electoral cycles'.[13] Electoral cycles refer to the timing of elections. Concurrent elections occur when the president and parliament are elected at the same time, whereas nonconcurrent elections are when the presidential and parliamentary elections are scheduled for different times. The timing of elections influences the political party or parties elected to the presidency and parliament because Shugart and Carey prove that 'the institutional design of plurality presidency and concurrent assembly by PR tends to support two major parties, plus some minor parties ... [while,] the holding of congressional elections apart from presidential elections encouraged parties to run independently of the presidents' parties [which resulted in more than two parties competing separately for the presidency and parliament]'.[14] The electoral rules and electoral cycles in Russia will be discussed in the next section.

## Electoral rules and cycles: Parliamentary and Presidential elections in Russia

### Parliamentary elections in Russia

The procedure for electing State Duma Deputies and Council of the Federation Members in December 1993 was established by a group of politicians, headed by Duma Deputy Viktor Sheynis.[15] This later became the basis of Yel'tsin's decree on 21 September 1993 on electing a Parliament.[16] The 1993 Russian Constitution established a four-year term for Duma Deputies and the President, but the Council of Federation Members' terms were to be decided in their respective regions.[17] Since the Council of the Federation is comprised of one executive head and one legislative leader from each of Russia's 89 regions, its Members are not directly elected in federal elections but are elected in regional elections, with the regional legislature deciding what positions will represent the region in the Council.[18] The Duma and President are directly elected, but in two different procedures.

A combined electoral system of PR and plurality votes determines the composition of the Duma. One-half (225) of the seats are allocated through registered parties' lists on a proportional basis of the votes that the party receives in elections, as long as the party obtains at least 5 percent of the vote. The other half (225) of Deputies are selected from a plurality vote in single-member constituencies.[19] A Deputy can run in both party list and single-member districts but must concede his/her party list position if he/she wins a seat via the plurality vote. Once elected, Deputies have the option of becoming affiliated with a political party. Table 3.1 illustrates that four new parties, Russia's Way, New Regional Policy, December 12 and Russia's Regions, were formed after the 1993 and 1995 elections by independents, Deputies from small parties and Deputies elected from single-member districts to gain full Duma privileges. Also, the table shows that a significant number of Deputies changed party affiliation in the months following the elections. This is because in order to be a registered party, factions must have at least 35 Deputies. Being a registered party is of great importance as it determines whether the faction is represented in committees and on the Council of the Duma, a Deputy's priority for recognition by the floor to speak during a session, and funding for staff and office expenses. According to Robert Moser, these electoral rules

> had very different and important consequences, advantaging or undermining parties as the chief vehicle of electoral competition and helping to determine winners and losers ... The electoral system has actually helped to establish or undermine the centrality of parties in the electoral arena. Just as creators of the electoral system had hoped, the PR system quickly established parties and electoral blocs as the central agents for structuring the electorate's voting choice ... Secondly, the electoral system has had a significant influence on the level of support for specific parties in Russia ... The LDPR provides the most dramatic example of how the electoral system shaped the distribution of power among parties [in 1993]. Without the PR half of Russia's electoral system the LDPR would not exist as a significant player in Russian politics. The Agrarian Party provides the opposite case. Its survival as a parliamentary party was sustained only because of its prowess in the plurality election.[20]

Table 3.1  Parliamentary election results, December 1993 and 1995

| Faction | 1993 PR party list | | | 1993 single-member constituencies | | 1993 total | | ***Total after changes in party affiliation in 1994 | | 1995 PR party list | | | 1995 single-member constituencies | | 1995 total | | ***Total after changes in party affiliation in 1996 | |
|---|---|---|---|---|---|---|---|---|---|---|---|---|---|---|---|---|---|---|
| | Vote % | Seats | % Seats | Seats | % Seats | Seats | % Seats | Seats | % Seats | Vote % | Seats | % Seats | Seats | % Seats | Seats* | % Seats* | Seats | % Seats |
| Russia's Choice | 15.5 | 40 | 17.8 | 30 | 13.3 | 70 | 15.6 | 73 | 16.2 | 3.9 | 0 | 0.0 | 9 | 4.0 | 9 | 2.0 | 0 | 0.0 |
| Liberal Democratic Party of Russia | 22.9 | 59 | 26.2 | 5 | 2.2 | 64 | 14.2 | 64 | 14.2 | 11.2 | 50 | 22.2 | 1 | 0.4 | 51 | 11.3 | 51 | 11.3 |
| Communist Party of the Russian Federation | 12.4 | 32 | 14.2 | 16 | 7.1 | 48 | 10.7 | 45 | 10.0 | 22.3 | 99 | 44.0 | 58 | 25.8 | 157 | 34.9 | 147 | 32.7 |
| Agrarian Party of Russia | 8.0 | 21 | 9.3 | 12 | 5.3 | 33 | 7.3 | 55 | 12.2 | 3.8 | 0 | 0.0 | 20 | 8.9 | 20 | 4.4 | 37 | 8.2 |
| Women of Russia | 8.1 | 21 | 9.3 | 2 | 0.9 | 23 | 5.1 | 23 | 5.1 | 4.6 | 0 | 0.0 | 3 | 1.3 | 3 | 0.7 | 0 | 0.0 |
| Yabloko | 7.9 | 20 | 8.9 | 3 | 1.3 | 23 | 5.1 | 28 | 6.2 | 6.9 | 31 | 13.8 | 14 | 6.2 | 45 | 10.0 | 46 | 10.2 |
| Party of Russian Unity and Accord | 6.8 | 18 | 8.0 | 1 | 0.4 | 19 | 4.0 | 30 | 6.7 | 0.4 | 0 | 0.0 | 1 | 0.4 | 1 | 0.2 | 0 | 0.0 |
| Democratic Party of Russia | 5.5 | 14 | 6.2 | 1 | 0.4 | 15 | 3.3 | 15 | 3.3 | | | | | | | | | |
| Democratic Reform Movement | 4.1 | 0 | 0.0 | 4 | 1.7 | 4 | 0.9 | 0 | 0.0 | | | | | | | | | |

| | | | | | | | | | |
| --- | --- | --- | --- | --- | --- | --- | --- | --- | --- |
| Dignity and Charity | 0.7 | 0 | 0.0 | 2 | 0.9 | | 0.4 | 0 | 0.0 |
| Civic Union | 1.9 | 0 | 0.0 | 1 | 0.4 | | 0.2 | 0 | 0.0 |
| Russia's Future | 1.3 | 0 | 0.0 | 1 | 0.4 | | 0.2 | 0 | 0.0 |
| New Regional Policy** | | | | | | 66 | 14.7 | | 0.0 |
| December 12** | | | | | | 26 | 5.8 | | 0.0 |
| Russia's Way** | | | | | | 14 | 3.1 | | 0.0 |
| Our Home is Russia | 10.1 | 45 | 20.0 | 10 | 4.4 | 55 | 12.2 | 66 | 14.7 |
| Russia's Regions** | | | | | | | | 42 | 9.3 |
| People's Power | 1.6 | 0 | 0.0 | 9 | 4.0 | 9 | 2.0 | 38 | 8.4 |
| Independents | | | | 78 | 34.7 | 78 | 17.3 | 23 | 5.1 |
| | | | | 141 | 64.4 | 141 | 31.3 | 11 | 2.4 |

* Deputies changed party affiliation in 1994 and 1996 because parties need 35 members for full privileges in the State Duma. Parties which originally won seats but whose deputies later left are not listed because 16 parties received between 1 and 9 seats but all elected members of these parties changed party affiliation after the 1995 election.

** Russia's Way, New Regional Policy and December 12 after the 1993 election and Russia's Regions after the 1995 election were formed by independents and deputies from small parties to gain full Duma privileges.

*** *Rossiyskaya gazeta*, 28 December 1993, p. 1 and 6 January 1996, p. 4–7. See *Spisok deputatov Gosudarstvennoi Dumy* (Moscow: Gosudarstvennaya Duma, 1996) for details about changes in affiliation after the 1993 and 1995 elections. Only those parties which gained seats are shown, though other parties received a small percentage of the vote.

The actual effect of the electoral rules on the outcomes of parliamentary elections in Russia is worth careful consideration.

Clearly, from Table 3.1, the electoral system with a separate party list and single district voting affects the political composition of the Duma. In each election, more Deputies elected under the plurality system are independents than from any other party. In 1993, 64.4 percent of Deputies and in 1995, 34.7 percent of those elected in the plurality vote were independents. The decrease in independent Deputies, from 1993 to 1995, elected under the single mandate system shows an increase in party development because an increasing number of Deputies in 1995 chose to associate themselves with a specific party prior to elections. Still, most of the independents formed their own parties or joined an established political party after the elections because of the advantages of being a registered party.

The 5 percent barrier, which all parties on the party list must obtain in order to be represented in the Duma, noticeably reduced the number of parties in 1993 and 1995. In the 1993 elections, eight parties passed the threshold, while only four parties did in 1995. The barrier helped to consolidate the number of parties gaining seats as seven parties in 1993 and 39 parties in 1995 won less than 5 percent of the vote in the party lists and did not gain seats by this means. So, the 5 percent barrier had the effect of eliminating small parties. It also hurt the power of liberal reform parties, those supporting democracy and market reform, in Parliament. Because these parties were fractionalized into various smaller parties, the 5 percent barrier resulted in Yabloko, with 5.1 percent of the seats, Russia's Choice, with 15.6 percent of the seats and the Party of Russian Unity and Accord, with 4 percent of the seats, being the only liberal reform parties to win seats in the party lists in 1993, with a total of 24.7 percent of Duma seats. Democratic Reform Movement polled only 4.1 percent of the vote and thus, it did not earn any seats in the Duma from the party list. Even though the pro-democracy group called the 'Liberal Democratic Union of December 12' was formed following the 1993 parliamentary election, it only constituted 5.8 percent of all seats. Liberal reform parties, after changes in party affiliation in 1994, had a total of 34.9 percent of the seats in the Duma. This is rather insignificant when the opposition and centrist parties won 62.6 percent of the seats, the remaining 2.4 percent belonging to independents. Since a simple majority vote of 50 percent is needed to pass bills in the Duma and a two-thirds majority is needed to override the President's or Council's veto, the opposition parties had a clear advantage.

In the 1995 election, even more liberal reform parties were unable to pass the 5 percent barrier. Yabloko, with 10 percent of the seats, and Our Home is Russia, with 12.2 percent of the seats, were the only two to have seats in the Duma. The pro-democracy group named 'Russia's Regions' was formed after the 1995 election by independents and Deputies from small parties, but it only had 9.3 percent of seats. Liberal reform parties held 34.2 percent of seats in 1996, accounting for changes in party affiliation. Similar to 1993, oppositionist groups controlled 60.6 percent of the seats, although now this was consolidated in four parties (an advantage for coalition-building). More importantly, numerous liberal reform parties won a small percentage of the vote but did not achieve 5 percent: Russia's Choice, with 3.9 percent; Russian Unity and Accord, with 0.4 percent; Christian Democratic Union, with 0.3 percent; and many others. If some of these parties had merged before the elections, democrats would have had greater representation and power in the Duma. Deputy Viktor Sheynis, author of the Duma's electoral law, maintained that the 5 percent barrier hurt pro-democracy parties for two reasons.

> First, the general weakness of democratic parties and, second, the inability to unite, as a result of which a significant amount of votes of democratic electors were lost. The votes were dispersed, but according to the law, 5 percent was required for overcoming the barrier. But, the smallest ambitious groups split the votes of democratic voters. This led to a weakening of the position of democratic parties in the Duma after the 1995 elections.[21]

It is clear that proportional representation leads to multipartism with several parties holding dominant roles, while the plurality system tends to favor bipartism with one group or two groups winning most seats and a few going to very small parties.[22] Electoral rules, along with electoral cycles, define the nature of the political system.

Electoral cycles facilitated the consolidation of political parties. A fractionalization calculation is the best method for determining the level of consolidation.[23] This is because fractionalization is the degree to which the party system is dominated by a few parties or divided among many parties. When fractionalization is relatively stable over time, the balance of strength between parties in the system is also relatively constant. In the second Russian parliamentary elections held in December 1995, only four political parties won seats in the Duma, whereas 12 parties won seats in 1993. After changes in party affiliation, there were 11 parties in 1993 (excluding independents) in the Duma and seven parties in 1995 (see Table 3.1). Still, more than one-quarter of Duma Deputies were re-elected, with 93 from single-member districts and 62 from party lists winning seats both in the 1993 and 1995 elections. An even better measure for assessing the consolidation of parties is the decline in the number of effective parties from 1993 to 1995. Using the Laakso–Taagepera index, we can determine the degree of fractionalization and number of significant, or 'effective', parties.[24] The index measures each party's relative size using the percentage of seats it holds. The formula is

$$N = \frac{1}{\sum_{i=1}^{n} p_i^2}$$

where $N$ is the number of effective parties with $p_i$ being the percentage of seats held by the $i$th party.[25] Political parties in the Duma appear to be greatly fractionalized when compared to other legislatures. The country with the closest degree of fragmentation to Russia after the 1993 elections is Belgium, with seven effective parties. Russia's score of 9.09 is highly unusual for most other legislatures in the world. After the 1995

*Table 3.2*   Effective number of parties contesting parliamentary and presidential elections

|  | Year |  | Effective number of parties | Total number of parties |
|---|---|---|---|---|
| Russia – Parliament ($N_p$) | 1995 |  | 5.66 | 8 |
|  | 1993 |  | 9.09 | 12 |
| Russia – President ($N_v$) | 1996 | (Round 1) | 3.89 | 10 |
|  |  | (Round 2) | 2.21 | 2 |
| *For Comparison – Parliament ($N_p$)*[a] |  |  |  |  |
| United States – Congress |  |  | 1.9 |  |
| France |  |  | 3.2 |  |
| Portugal |  |  | 3.6 |  |
| Switzerland |  |  | 5.4 |  |
| Belgium |  |  | 7.0 |  |

[a] Calculated by Alfred Stepan and Cindy Skach, 'Constitutional Framework and Democratic Consolidation: Parliamentarism versus Presidentialism', *World Politics* 46, 1 (October 1993): 8, table 1. Stepan and Skach calculate the effective number of parties in 44 countries but since the article was published in 1993, the 1993 and later Russian elections are not included in their analysis.

*Source*: Author calculated the data using the Laakso and Taagepera index formula. Markku Laakso and Rein Taagepera, 'Effective Number of Parties: A Measure with Application to West Europe', *Comparative Political Studies* 12, 1 (1979): 3–27.

elections, I found that the number of significant parties declined to 5.66 which is much closer to Switzerland (5.4) and Finland (5.1), as calculated by Stepan and Skach.[26] Still, even at 5.66, Russia has a highly fragmented party system. The effect of this is that there is not a majority in Parliament, which makes coalition-building very important.

Coalitions are an essential way of securing enough votes on an issue to ensure its passage or rejection by parliament. The 1996–98 Parliament has been more effective at organizing coalitions than the 1994–95 Parliament primarily because the Communist Party received such a high percentage of the vote in 1995 (32.7 percent), which is greater than the percentage of all democratic parties combined. Due to similarities in ideology and anti-Yel'tsin party platforms, the Communist Party formed a coalition with People's Power and the Agrarian Party, yielding a combined total of 49.3 percent of the seats in the Duma. If just three of the 23 independents or Deputies from other parties vote in line with this coalition, any bill can be passed (a 50 percent vote of all Deputies is required), assuming the coalition votes go according to party line. This is a powerful bargaining tool for Parliament against the President. When the Communist–Agrarian–People's Power coalition couple their votes with the other opposition parties of Yabloko (10.2 percent) and Russia's Regions (9.3 percent), they can override vetoes of the President or Council of the Federation with a 68.8 percent vote (a 66 percent majority vote is required). This gives the Duma great bargaining power since the President is not associated with any party and the only pro-Government party is Our Home is Russia, with 14.7 percent of seats. Often, the Liberal Democratic Party of Russia, while claiming to be oppositionist, maintains a pro-Government stance on issues and it is usually the first party, after Our Home is Russia, to negotiate or bargain with the President and/or Government.

Coalitions in the 1994–95 Parliament were much more difficult to form because the seats were more evenly dispersed between parties. Russia's Choice received the most seats, but this was only 16.2 percent of the total. As previously mentioned, democratic parties held 34.9 percent of seats, while the main opposition parties (Liberal Democratic Party, more anti-Government in their voting patterns before the 1995 elections, Communist Party, Agrarian Party and Russia's Way) gathered 39.5 percent of seats. The deciding votes in most cases belonged to the centrist parties of Women of Russia, Democratic Party of Russia, New Regional Policy and the independents, which together controlled 25.6 percent of Parliament.[27] Moreover, since most of the parties were only just formed in late 1993, strong alliances between parties did not have much time to develop in the first Duma which only had a two-year term. Party ideology, bargaining and personal contacts take time to become established and institutionalized. Thus, greater fragmentation and ideological division among parties, along with the newness of the parties themselves, caused coalitions to be less powerful from 1994 to 1995.

Another important consideration is the disproportionality in election results in Russia. Disproportionality is a calculation of the share of votes to the share of seats a party obtains. Taagepera and Shugart devised a formula, $D = (0.5) \Sigma |S_i - V_i|$, for calculating disproportionality where D is the measure of disproportionality, $\Sigma$ is the summation over all parties involved, $S_i$ is the percentage of seats held by the $i$th party and $V_i$ is the percentage of votes received by the $i$th party.[28] Since there was only one presidential race between 1994 and 1999 we cannot accurately judge disproportionality at the presidential level. The State Duma is extremely disproportional, as shown in Table 3.3. When taken as a percentage and analyzed against other systems, the disproportionality in Russia of 49 percent in 1995 is the highest level of any country holding democratic PR elections.[29] France is the only country with a relatively similar level of disproportionality because their electoral law excluded extreme right

*Table 3.3*   Disproportionality in election results

|  | Year | Percentage of disproportionality |
| --- | --- | --- |
| Russia | 1995 | 49 |
|  | 1993 | 15 |
| *For comparison:*[a] |  |  |
| France | 1993 | 41 |
| Poland | 1993 | 34 |
| Hungary | 1994 | 22 |
| Romania | 1992 | 19 |
| Britain | 1992 | 17 |
| United States | 1992 | 9 |
| Western Europe PR mean |  | 6 |

[a] Richard Rose, *What is Europe?* (New York: Longman, 1996), table 8.3. Rose calculated disproportionality in European and other Western countries. These results are used for comparison.

*Source*: Author calculated the data from Table 3.1 using the Rein Taagepera and Matthew Shugart measure of disproportionality (*Seats and Votes: The Effects and Determinants of Electoral Systems* (New Haven: Yale University Press, 1989)).

and left-wing parties. A score of 15 for Parliament after the 1993 elections is consistent with that of most Western countries. As previously mentioned, this is because more parties won seats and the votes were more evenly dispersed between parties. Table 3.1 shows the great disproportionality in the 1995 elections, as the Communist Party won more than twice as many seats as any other party and the seats among other parties were unevenly distributed. Duverger found that disproportionality is the factor which would induce underrepresented parties to dissolve.[30] If this were true, one would expect that with the current extreme level of disproportionality, in the next parliamentary elections in December 1999 fewer parties would win seats. This would be very beneficial because it would, most likely, reduce the degree of fragmentation by lowering the number of effective parties. As a result, coalitions would be easier to form and the Duma as a whole would be more efficient, thereby increasing its bargaining power with the President and Government.[31] The discussion of coalitions proved that this has held true from the increase in disproportionality from 1993 to 1995, which aided the creation of a majority coalition in the Duma.

One problem with fragmentation and disproportionality indexes is that they do not indicate whether support for each party came from the same group of voters. The scores do not take account of instances when, for example, all Liberal Democratic supporters voted for the Communist Party in alternate elections. In relation to shifting voters, volatility is the degree to which electoral results by party are stable from one election to the next.[32] The measure of volatility, developed by Adam Przeworski and John Sprague, represents the net transfer of votes from one party to another between two elections. It is found by taking the absolute value of the sum of the percentage of votes added or lost by each party in the current election, as compared to the previous election, and dividing by two.[33] A new party adds all of its votes, while an old party subtracts all of its previous votes. For example, if Yabloko won 15 percent in 1993 and 20 percent in 1995 of the vote, then five would be added to the difference in electoral results for the other parties and then divided by two. Russia is highly volatile because a score of 47.1 is significantly greater than any other democracy; only Japan (1948 to 1959) with 37.4 comes close, as illustrated in Table 3.4. This extreme volatility can be explained by the disproportionality and fractionalization of the system, since the greater the percentage of fractionalization and disproportionality, the higher the level of volatility. It will take several electoral cycles for the volatility to significantly decrease because successive elections enable a political party to establish credibility and support at both federal and

*Table 3.4*   Volatility of democratic party systems

| Country | Volatility |
|---------|------------|
| Russia (1993–95) | 47.1 |
| *For comparison:*[a] | |
| United States | 3.2 |
| France | 10.6 |
| Japan (1948–59) | 37.4 |

[a] Calculated by Russell Dalton, Scott Flanagan, James Alt and Paul Beck, *Electoral Changes in Advanced Industrial Democracies: Realignment or Dealignment?* (Princeton: Princeton University Press, 1984), 10. This is provided for comparison.

*Source*: Author calculated the data from Table 3.1 using a measure developed by Adam Przeworski and John Sprague, *Paper Stones: A History of Electoral Socialism* (Chicago: University of Chicago Press, 1986).

local levels. This is particularly what helped the Communist Party to gain the largest percentage of the vote in 1995, as it was the most organized party with a developed system of party branches and networks in regional areas.[34] Therefore, after several more parliamentary elections in Russia, the degree of fragmentation, disproportionalism and volatility should decrease substantially.

### Presidential elections in Russia

Although Parliament is elected by plurality and PR, the presidential race is solely determined by plurality vote. Requiring two rounds of voting, the two presidential candidates with the highest percentages of the vote in the first round advance to a second, run-off round. In the second round, a candidate must secure at least 50 percent plus one vote to be elected. Table 3.5 shows that Yel'tsin won the second round of the 1996 presidential election with 53.8 percent of the vote.[35] Tables 3.5 and 3.6 illustrate that the two-round plurality system encourages many candidates to run in the first round, while the second round is bipartisan in nature. Indeed, Duverger found in his seminal study of political parties that majority runoffs are associated with multiparty systems.[36] The presidential and parliamentary elections from 1994 to 1999 were scheduled at different, or nonconcurrent, times of the year. Parliamentary elections took place in December 1993 and 1995, as the first parliament was given a two-year trial period. Presidential elections were held in June and July 1996.

*Table 3.5*  First-round presidential election results, 16 June 1996

| Candidates | Percentage vote |
|---|---|
| Boris Yel'tsin, Independent | 35.3 |
| Gennadiy Zyuganov, Communist Party | 32.0 |
| Aleksandr Lebed, Independent | 14.5 |
| Grigoriy Yavlinskiy, Yabloko Party | 7.3 |
| Vladimir Zhirinovskiy, Liberal Democratic Party | 5.7 |
| Svyatoslav Fedorov, Workers' Self-Government Party | 0.9 |
| Mikhail Gorbachev, International Fund for Socioeconomic and Political Research | 0.5 |
| Martin Shakkum, Socioeconomic Reform Party | 0.4 |
| Yuriy Vlasov, National Patriotic Party | 0.2 |
| Vladimir Bryntsalov, Russian Socialist Party | 0.2 |
| Against all candidates | 1.5 |
| Total valid vote | 68.7 |

Source: *Rossiyskaya gazeta*, 22 June 1996, 1.

*Table 3.6*  Second-round presidential election results, 3 July 1996

| Candidates | Percentage vote |
|---|---|
| Boris Yel'tsin, Independent | 53.8 |
| Gennadiy Zyuganov, Communist Party | 40.3 |
| Against all candidates | 4.8 |
| Total valid vote | 68.1 |

Source: *Rossiyskaya gazeta*, 10 July 1996, 1.

Electoral cycles and electoral rules in Russia had a devastating effect on executive–legislative relations. According to Shugart and Carey:

> because PR encourages a multiparty system, some presidents under plurality rule may be endorsed by considerably less than a majority. Ironically, however, majority runoff, the institutional fix frequently chosen to redress this problem, tends to increase fragmentation rather than induce consensus. Worse, it makes lack of presidential-congressional harmony highly likely, as do nonconcurrent electoral cycles.[37]

Thus, nonconcurrent elections and majority runoffs increase both fragmentation and the likelihood that the president and the majority or largest political party in Parliament are from different parties. This is particularly evident from Table 3.2 where the effective number of parties in the presidential race ($N_p$) was 3.89 and in the parliamentary elections ($N_v$), 9.09 and 5.66 in 1993 and 1995, respectively. Shugart and Carey found similar results of this disparity between the effective number of parties in presidential and parliamentary elections when they were held nonconcurrently. The average difference between $N_v$ and $N_p$ in democratic systems was 2.3, which Shugart and Carey call 'enormous'.[38] In Russia, the difference between $N_v$ and $N_p$ was 5.2 in the 1993 elections and 1.77 in the 1995 vote. The former is a remarkable figure in that only Chile from 1933 to 1973 came close to this level of fragmentation with a disparity of 4.2. Nonconcurrent elections with majority runoffs encourage party systems for the two branches that are almost entirely different from one another.[39] This was precisely the result in Russia.

There are, however, advantages to the two branches being composed of different parties. Although similar parties in both branches would tend to mean that the President and Parliament cooperated regularly and there would be less conflict, the oppositionist-led Duma and the pro-reform President has the effect of enabling Parliament to function as an independent body. Indeed, even though the Communist–Agrarian–People's Power bloc sometimes fails to obtain the two-thirds majority vote necessary to overturn the President's veto,[40] if the President and the party with a majority in Parliament were of the same party, Parliament would probably be a rubber-stamp body, given the constitutional powers of the President in Russia. Opposition parties in the Duma at least attempt to challenge the power of the President and Government. With a President who strives to be 'all-powerful', a Parliament which supports the President would just give him more power and it would be just an extension of the executive branch.

## Legislative and executive committees

The importance of stable, permanent committees in a legislature and executive, as a means of enabling each branch to be more autonomous, is well established in the existing literature. Olson and Norton explain that:

> committees vary greatly, with two attributes defining their ability to function in the policy process. Committees which are permanent rather than temporary, and committees which parallel rather than cross-cut the administrative structure, have increased ability to both know and act in the policy process independently of the executive.

Committees can also facilitate greater independence in that partisanship can be relaxed. The lack of publicity, relative to the chamber, may permit greater candor in voice and vote, personal friendships may form across party lines and working together over time may encourage a common view to develop. Such committees can also become means by which parties negotiate with one another ... Where committees are permanent, continuing service by incumbents may build up both a collective expertise and a more independent ethos. The absence of such characteristics may limit the capacity of committees to operate independently.[41]

Although Olson and Norton refer to the power of legislative committees as improving the legislature's 'ability to function in the policy process', I believe that the same is true for executive committees. Any structural framework, whether in the legislature or executive, which is permanent, facilitates negotiations, is relatively nonpartisan, and serves to divide the functions of the branch into specialized committees which parallel the administrative structure would tend to improve the organization, bargaining power and ability to participate in policy-making. Indeed, when executive committees are similar in focus and work to the same or similar ends as legislative committees, negotiations and relations between branches would be inclined to improve.

### Standing committees in the State Duma

The State Duma elected in December 1993 voted to have 23 permanent standing committees, varying in size from 10 to 43 members, with the Chairman, Vice-Chairmen and members from different political parties. Standing committees are intended to be substructures which debate and consider legislation before submitting it to the floor of the Duma for a first reading. Amendments are first considered in the committees and then included in the second reading of a bill. These two functions make the committees an important initial stage in the policy process. Duma committee members can decide whether a bill will be debated during a given parliamentary session. This gives Deputies the power to postpone debates on legislation they disagree with, which can affect their current position or their power, or when they hope to gain something (concessions) by delaying the debates. For example, in the case of the START II Treaty, debates were delayed for over five years, despite Yel'tsin's repeated requests for the Duma to ratify the treaty. This, also, partly explains why some of the provisions in the 1993 Russian Constitution which must be determined by a federal constitutional law have still not been passed or decided on.

Committees in the Duma are specifically structured to provide checks and balances between parties, coalitions and power.[42] According to Oleg Medvedev:

> in distributing key parliamentary posts, the members of the State Duma tried to create an intrachamber system of checks and balances in order to provide the maximum insurance against dominance by one bloc or another. The influence of speaker Ivan Rybkin, from the Agrarian Communist bloc, is held in check by the counterinfluence of his first Deputy, Mikhail Mityukov [Russia's Choice] and by the committee on organizing the work of the State Duma, headed by Vladimir Bauer [Russia's Choice]. If a committee is headed by a figure who has irreconcilable opponents, an antagonist to that figure is included in the committee's Vice-Chairmen. For example, Mikhail Poltoranin is balanced by the Communist Gennadiy Seleznyov, and the Communist Viktor Ilyukhin is balanced by Viktor Pimenov, a radical Deputy from Russia's Choice.[43]

Committee positions were distributed using a token system. Parties were given tokens in relation to the percentage of seats they won. Chairmanships of committees would be worth more tokens than Deputy Chairman positions, with committee membership being worth the least amount. Faction and party leaders are not on any of the standing committees because they are represented separately in the Council of the Duma. As a result, the total number of Deputies on committees is 430 instead of 450. Table 3.7 shows how membership in the Duma's committees was divided among factions and parties. Russia's Choice, the party which won the most parliamentary seats in 1993, has the greatest number of Deputies on committees. The table is based on membership in political parties in August 1995 because Deputies changed parties between January 1994 and August 1995 (see Table 3.1). Still, the largest parties in the Duma have the most Chairmen and Deputy Chairmen of committees.

There is also a correlation between policy issues, political parties and representation in certain committees. If a party's platform centers around one or more specific policy issues which come under the heading of one of the committees, that political party will have a large representation on the given committee and most likely, the Chairman will come from that party. The Agrarian Party's platform is largely concerned

Table 3.7  State Duma committee membership by faction, 1994–95

| Committee | Political faction | | | | | | | | | | | | |
|---|---|---|---|---|---|---|---|---|---|---|---|---|---|
| | Russia's choice | Liberal Democratic Party | New regional policy | Agrarian Party | Communist Party | Party for stability | Party of Russian Unity and accord | Yabloko | Women of Russia | Democratic Party of Russia | Liberal Democratic Union – Dec. 12 | Independent | Total |
| Agrarian Questions | 2 | 1 | 1 | 20 | 1 | 1 | 0 | 0 | 0 | 0 | 0 | 0 | 26 |
| Budget, Taxes, Banks, and Finance | 5 | 4 | 9 | 4 | 2 | 5 | 4 | 3 | 2 | 1 | 4 | 0 | 43 |
| CIS and Liaisons with Compatriots | 1 | 1 | 0 | 1 | 2 | 1 | 3 | 2 | 1 | 0 | 0 | 1 | 13 |
| Defense | 3 | 3 | 2 | 1 | 2 | 0 | 0 | 1 | 1 | 1 | 0 | 1 | 15 |
| Ecology | 1 | 4 | 1 | 0 | 0 | 2 | 0 | 1 | 0 | 0 | 0 | 5 | 14 |
| Economic Policy | 2 | 2 | 5 | 2 | 1 | 1 | 1 | 3 | 1 | 1 | 3 | 1 | 23 |
| Education and Science | 6 | 2 | 6 | 1 | 2 | 1 | 1 | 2 | 2 | 0 | 0 | 1 | 24 |
| Federation Affairs and Regional Policy | 5 | 1 | 2 | 1 | 2 | 0 | 2 | 0 | 0 | 1 | 0 | 3 | 17 |
| Geopolitical Affairs | 1 | 6 | 1 | 0 | 1 | 3 | 0 | 0 | 1 | 0 | 0 | 1 | 14 |
| Health Care | 1 | 0 | 1 | 1 | 1 | 1 | 0 | 0 | 3 | 3 | 0 | 0 | 11 |
| Industry, Construction, Transportation, and Energy | 2 | 6 | 5 | 0 | 3 | 3 | 3 | 1 | 0 | 1 | 0 | 2 | 26 |
| Information Policy and Communications | 4 | 2 | 1 | 1 | 4 | 0 | 0 | 2 | 0 | 0 | 0 | 0 | 14 |
| International Affairs | 4 | 5 | 3 | 1 | 3 | 1 | 2 | 2 | 1 | 1 | 2 | 1 | 26 |
| Labour and Social Support | 2 | 2 | 1 | 1 | 3 | 1 | 1 | 2 | 1 | 0 | 0 | 0 | 14 |

Table 3.7 continued

| Committee | Political faction | | | | | | | | | | | | |
|---|---|---|---|---|---|---|---|---|---|---|---|---|---|
| | Russia's choice | Liberal-Democratic Party | New regional policy | Agrarian Party | Communist Party | Party for stability | Party of Russian Unity and accord | Yabloko | Women of Russia | Democratic Party of Russia | Liberal Democratic Union – Dec. 12 | Independent | Total |
| Legislation and Judicial-Legal Reform | 4 | 2 | 2 | _2_ | 1 | 1 | 1 | 3 | 1 | 0 | 0 | 2 | 19 |
| Local Self-Government | 1 | 0 | 3 | 3 | 2 | 0 | _3_ | 0 | 0 | 1 | 2 | 1 | 16 |
| Nationality Affairs | 3 | 0 | 2 | 0 | 1 | 4 | 2 | 0 | 0 | 0 | 0 | 1 | 11 |
| Natural Resources and Environmental Management | 1 | 2 | 1 | 3 | 1 | 1 | 1 | 0 | 0 | 0 | 0 | 0 | 10 |
| Organizing the Work of the State Duma | 1 | 3 | 4 | 1 | 3 | 3 | 2 | 0 | 1 | 0 | 0 | _2_ | 20 |
| Property, Privatization and Economic Activity | 7 | 6 | _3_ | 2 | 3 | 1 | 1 | 2 | 0 | 1 | 0 | 0 | 26 |
| Security | 2 | 2 | 2 | 1 | _2_ | 6 | 1 | 0 | 1 | 1 | 0 | 3 | 21 |
| Social Associations and Religious Organizations | 3 | 2 | 1 | 2 | _2_ | 0 | 1 | 1 | 0 | 1 | 1 | 3 | 16 |
| Women, the Family and Young People | 1 | 1 | 0 | 1 | 2 | 0 | 0 | 0 | _5_ | 0 | 0 | 0 | 11 |
| Mandate Commission | N/A | | | | | | | | | | | | |
| Total | 62 | 57 | 56 | 49 | 44 | 36 | 29 | 25 | 21 | 13 | 12 | 28 | 430 |
| Chairmanships | 3 | 4 | 3 | 2 | 2 | 1 | 3 | 2 | 1 | 1 | 0 | 1 | 23 |
| Deputy Chairmanships | 10 | 11 | 12 | 9 | 8 | 4 | 6 | 6 | 1 | 3 | 1 | 3 | 74 |

An underlined number indicates that the chairman for the given committee is from the given political party.

Source: Author calculated these data from Gosudarstvennaya Duma Federal'nogo Sobraniya Federatsii: Vtorogo Sozyva, (Moscow: Gosudarstvennoy Dumi (published by the Russian State Duma)), 1996.

with agrarian issues. Since parties decide which committees they want to have membership in, the Agrarian Party in 1994 lobbied for 20 members (out of its 49 committee posts) to be on the Committee on Agrarian Questions and also for the Chairman to come from their party. Similarly, the party, Women of Russia, had more seats on the Committee for Women, the Family and Young People than it had on any of the other committees, with five of its 21 posts on that committee. Also, the Chairwoman of that committee was from the Women of Russia Party.

Moreover, there is a relation between specialized knowledge of a given subject and committee posts. Olson and Norton claim that this is important because

> the composition of the membership of committees is another independent variable [for determining how they function in the policy process]. Members may be chosen because of their knowledge of the sector covered by the committee. They may be chosen because of their seniority in the chamber or parliamentary party.[44]

The committee Chairperson assignments clearly illustrate that both expertise and seniority influenced the appointments. For example, in the 1994–95 State Duma, Sergey Glazyev, Head of a laboratory at the Central Institute of Mathematical Economics, was Chairman of the Committee on Economic Policy; Bela Denisenko, a cardiologist, professor and the Russian Deputy Minister of Public Health (1990–91), was Chairman of the Committee on Health Care; and Mikhail Poltoranin, former Russian Minister of the Press and Information and former Director of the Federal Information Center, was Chairman of the Committee on Information Policy and Communications.[45] Many of these key committee posts are not only assigned based on expertise and seniority, but have also been held by the same people for two terms (five years to date). Several examples are Mikhail Zadornov, leading research associate at the Center for Economic and Political Research, who was Chairman of the Committee on the Budget, Taxes, Banks and Finance in the Duma from 1994 to 1998; Vladimir Lukin, former Russian Ambassador to the United States from 1992 to January 1994, is Chairman of the Committee on International Affairs; and Viktor Ilyukhin, former staff member of the USSR Prosecutor General's Office, continued as Chairman of the Committee on Security. Thus, there is an opportunity in the State Duma for collective expertise and more of an 'independent ethos' which, as Olson and Norton argued above, improves the committees' power.

There are several notable differences in the Duma's committee structure and composition from the 1994 to 1996 Dumas, in Tables 3.7 and 3.8. First, five new committees were added after the December 1995 parliamentary elections making the total number of Duma committees 28, plus the Mandate Commission, each varying in size from 9 to 48 members. The new committees were the Committee on Conversion and High Technologies, Committee on War Veterans' Affairs, Committee on Tourism and Sport and Committee on Problems in the North, and the Committee on Culture became a separate committee instead of a subcommittee. Also, another difference is that quite a few Deputies are on several committees as the total number of committee memberships increased from 430 to 463 (there are only 450 Deputies in total), with the party leaders still absent from committees. Table 3.8 shows that committee Chairmanship positions are distributed more according to the percentage of seats each party has in the Duma than previously, with the Communist Party having 10 of the 29 Chairmanships (34.5 percent) and 32.7 percent of the seats and Our Home is Russia, the second largest party, with 4 Chairmanships (13.8 percent) and 14.7 percent of the seats. The four political parties with the greatest number of seats, Communist Party, Our Home is Russia, Yabloko and the Liberal-Democratic Party, all have (approximately) one Chairman or Vice-Chairman on each committee. This also allows for greater checks and balances, as mentioned before, because the main parties can balance their views with equal representation as either Head or Deputy Head of committees. Another important difference in the committee structure from 1994–95 and 1996–99 is that in the latter period the top four parties have Chairmen in the most influential committees, while in the former time period, chairmanships of the most powerful committees are distributed more equally. Despite the addition of five new committees, the State Duma committees are permanent structures which parallel the administrative structure and party system.

Olson and Norton also consider two other factors important to committee strength: facilitating 'relaxed' partisanship and negotiation between parties and receiving evidence from external sources.[46] According to Thomas Remington and Steven Smith:

> generally factions do not dictate the behavior of their members in committee. In fact, Deputies from across the ideological spectrum described the relationship between committees and factions to us by distinguishing the political aspects of the legislative process from the process of drafting good laws. Some Deputies and committee Chairs

Table 3.8  State Duma committee membership by faction, 1996–98

| Committee | Political faction | | | | | | | | |
|---|---|---|---|---|---|---|---|---|---|
| | Communist Party | Our Home is Russia | Liberal Democratic Party | Yabloko | Russia's Regions | People's Power | Agrarian Party | Independent | Total |
| Agrarian Questions | 3 | 2 | 1 | 0 | 0 | 0 | 15 | 0 | 21 |
| Budget, Taxes, Banks and Finance | 5 | 8 | 2 | 6 | 11 | 6 | 2 | 8 | 48 |
| CIS and Liaisons with Compatriots | 4 | 1 | 1 | 3 | 0 | 4 | 2 | 0 | 15 |
| Conversion and High Technologies | 7 | 1 | 1 | 1 | 0 | 2 | 0 | 0 | 12 |
| Culture | 6 | 2 | 1 | 1 | 0 | 2 | 0 | 0 | 12 |
| Defense | 5 | 3 | 3 | 1 | 1 | 1 | 1 | 3 | 18 |
| Ecology | 2 | 1 | 1 | 2 | 1 | 1 | 0 | 1 | 9 |
| Economic Policy | 6 | 1 | 1 | 2 | 0 | 2 | 2 | 0 | 14 |
| Education and Science | 7 | 2 | 1 | 1 | 0 | 1 | 0 | 0 | 12 |
| Federation Affairs and Regional Policy | 7 | 5 | 1 | 1 | 4 | 1 | 0 | 0 | 19 |
| Geopolitical Affairs | 2 | 1 | 8 | 0 | 0 | 0 | 1 | 1 | 13 |
| Health Care | 2 | 3 | 1 | 1 | 2 | 1 | 1 | 1 | 12 |
| Industry, Construction, Transportation, and Energy | 5 | 4 | 4 | 1 | 2 | 5 | 1 | 0 | 22 |
| Information Policy and Communications | 4 | 1 | 4 | 2 | 2 | 0 | 0 | 0 | 13 |
| International Affairs | 6 | 1 | 5 | 3 | 3 | 2 | 1 | 3 | 24 |
| Labor and Social Support | 6 | 2 | 2 | 3 | 0 | 2 | 1 | 0 | 16 |
| Legislation and Judicial-Legal Reform | 5 | 1 | 1 | 3 | 1 | 1 | 1 | 2 | 15 |
| Local Self-Government | 4 | 2 | 1 | 2 | 1 | 0 | 1 | 0 | 11 |
| Nationality Affairs | 6 | 4 | 1 | 0 | 1 | 0 | 0 | 0 | 12 |
| Natural Resources and Environmental Management | 2 | 1 | 1 | 2 | 3 | 1 | 2 | 0 | 12 |

Table 3.8 continued

| Committee | Political faction | | | | | | | | |
|---|---|---|---|---|---|---|---|---|---|
| | Communist Party | Our Home is Russia | Liberal Democratic Party | Yabloko | Russia's Regions | People's Power | Agrarian Party | Independent | Total |
| Organizing the Work of the State Duma | 5 | 2 | 1 | 1 | 2 | 0 | <u>2</u> | 0 | 13 |
| Problems in the North | 3 | 3 | 1 | 1 | <u>2</u> | 1 | 0 | 1 | 12 |
| Property, Privatization and Economic Activity | 6 | <u>5</u> | 2 | 3 | 1 | 2 | 0 | 1 | 20 |
| Security | <u>6</u> | 3 | 2 | 2 | 5 | 2 | 1 | 1 | 22 |
| Social Associations and Religious Organizations | <u>6</u> | 1 | 1 | 1 | 1 | 0 | 1 | 1 | 12 |
| Tourism and Sport | <u>8</u> | 1 | 1 | 0 | 0 | 0 | 1 | 1 | 12 |
| War Veterans | <u>7</u> | 1 | 1 | 1 | 0 | 0 | 0 | 0 | 10 |
| Women, the Family and Young People | <u>8</u> | 2 | 1 | 1 | 0 | 0 | 0 | 0 | 12 |
| Mandate Commission | <u>7</u> | 3 | 3 | 1 | 1 | 2 | 3 | 0 | 20 |
| Total | 150 | 67 | 54 | 46 | 44 | 39 | 39 | 24 | 463 |
| Chairmanships | 10 | 4 | 4 | 4 | 2 | 3 | 2 | 0 | 29 |
| Deputy Chairmanships | 16 | 23 | 25 | 20 | 7 | 7 | 9 | 1 | 108 |

An underlined number indicates that the chairman for the given committee is from the given political party.

Source: Author calculated these data from Gosudarstvennaya Duma Federal'nogo Sobraniya Federatsii (Moscow: Gosudarstvennoy Dumi (published by the Russian State Duma)), 1998.

report that faction politics was supposed to be, and to a large extent was, held separate from committee deliberation on bills, while political decisions, such as whether and when a controversial piece of legislation should be reported and what the shape of a compromise should be, were decided by the faction leaders in the Council of the Duma.[47]

Vice-Chairman of Our Home is Russia and the First Deputy Speaker in the Duma, Vyacheslav Kuznetsov, confirmed this by stating that even on the Duma's most powerful committee, the Committee for Budget, Taxes, Banks and Finance, of which he is a member:

> when professionals discuss professional issues they often, as a rule, forget about their political affiliations. In the activities of the State Duma's Budget Committee, although all factions of Deputies are represented in this committee, I have very rarely heard members of our committee saying that I am from the Communist Party and therefore I think this, this, and this. These are financial issues, issues of the budget, and therefore professionalism is put in the main corner and politics is put far, far on the side.[48]

Duma Deputy Vladimir Averchev, a member of the Duma's Committee on International Affairs and from the Yabloko Party, confirmed that even in international affairs, 'coalitions and political parties are not very important in committees'.[49] Thus, Duma committees create an environment with relaxed partisanship which helps to increase the strength of committees and their power to negotiate with the executive.

Moreover, committees have their own expert staff who advise them on any issue. Outside experts also assist in drafting the specific or technical parts of legislation. For example, Aleksey Avtonomov, Director of the Legal Department at the Foundation for the Development of Parliamentarism in Russia and Legal Advisor to the State Duma, was

> cooperating with the State Duma Committee on Public Associations and Religious Organizations, with the Committee on Legislation and Judicial-Legal Reform, and the Moscow City Duma and Moscow Government along with its public associations [to draft legislation]. I am also the member of an expert Council of Advisors organized by the Legal Department of the State Duma's staff. There are different expert councils and we are discussing different laws. Just now in the State Duma I am preparing a draft law on not-for-profit foundations.[50]

While the budget resources for financing a committee's advisors and external staff are quite large, with some committees having over 100 advisors, it is not as large as committees' resources in many Western countries, such as the United States. Still, the budget resources coupled with the expert knowledge of many Deputies, enables the Duma to build a collective expertise and operate more independently from the executive. Thus, it appears that the structure of State Duma committees makes them, using Olson and Norton's classification, very 'able to both know and act in the policy process independently of the executive'.[51]

### Committees in the Federation Council

After a bill is passed by the Duma, it is sent to the respective committee in the Council of the Federation. Because the Council of the Federation is only a part-time body[52] and its responsibilities are slightly different from the Duma's, it has fewer committees and they vary in scope from the Duma's. It is not possible to create a separate chart with the Council's committee membership by faction because since the Council is composed of executive and legislative heads of Russia's 89 subjects, many of the Members are not associated with a political party. Indeed, in the first election of Council Members under the 1993 Constitution, almost half of those elected did not give any party affiliation after they were elected. As shown in Table 3.9, the Council has 12 committees,

*Table 3.9*   The committees of the Council of the Federation

| Committee |
| --- |
| Agrarian Questions |
| Budget, Taxes, Finance and Credit Regulations |
| CIS Affairs |
| Constitutional Laws and Judicial-Legal Reform |
| Defense and Security |
| Economic Policy |
| Education, Science, Culture and Ecology |
| Federation Affairs and Regional Policy |
| International Affairs |
| Problems in the North and Small Areas |
| Regulations and the Parliamentary Process |
| Social Policy |

*Source*: Author's translation from *Federal'noe Sobranie: Sovet Federatsii i Gosudarstvennaya Duma* (*Federal Assembly: Council of the Federation and the State Duma*) (Moscow: Fond Razvitiya Parlamentarizma v Rossii, 1995), 28–36.

ranging in size from nine to 31 members (with the Budget Committee being the largest, just as in the Duma). Another reason for the smaller number of committees in the Council is that there is less partisanship. Originally, the Duma was intended to have only a small number of committees but when debates over the distribution of committee assignments ensued, Deputies decided to create more committees to divide power more proportionally among political parties and factions. Since the Federation Council Members work on only a part-time basis and most are not affiliated with parties, there was little reason to increase the number of committees. As far as resources are concerned, the Council's committees have their own budget, but they tend to share support staff and external advisors with their partner committee in the Duma. Moreover, committees are the main mechanism for interaction between the Duma and Council of the Federation. According to Viktor Sergeyev, Advisor on the Duma's Committee on Science and Education:

> usually committees of the State Duma and committees of the Council of the Federation have good relations and they enjoy them permanently. I worked for the Committee on Science and Education. For this Committee, there is a permanent connection between the Committee in the State Duma and the Committee in the Council of the Federation. There are very strong personal relations between people who know each other well and have permanent formal and informal contacts.[53]

Since many Council Members do not belong to political parties, the committees are used more often for negotiation between branches. Many committee members in the 1994–95 and 1996–99 Council of the Federation are/were leading experts in the area of their committee, such as the following: Aleksandr Lebed, former Head of the Security Council (1996), on the Defense and Security Committee; Isa Kostoev, General Prosecutor of the Soviet Union for ten years, as Chairman of the Committee on Constitutional Law; and Aleksandr Titkin, President of the finance and investment company called 'Technology and Investment in Russia', as Deputy Chairman of the Budget, Taxes, Finance and Credit Regulations Committee. Thus, similar to the Duma, the Council's committees are permanent structures, which parallel the administration; they have little, if any, partisanship; and many are composed of Council Members who are experts in the area. This lends support to the independent power of the legislature in the policy process, using Olson and Norton's analysis.

## Relations to executive committees and the level of autonomy

Like the legislature, the executive branch in Russia has a formal system of permanent committees, commissions and councils, as illustrated in Table 3.10. One of the main committees is known as 'the Supreme Council' or 'Big Four' because it is comprised of the President, Prime

*Table 3.10*   Councils, commissions and committees of the Russian President

*Councils of the President*
Supreme Council (or, Council of Four)
Security Council
Defense Council
Council on Religious Associations
Council on Public Associations of Veterans and Reserve and Retired Military
 Officers
Council on Questions of Justice
Council on the Affairs of Disabled People
Council on Culture and Art
Council on Local Self-Government
Council on Federal and National Policy
Political Consultative Council
State Expert Council on Especially Valuable Cultural Items of the Russian People

*Commissions of the President*
Commission on Tax Collection and Budget Discipline
Commission on the Chechen Republic
Commission on Preparing Agreements on Divisions of Power Between Federal
 Organs of State
Power and Organs of State Power in Subjects of Russia
Commission on Questions of Citizenship
Commission on Countering Political Extremism
Commission on the Rights of People
Commission on State Prizes of Russia in the Subjects of Literature and Art
Commission on Pardons
Commission on Public Activities
Commission on Questions of Women, the Family and Demography
Commission on the Rehabilitation of Victims of Political Repression
Commission on the Interactions Between Federal Organs of State Power and
 Organs of State
Power in Subjects of Russia in Constitutional-Legal Reform in the Subjects of
 Russia

*Committees of the President*
Committee on the Problems of Conventional Chemical and Biological Weapons

*Source*:  Author's translation from Lev Okun'kov, *Prezident Rossiyskoy Federatsii: Konstitutsiya i Politicheskaya Praktika* (Moscow: INFRA.M–NORMA Group, 1996), 141–59.

Minister and the Chairmen of the Duma and Council of the Federation. While this is a joint committee with the legislature, it structurally falls under the executive branch because the President heads it and decides its composition. In 1996, this committee expanded to include leaders of parliamentary factions and others. Gennadiy Zyuganov, Leader of the Communist Party of Russia and a member of this committee, in 1997 stated that:

> there is an understanding [between the executive and legislature] that a compromise should be found on the basis of dialogue. I think now when we are trying to exit from the difficult crisis it is important to suggest this form of dialogue. The Big Four will be gathering, the President, Prime Minister, Chairmen of the Council of the Federation and Duma. G-8 meets and in our country four leaders cannot meet to agree how to act further – it is an abnormality – so we agreed it will be regular, this 'G-4'. We agreed to create a big round-table. It has big authorities, the representation is rather solid (eight people from the State Duma, seven leaders of fractions and groups and the Chairman of the Duma, the Chairman of the Council of the Federation and seven leaders of regional areas (Siberia, Big Volga, Northern Caucusus, center of Russia, etc.), three members of Government and two leaders of the biggest trade unions). Having gathered around such a big table, it is possible to agree and to accept a decision. It is easier than passing a law in the Duma and Council of the Federation, or passing an act of the Government because people around this table are high authorities.[54]

Partly, however, as a result of President Yel'tsin's health, this committee has not held regular meetings since the beginning of 1998.[55] From September 1998, Prime Minister Yevgeniy Primakov – until his dismissal by Yel'tsin in May 1999 – created his own committee with parliamentary leaders in its place. Primakov's committee, in contrast to Yel'tsin's 'Big Four', met frequently and was more apt to reach agreements. Besides this council, the majority of such bodies under the President are similar in scope to those of the Duma and Council. Of the 24 executive councils, commissions and committees, 17 are similar in scope to the committees in the Duma and to the related committees in the Council of the Federation. As a result, these bodies provide an established structure for communication between the executive and legislative. Vladimir Lukin, Chairman of the Duma's Committee on International Affairs and

Vice-Chairman of the Yabloko Party, stated that:

> we (the Committee on International Affairs) are permanently connected with the executive power, the main executor of foreign relations. We are involved daily in foreign policy with the part of the administration of the President which covers these issues. For meetings of our (International Affairs) Committee, people from the executive power who became involved in the issues of such and such a treaty prepared it for ratification with our Committee.[56]

The bodies which are unique to the executive are the following: Commissions on the Rights of People, Pardons, State Prizes, Public Activities, Rehabilitation of Victims of Political Repression, Countering Political Extremism and Agreements on Divisions of Power Between Federal Organs of State Power and Organs of State Power in Subjects of Russia. These bodies are particular to the executive branch because they are non-legislative in function and are either the President's constitutional responsibility, such as awarding state prizes and pardons, or relating to upholding the constitution, such as ensuring the protection of the rights of people and victims of repression. The bodies which parallel those in the Duma and Council tend to coordinate their work with each other. For example, the Council on Culture, the Council on Federal and National Policy and the Commission on Women and the Family, work together with Duma and Council committees on drafting legislation, sharing expert advice and negotiating deals in cases of disagreement, depending on the importance of the issue. Since the executive's scope in the political process is slightly different from the legislature's, there are differences in the areas of specialty for some committees and others are more specific in nature, such as the Committees on Problems of Conventional Chemical and Biological Weapons which would be covered under the Committee for Defense or International Affairs in the Duma, from those in Parliament. Still, there is a great degree of symmetry in function, permanence and scope of committees in the executive and legislature which enables the policy process to be better organized and informed than it would otherwise be. Of course, the committees in the Duma tend to be oppositionist as a whole, but this only helps to make them more autonomous structures from executive control. Despite the similarities between branches, the committees in both the executive and legislature are autonomous structures in that they are responsible only to their given branch and not to other bodies or political parties.

## The Chamber

The length of sessions, autonomy of agenda-setting and availability of resources can influence the power of the legislative and executive branches. According to Olson and Norton:

> characteristics of the chamber itself affect the capacity of a legislature to shape public policy. Some legislatures have carved out some capacity for agenda setting, even in strong party systems ... Another chamber variable is that of resources for both the chamber and individual members ... Some legislatures have increased resources in recent years, though substantial resources do not by themselves lead to increased parliamentary activity and independence of the executive.[57]

Parliamentary activity is also illustrated by the number and length of sessions held by parliament. In the unreformed Soviet Union, the legislature called the 'Supreme Soviet' met infrequently, convening only twice a year for two or three-day sessions. As a result, it was not a full-time legislature 'and rubber-stamped legislation at the behest of the executive ... [After the Gorbachev reforms of 1989,] a bicameral Supreme Soviet, which would be the standing legislature, meeting for some eight months of the year',[58] was established. Parliaments which meet infrequently are inherently less powerful and obviously less able to influence the policy process. The main reasons are the following: timing, because a legislature rarely meets, it will have less time to oppose or negotiate with the executive branch; responsibilities, if it assembles infrequently, it will tend to not have great responsibilities on a day-to-day basis and in the constitution; and, bargaining power, infrequent and sporadic parliamentary meetings mean there is less opportunity to establish coalitions, develop relations among parties and have issues on which to bargain with the executive. A very good example of this is the comparison between these factors and length of sessions between the Duma and Council of the Federation. Thus, the more frequently a legislature meets, the more resources it has and the more power it is given to set the agenda, the more powerful and autonomous the legislature will be from the executive.

### Length of Parliamentary sessions

According to the 1993 Constitution, the Duma is a full-time body, while the Council of the Federation functions only part-time. Table 3.11

*Table 3.11*   Frequency of the sessions of the State Duma and
Council of the Federation

|  | Year | Number of sessions |
|---|---|---|
| State Duma | | |
| | 1998 | 83 |
| | 1997 | 76 |
| | 1996 | 70 |
| | 1995 | 64 |
| | 1994 | 77 |
| | Total | 370 |
| Council of the Federation | | |
| | 1998 | 19 |
| | 1997 | 18 |
| | 1996 | 27 |
| | 1995 | 43 |
| | 1994 | 51 |
| | Total | 158 |

*Source*: Author calculated data from *Gosudarstvennaya Duma:
Stenogramma zasedaniy* (Federal'nogo Sobraniya Rossiyskoy Federatsii,
Moscow: Izvestiya, 1994 to 1998) for the State Duma and *Sovet
Federatsii: Stenogramma zasedaniy* (Federal'nogo Sobraniya Rossiyskoy
Federatsii, Moscow: Izvestiya, 1994 to 1998) for the Council of the
Federation.

illustrates the latter's part-time nature. The Duma, from 1994 to 1999,
met on average almost two and a half times as often as the Council.
From 1997 to 1998, the Duma met more than four times as frequently.
During the period from 1996 to 1998, the Council met on average less
than two days a month. The Duma, during the same period, convened
for more than six times a month. Plenary sessions in the Council were
more numerous from 1994 to 1995 when it met about four times a
month because it was only just established and had to set up its internal
rules and regulations. Moreover, the Council must meet to discuss a bill
passed by the Duma within 14 days of receiving it. As a result of the
number of bills passed by the Duma in 1994 and 1995 (see the table in
Chapter 4), the Council was obliged to assemble more regularly to consider them, otherwise bills would be forwarded directly to the President
for approval. Since the data in Table 3.11 are presented by years, it does
not show certain facts about the Duma's and Council's schedule. The
Duma Deputies are expected to be in the Duma from the second week to
fourth week of the month. During the first week of every month,
although it usually falls on the calendar as the last days of the month

and first few days of the next month, the Deputies are expected to be in their home constituencies.[59] They also have vacation periods for several weeks over the Christmas and New Year period, around Easter time and for several months over the summer. The Council Members and President usually take holiday breaks at similar times to the Duma Deputies. Even during their holiday time, the Duma and Council can be, and have been, called in for emergency sessions. Council Members, due to their responsibilities and main priorities in their constituencies, spend most of their time in the regions and often only return for one week a month to Moscow.

In the 1993 Constitution, as analyzed in Chapter 2, the Duma is granted considerably more powers than the Council. This is partially the reason for the infrequent sessions of the Council because it constitutionally has less responsibility. The Duma is the full-time and more powerful branch of the legislature, not only because of the frequency of plenary sessions, but also because it is constitutionally given more extensive duties, as shown in the previous chapter. From the discussion above on political parties and coalitions, it is evident that since the Council is focused more on regional issues than partisanship and because it meets sporadically, it has less interest in and ability to develop coalitions and establish ties between parties and individual Members. Conversely, the regularity of Duma sessions has the effect of strengthening coalitions and opposition forces, its bargaining power with the executive, and therefore, its power to influence the policy process in Russia.

## Autonomy of agenda-setting

According to the 1993 Russian Constitution, both the executive and legislative branches have the power to initiate legislation.[60] The extent to which they exercise this power is discussed in the next chapter. Although the President and Government can submit bills to the Duma for consideration, the Council of the Duma solely determines which bills to send to committees for consideration. Then, the Duma committees decide whether a bill should be debated in a plenary session or disregarded. Once it is at the plenary session, it must pass in three readings before going to the Council of Federation for consideration. The Duma and Council of the Federation also have the power to delay legislation, as previously mentioned, and on areas which the President cannot issue a decree, such as ratifying treaties. This is a very powerful tool. Thus, the Duma has great power in agenda-setting, though the President can bypass the Duma and issue decrees in many policy areas. These decrees, however, cannot contradict existing laws, and become void after a parliamentary law is passed on that issue. Therefore, both branches have significant powers in the policy process to set the political agenda.

## Conclusions

The State Duma has significant structural powers which enhance its ability to participate in and affect the policy process in Russia. The Council of the Federation, in contrast, is more limited in its structural powers, which has an impact on the policy process. Still, it is responsible for passing (or vetoing) legislation before the President can sign or veto it. Political parties are becoming more consolidated in the Duma and a coalition of Deputies holds a simple majority in the 1995–99 Duma giving it greater power to oppose the executive and to uphold its own policy position. While the President is not affiliated to any party, the pro-Government party, Our Home is Russia (from 1996 to Summer 1998), had a very small percentage of the seats in the mostly oppositionist Duma, forcing the President and Government to negotiate and bargain with Deputies on important issues. Duma committees' structure and composition, because of their permanence, nonpartisan nature, expert advice and resources, are important for developing greater bargaining power with the executive and Council of the Federation and to further their policy-making capacity. Moreover, the Duma, to a great extent, sets the agendas for policy discussions. Although the President can issue decrees and bypass Parliament, it appears in the next chapter that he was doing this less frequently after the December 1995 elections than when the Federal Assembly first convened in 1994. The Duma and President both have significant structural powers, allowing one to conclude that the political system in Russia, in this regard, is more semipresidential than presidential or superpresidential. The following four chapters will elaborate on the extent to which the political system is semipresidential in relation to the actual powers exercised by the President and Parliament.

# 4
# Actual Legislative Powers of the Russian President and Parliament: Parliamentary Laws versus Presidential Decrees

Following the discussions of constitutional and structural powers, I will examine the actual powers exercised by the Russian President and Parliament from 1994 to 1999 in this and the remaining chapters. As Maurice Duverger demonstrated and I explained in Chapter 1 of this study, there can potentially be great differences between the constitutional powers granted to a president or parliament and the extent to which these are employed in reality. As a result, a study of presidential and parliamentary powers cannot be based solely on their written powers but must also consider the degree to which each body exercises them. Drawing on the factors from Figure 2.1 in Chapter 2, I will analyze those which the Russian President and Parliament have actually used, and not just threatened to use, from 1994 to 1999. These include adopting parliamentary laws versus presidential decrees, issuing vetoes and veto overrides, forming and dismissing the Government, and influencing the budgetary process. An in-depth analysis of each of these constitutes a separate chapter.

The focus of this chapter is the Russian President's use of his decree power and Parliament's ability to pass parliamentary laws. Laws approved by the Duma and Council of the Federation are more powerful than decrees because decrees cannot contradict parliamentary laws, but parliamentary laws can contradict, and thus override, decrees. Empirical data on the frequency of adopting laws and decrees illustrate the extent to which these powers are exercised in Russia and any trends in their usage will be highlighted. The constraints on employing these powers, the influence of the President's health, and the President's and Parliament's incentives to utilize these powers are also considered. An examination of the number of decrees issued by Yel'tsin versus legislation passed by Parliament will show the extent to which Yel'tsin rules by decree and the extent to which he negotiates policies with Parliament, or allows them to decide on issues themselves.

## Actual powers: theories and significance

Analyzing actual powers is particularly important for determining how political actors function in a political system. A president might constitutionally have significant powers while the parliament might be much more restricted by the constitution, but if the president rarely exercises these powers while the parliament regularly uses its powers to their full extent, one would have to rethink a classification of superpresidentialism for this regime type. Within the boundaries established by a constitution, the decision of the president and parliamentarians to employ their powers depends on their own personalities, interests and incentives. As James March and Johan Olsen were quoted in Chapter 1 as stating, political outcomes are a function of three main factors: interests, powers and constitutions.[1] In the discussion for each of the actual powers in this and subsequent chapters I hypothesize about the incentives for the Russian Parliament and President to exercise their powers. The primary motivations which are considered are public opinion and improving one's own chances of being re-elected;[2] the decision whether to oppose the president and government;[3] the relative importance of the policy issue area itself;[4] concessions, bribes and related forms of influence; and the personalities of the president and parliament (including the effect of Yel'tsin's health).[5] Given these possible incentives, I then apply them to actual events to determine how and why the Russian President and Parliament act in the policy process.

Thus, in categorizing regime type on the basis of actual powers one must determine the frequency and the extent to which constitutional powers are used and to what degree this challenges or restricts the power of the other branch. When a president exercises considerable powers in the areas considered in Figure 2.1 and the parliament has very limited or no redress to limit his/her actions, this system is characterized as superpresidential. If the opposite were true, it would be a superparliamentary system. When the president is limited to some degree by parliament in using his/her constitutional powers on some of the factors in Figure 2.1, this would be classified as presidential. The reverse is termed parliamentary. In systems where the president exercises more power than the parliament but parliament can check all of his powers to some degree, this is termed semi-presidential. The opposite would be semi-parliamentary. When the parliament and president use their constitutional powers to the same degree, this is a system of dual powers. I will now apply these characterizations to Russia to assess the type of political system based on the actual powers of the President and Parliament.

## The actual powers of the Russian President: decree power

At the beginning of 1994 Yel'tsin was compelled to rule by decree until the Duma and Council of the Federation established the internal rules and procedures for approving legislation and they were able to secure the simple majority needed to pass bills. The first law, 'On Financing Expenditures of the Federal Budget in the Second Quarter of 1994,' was signed by the President on 10 April 1994.[6] It was not until August 1994 that more than four laws were passed in a month and more than 12 laws overall were signed by the President, as shown in Table 4.2. As a result, for reforms to continue and at least some policies to be enacted, the President made numerous decrees from January to August 1994. It is unclear from Table 4.1 just how many normative decrees were signed during this period because the official publication of decrees did not disclose this information. There is no explanation why the decrees from January to mid-April 1994 were not published.[7] One can assume that because the total number of decrees was higher during this period than for any other similar time from 1994 to 1999 and because no parliamentary laws were adopted before April that the President issued numerous normative decrees on significant policy issues. It is also apparent from Table 4.1 that the President made 467 more decrees overall in 1994 than in any other year. Even though the number of normative decrees for 1994 only appears to be 193, less than any other year, this is because the decrees before mid-April were not published so it is impossible to determine how many there were during this time. One would expect, however, the number to be quite high. It is obvious from Table 4.1 and Figure 4.1 that the President issues significantly more non-normative decrees than normative ones.[8] In fact, from 1994 to 1998, there were 1404 non-normative decrees on average each year, but for all five years there were only 1420 normative decrees in total. Figure 4.1 graphically illustrates the huge division between the number of normative and non-normative decrees each month during this five-year period. It is interesting to note the large increase in the number of normative decrees in the four months preceding the June/July 1996 Presidential elections. Indeed, in the month of June 1996 there were

*Table 4.1* Normative and non-normative decrees issued by the President, 1994–98

| Month/ Year | Number of published normative decrees | Number of published (and total published and unpublished) non-normative decrees | | Total number of published and unpublished decrees* | Month/ Year | Number of published normative decrees | Number of published (and total published and unpublished) non-normative decrees | | Total number of published and unpublished decrees* |
|---|---|---|---|---|---|---|---|---|---|
| **1998** | | | | | **1995** | | | | |
| January | 27 | 60 | (93) | 120 | January | 18 | 32 | (72) | 90 |
| February | 7 | 42 | (88) | 95 | February | 18 | 54 | (120) | 138 |
| March | 26 | 46 | (93) | 119 | March | 25 | 34 | (65) | 90 |
| April | 17 | 83 | (132) | 149 | April | 20 | 50 | (97) | 117 |
| May | 21 | 92 | (130) | 151 | May | 28 | 47 | (90) | 118 |
| June | 18 | 61 | (102) | 120 | June | 19 | 35 | (87) | 106 |
| July | 17 | 71 | (142) | 159 | July | 23 | 54 | (110) | 133 |
| August | 23 | 62 | (108) | 131 | August | 21 | 39 | (78) | 99 |
| September | 6 | 83 | (123) | 129 | September | 34 | 33 | (76) | 110 |
| October | 14 | 51 | (129) | 143 | October | 13 | 27 | (52) | 65 |
| November | 13 | 67 | (105) | 118 | November | 28 | 57 | (112) | 140 |
| December | 22 | 51 | (200) | 222 | December | 28 | 48 | (110) | 138 |
| Total | 211 | 769 | (1445) | 1656 | Total | 275 | 510 | (1069) | 1344 |
| **1997** | | | | | **1994** | | | | |
| January | 23 | 32 | (51) | 74 | January–April** | | | | 811 |
| February | 9 | 38 | (67) | 76 | April (part) | 5 | 23 | (32) | 37 |
| March | 16 | 51 | (107) | 123 | May | 27 | 162 | (237) | 264 |
| April | 27 | 88 | (142) | 169 | June | 30 | 136 | (242) | 272 |
| May | 28 | 40 | (72) | 100 | July | 20 | 146 | (176) | 196 |
| June | 21 | 68 | (99) | 120 | August | 25 | 152 | (189) | 214 |
| July | 35 | 67 | (116) | 151 | September | 16 | 130 | (148) | 164 |
| August | 30 | 65 | (114) | 144 | October | 20 | 43 | (70) | 90 |
| September | 24 | 65 | (81) | 105 | November | 19 | 44 | (69) | 88 |
| October | 14 | 28 | (69) | 83 | December | 31 | 38 | (92) | 123 |
| November | 18 | 59 | (100) | 118 | Total | 193 | 1685 | (2066) | 2259 |
| December | 21 | 53 | (108) | 129 | | | | | |
| Total | 266 | 654 | (1126) | 1392 | | | | | |
| **1996** | | | | | | | | | |
| January | 35 | 61 | (96) | 131 | | | | | |
| February | 25 | 63 | (139) | 164 | | | | | |
| March | 48 | 48 | (95) | 143 | | | | | |
| April | 57 | 70 | (131) | 188 | | | | | |
| May | 50 | 56 | (113) | 169 | | | | | |
| June | 68 | 85 | (144) | 212 | | | | | |
| July | 29 | 42 | (85) | 114 | | | | | |
| August | 67 | 73 | (123) | 190 | | | | | |
| September | 26 | 50 | (69) | 95 | | | | | |
| October | 29 | 53 | (76) | 105 | | | | | |
| November | 21 | 50 | (78) | 99 | | | | | |
| December | 20 | 83 | (162) | 182 | | | | | |
| Total | 475 | 734 | (1317) | 1792 | | | | | |

*Table 4.1    continued*

| Month/ Year | Number of published normative decrees | Number of published (and total publishedand unpublished) non-normative decrees | Total number of published and unpublished decrees* | Month/ Year | Number of published normative decrees | Number of published (and total published and unpublished) non-normative decrees | Total number of published and unpublished decrees* |
|---|---|---|---|---|---|---|---|
| *1996–98* | | | | *1994–95* | | | |
| Overall total | 952 | 2157 (3888) | 4840 | Overall total | 468 | 2195 (3135) | 3603 |

** From January to mid-April 1994, presidential decrees were not divided into normative and non-normative categories.

*Source*: Data were calculated by the author from the official publication of presidential decrees, *Sbornik Federal'niykh Konstitutsionnykh Zakonov i Federal'nykh Zakonov* (Moscow: Izvestiya, 1994 to 1998). Decrees are officially divided into normative (on similar policy areas as parliamentary laws) and non-normative (on such administrative matters as appointments and dismissals of Government officials, similar to the Government's or Parliament's resolutions) categories in this publication. There are numerous decrees which are not published but, as shown in Chapter 4, they are always non-normative. The total number of published and unpublished decrees is calculated from the last published decree each year.

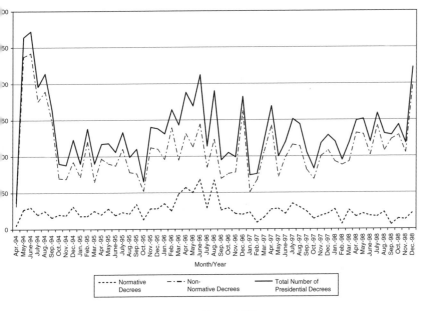

*Figure 4.1*   Presidential decrees from 1994 to 1998.

more normative decrees issued than in any other month between 1994 and 1998. This was the result of political favors and election promises. Viktor Luchin, a Constitutional Court judge, explained that 'in many instances, decrees issued by the President use alluring promises in a calculated attempt to win the sympathies of broad segments of the population'.[9] However, although the number decreases in July 1996 to 29, it peaks again in August to 67, just one less than in June. The reason for this is that Yel'tsin issued normative decrees which retracted previous ones that he made to facilitate his re-election to the presidency.[10]

The overall number of normative decrees has been steadily declining. Following the rise in 1996 because of the presidential elections when 475 normative decrees were made, only 266 were issued in 1997 and 211 in 1998. Withstanding the 1996 (because the elections distorted the numbers) and 1994 (because there are incomplete data) totals, in 1995 the total number was 275 which then fell to 266 in 1997 and 211 in 1998. The reason for this is that as Parliament passes more and more laws, the President is restricted by the areas in which he can issue decrees, as will be further examined later. Additionally, during the August and September 1998 crisis, there were significantly fewer normative decrees than might be expected, only 23 in August and six in September because the President let the Duma approve the stabilization program and other economic laws. This is illustrated in Figure 4.2 by the large increase in parliamentary laws during the same period.

The peaks in the number of non-normative decrees also deserve examination. The most significant rise from January to September 1994 is because Yel'tsin needed to establish the composition of the executive branch and the structure and function of all executive bodies under the President.[11] The lowest number of non-normative decrees (51) was in January 1997 when the President was incapacitated with double pneumonia. Another low period was between September and November 1996 when Yel'tsin suffered a heart attack, had heart surgery, and was recovering. The increase in December 1996 was due to his recovery before he contracted double pneumonia. Other trends were the decline in number of both normative and non-normative decrees when the President suffered a heart attack in July 1996. Moreover, the increase in non-normative decrees from April to December 1998 was due largely to the dismissals of Prime Minister Viktor Chernomyrdin in March 1998 and Sergey Kiriyenko in August 1998 and the need to issue decrees on the composition of the new Government. Non-normative decrees were beginning to decline from 1317 in 1996 to 1126 in 1997, but for this reason the number rose again in 1998 to 1445. Chapter 5 also examines similar trends (and explanations) during this and other periods in the President's use of his veto powers. The exact timing and reasons for appointing and dismissing Government officials via non-normative decrees is considered in greater detail in Chapter 6.

Even though the President is constrained by several policy areas in which he cannot issue normative decrees, there are many other spheres in which he can. Thomas Remington, Steven Smith and Moshe Haspel found that most normative decrees were issued in the areas of administrative reorganization, social welfare, economic policy, sectoral support, state programs, and national defense. In 1994, 23 percent of the normative decrees concerned administrative reorganization, 12 percent were on national defense, 10 percent on economic policy, and 8 percent on social welfare. The focus shifted more towards economic policy and state programs in 1995 with 16 percent on administrative reorganization, 12 percent on economic policy, 11 percent on defense, and 7 percent on state programs. Results were similar in 1996 with 20 percent on administrative reorganization, 10 percent on sectoral support, 10 percent on economic policy, and 9 percent on national defense.[12] Furthermore, Gennadiy Seleznyov, Chairman of the State Duma, discovered that from 1 January 1996 to 20 May 1997, 38 percent (rounding up) of normative decrees were on finances and credits, while 46 percent concerned the fundamentals of the constitutional system, 15 percent were on civil law, and 11 percent on social welfare.[13] Besides Scott Parrish's case studies of presidential decrees from 1994 to 1996,[14] there is a lack of information and statistics available on the policy issues in which normative decrees were issued.

Thus, as I have demonstrated, there was a gradual decline in the number of normative decrees made by the President from 1996 to 1998. In the next section I will show that this is because as increasing numbers of parliamentary laws were passed, the President was restricted by the areas in which he could issue normative decrees.

## The actual powers of the Russian Parliament: parliamentary laws

The Duma and Council of the Federation's ability to adopt parliamentary laws restricts the degree to which the President can rule by decree. Table 4.2 and Figure 4.2 show the gradual increase in the legislation passed by Parliament and signed into law by the President from January 1994 to December 1995. The peak in December 1995 is explained because it was the month when new elections to the Duma were held

*Table 4.2*   Laws passed by the State Duma and signed by the President, 1994–98

| Month/ Year | Number of laws passed in the Duma, 1996–98 | Month/ Year | Number of laws passed in the Duma, 1994–95 |
|---|---|---|---|
| *1998* | | *1995* | |
| January | 13 | January | 10 |
| February | 16 | February | 16 |
| March | 25 | March | 13 |
| April | 12 | April | 30 |
| May | 16 | May | 15 |
| June | 12 | June | 15 |
| July | 62 | July | 22 |
| August | 0 | August | 33 |
| September | 2 | September | 1 |
| October | 11 | October | 3 |
| November | 13 | November | 32 |
| December | 11 | December | 37 |
| Total | 193 | Total | 228 |
| *1997* | | *1994* | |
| January | 24 | January | 0 |
| February | 21 | February | 0 |
| March | 21 | March | 0 |
| April | 9 | April | 1 |
| May | 12 | May | 2 |
| June | 8 | June | 5 |
| July | 28 | July | 4 |
| August | 0 | August | 15 |
| September | 4 | September | 0 |
| October | 10 | October | 4 |
| November | 9 | November | 21 |
| December | 13 | December | 27 |
| Total | 159 | Total | 79 |
| *1996* | | | |
| January | 16 | | |
| February | 5 | | |
| March | 3 | | |
| April | 16 | | |
| May | 21 | | |
| June | 22 | | |
| July | 22 | | |
| August | 23 | | |
| September | 0 | | |
| October | 0 | | |
| November | 20 | | |
| December | 15 | | |
| Total | 163 | | |
| 1996–98 total | 515 | 1994–95 total | 307 |

*Source*: Data were calculated by the author from the official publication of federal laws, *Vedomosti Federal'nogo Sobraniya Rossiyskoy Federatsii* (Federal'nogo Sobraniya Rossiyskoy Federatsii, Moscow: Izvestiya, 1994 to 1998).

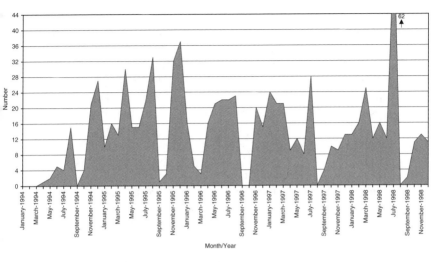

*Figure 4.2* Laws passed by the State Duma and signed by the President, 1994–98.

and Deputies and Council Members adopted more laws than previously so they would be enacted when the new Duma came to power. Unlike decrees which cannot be transferred when a new President enters office, parliamentary laws are set and cannot be altered without the approval of a new law. Parliamentary laws signed by the President dropped to one or zero in September 1994, 1995, 1996 and August 1997, 1998 because these were the periods when the Duma and Council were on vacation. There is often a short gap between when the Duma passes a bill and when the President signs it since it is forwarded to the Council first, which has two weeks to vote on it. Thus, vacations might not have been exactly in August or September but less than a month prior.

After the December 1995 Duma elections, the number of laws slowly began to increase again. In January 1996 there were 16 laws signed by the President but these were bills approved by the previous Duma as the new Duma did not hold its first session until the middle of the month. The decline in the number of laws adopted by the President from April to June 1997 is due to the large number of vetoes he issued, especially in April and June 1997 (see Figure 5.2 and further analysis in the next chapter). Because a greater proportion of bills were vetoed, there were fewer possible bills for Yel'tsin to approve during this time. After this period, the number of laws peaks in July 1997 as Duma Deputies and Council Members try to pass more bills than usual before the summer holidays. Following the vacation, the trend continues its gradual increase until March 1998. The decline in the laws signed from April to June 1998 is explained by the intense period of confrontation which existed between the executive and legislature after Sergey Kiriyenko's appointment as Prime Minister in April 1998. The President vetoed more bills during Kiriyenko's Government than in any other period from 1994 to 1998, as explained in Chapter 5. The highest peak occurred in July 1998 because the Duma and Council of the Federation, despite Yel'tsin's numerous vetoes, overrode approximately 50 percent of them so Yel'tsin was forced to sign the bills into law (Figure 5.2). Then there is a decline for the summer holidays which is followed by a rise when the Duma and Council reconvened.

The Duma has significant powers to delay legislation to secure concessions from the executive. Because this can be an effective method of challenging and restricting the President's power, I will examine the ratification of the START II Treaty as a case study of how this can be used.

## Case study on the ratification of the START II Treaty

'The Treaty between the United States and the Russian Federation on Further Reduction and Limitation of Strategic Offensive Arms (the START II Treaty)' was signed by Presidents Boris Yel'tsin and George Bush on 3 January 1993 in the Kremlin. It was a continuation of the nuclear weapons disarmament that was agreed on in the START Treaty, signed by Presidents Mikhail Gorbachev and George Bush on 31 July 1991, but START II calls for both countries to reduce nuclear arms to less than a half of what was allowed in the first START Treaty, that is, to between 3000 and 3500 total warheads each. Before START II can be implemented it must first be ratified by both the US Congress and Russian Parliament, where it has met with hostility. Because START II has yet to be ratified by Duma Deputies, despite concessions from the executive and pressure from the United States, an analysis of the more than six years that they have postponed it will illustrate how the Duma can gain power in the legislative process by delaying legislation.

Duma Deputies have been very reluctant to approve this treaty because most of them believe that it would greatly undermine Russia's power since nuclear parity between Russia and the United States is Russia's last claim to its former superpower status. Vladimir Lukin, Chairman of the Duma's Committee on International Affairs, stated that:

> 'today the atmosphere in the Duma is not right for ratification of START II' ... [Yuriy Golotyuk argues that] this atmosphere arose because of a sharp decline in trust in the United States, [due to the]

'strategically incorrect or overly self-reliant direction' of this country. And, judging by yesterday's hearings, a change in the atmosphere in the State Duma is not foreseeable in the near future.[15]

Moreover, by delaying ratification of the Treaty, Duma Deputies are using it as a bartering piece both with the executive branch and the United States for issues such as NATO expansion and domestic policy concerns.

> The [former] head of the Duma's Defense Committee, Lev Rokhlin, said that Russia should not consider ratifying START II at all until the Russian authorities have resolved national security issues associated with eastward NATO expansion. Rokhlin called START II a treaty that is of absolutely no benefit to Russia, one that would reduce the effectiveness of the country's strategic arsenals and upset the balance of forces.[16]

With NATO's efforts to expand its membership to include former countries of the Soviet Union, the Duma has become even more hesitant to adopt the treaty. Sergey Shakhray, the deputy head of the President's administration and Duma Deputy, stated that 'the admission of new members to NATO could make the ratification of the START II Treaty by the State Duma unrealistic'.[17]

Yel'tsin and the executive branch strongly support the Duma's ratification of the Treaty, since the President already signed the document in 1993. Immediately after signing the Treaty he said that it:

> 'surpasses all other treaties that have ever been signed on disarmament questions' and 'becomes the core of the system of guarantees of global security' ... the President gave his unambiguous assurances that the signed treaty does not weaken Russia's security but strengthens it, and that its implementation 'will not be economically destructive for Russia' ... President Boris Yel'tsin is confident that the Russian Parliament will ratify the Russian–American START II Treaty, despite the obvious opposition of some of the corps of Deputies.[18]

Although some doubts were raised about the Treaty within the executive after August 1997, the executive tended to endorse it. In 1996, the Russian Minister of Defense, Igor Rodionov stated that he 'not only supports the START II Treaty but also advocates considering a subsequent treaty, START III, which would be aimed at further cuts in strategic weapons'.[19] At the March 1997 Summit Meeting in Helsinki between Yel'tsin and Bill Clinton, revisions to the START II Treaty were agreed upon which were demanded by the Duma. Some of the main objections and demands from Duma Deputies were met in these revisions and Yel'tsin even pushed for them because he knew that he needed the Duma's support to ratify the Treaty.[20] They agreed to drafting a START III Treaty as soon as START II was ratified to further reduce nuclear arms on both sides, preserving the ABM Treaty, and extending the deadlines for destroying delivery vehicles by four years, to 2007. This last concession that Clinton made is of great advantage for Russia because it means that Russia can just let its weapons expire, as many will between 2005 and 2007, without having to invest money to destroy them prematurely. Even with these concessions to the Duma, Sergey Rogov wrote the day after the Summit:

> it can be assumed that it will be very difficult to get the Duma to ratify [the START II Treaty]. One would like to hope that the participants in the future debates will still be guided by the interests of Russia's national security. But that will be possible only if the government will at last present a clear and well-thought-out program for the development of Russia's strategic forces in the coming 10 years. For the time being, the discussions of the defense budget and military doctrine have such an obvious pretentious character that they lend themselves to a wide variety of demagoguery.[21]

It took more than seven years for the Duma to sign the Treaty. It was scheduled for debate in plenary sessions, but it was removed at the start of the Kosovo War in Spring 1999. On 14 April 2000 Deputies ratified it after President Putin attended the Duma debate and they realized that most Russian missiles were old and would be scrapped soon anyway. This is significant because it is an issue not only of domestic but also international concern. Duma Deputies' unwillingness to submit to Yel'tsin or Clinton shows that they can and do challenge the executive on important legislation by delaying debates. A further example of this is given in Chapter 7 on the approval of the federal budget each year, which Duma Deputies postpone for at least several months, except for the 1999 Budget, forcing the executive to meet at least some of the Duma's demands.

## Laws versus decrees

Finally, it is important to compare parliamentary laws and normative decrees since they are similar in scope and function. Figure 4.3 shows,

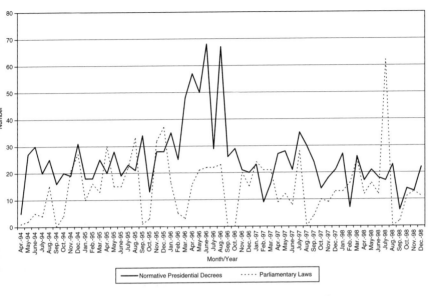

*Figure 4.3* Presidential normative decrees versus Parliamentary laws.

when Figures 4.1 and 4.2 are combined, that despite the large number of normative decrees prior to and just after the 1996 Presidential elections, there are approximately the same number of parliamentary laws and normative decrees. The y-axis of Figure 4.3 illustrates that despite some rises and falls from 1994 to 1998 the number of parliamentary laws and normative decrees remained similar. Evidence of this is that in 1998 the President signed 211 normative decrees while Parliament passed 193 laws. In 1995, for example, Yel'tsin issued 275 decrees on policy issues, but 228 parliamentary laws were signed. This is particularly important because one of the misconceptions about the President's decree power is that he issues many more decrees than laws. As I have shown, this must be qualified because the vast majority of his decrees are non-normative and do not concern policy issues. Scott Parrish also found that 'without a careful examination of Yel'tsin's decree output, one could easily leap to the conclusion that he totally overshadowed the assembly in terms of producing new policy initiatives ... The ratio [of normative decrees to laws] indicates a much lesser extent of executive dominance.'[22] From Figure 4.3 it appears that on average the President signed between 20 and 30 normative decrees a month, but this declined to between 10 and 20 from April to December 1998. Similarly, the Duma and Council passed an average of between 20 and 30 laws from October 1994 to

January 1996 and 15 to 25 laws between February 1996 and December 1998, excluding summer recesses and the 62 laws in July 1998. Thus, the President did not exercise his decree power to the extent that was previously believed, as almost the same number of normative decrees were issued as parliamentary laws each year.

## Conclusions

In conclusion, the President has considerable constitutional power to sign decrees into law. A close analysis, however, found that he did not employ his normative decree powers to the extent that one would expect from a President who has been described as an 'authoritarian leader ruling by decree'. In fact, the Duma and Council challenged the President's decree power by passing federal laws which replaced decrees and which limited the areas in which the President could issue new decrees. From 1996 to 1998 there was a significant decline in the number of normative decrees from the President but the number of parliamentary laws increased slightly during this period. Moreover, besides approving parliamentary laws, the Duma can also postpone bills on which the President cannot make decrees so the executive is forced to negotiate with Duma Deputies in order for them to be approved. The START II Treaty was described as one such example. In addition, I compared normative decrees with parliamentary laws to show the similarity in number, thereby demonstrating that the President did not have as much influence over the policy process as Stephen Holmes and others have claimed. Because the Duma and Council can challenge and restrict the President's decree power and force the executive to submit to the Duma's demands by stalling important legislation outside the President's area of decree power, the political system in Russia is more semi-presidential in terms of actual powers. The subsequent chapters on actual powers will examine the extent to which this is the case for other aspects of the policy process.

# 5
# Vetoing and Overriding Vetoes on Legislation in Russia

Although the number of laws adopted by the Duma, Council of the Federation, and President was the subject of the previous chapter, it is also important to analyze the stages of the legislative process before the President signs a bill into law. Numerous bills are withdrawn or delayed each year following a veto by the Council of the Federation or President.[1] The President's and Council of the Federation's power to issue vetoes serves as a check on the Duma's authority in law-making, but the Duma can override them with a two-thirds supermajority vote.

This chapter examines the following question: How often, to what extent, and why did the Russian President and Parliament utilize their constitutional powers to deliver vetoes or overturn them from 1994 to 1999? The theoretical framework from the previous chapter is employed to evaluate these issues. Empirical data on the number of the President's and Council of the Federation's vetoes each month and year are compared with Parliament's success at overriding, and thus retracting them. Because it is unclear from these data why vetoes were made or overturned, a detailed explanation of the rationale for exercising these powers is given. By analyzing the incentives of the President and Parliament to employ their veto powers, their ability to command majorities to vote in favor or against veto overrides, and the influence of the electorate, we can further understand why the President and Council of the Federation used their veto power and the Duma overturned vetoes in certain instances and not in others.

## Constitutional powers of the Russian President and Parliament in vetoing legislation

In Chapter 2, the veto powers of both the President and Parliament were given a score of 2 (out of 4) because the Duma and Council of the Federation can override the President's vetoes with a two-thirds vote of the total number of Deputies in each house.[2] There is no set time frame in which they must be overturned, so often there are large gaps between when legislation is vetoed and when it is reconsidered by Parliament. Before bills are sent to the President, they must be adopted by the State Duma. Once passed by the Duma, they are then forwarded to the Council of the Federation which can choose to veto, not consider, or approve them.[3] If Council Members veto a bill, it is resubmitted to the Duma for a decision.[4] To override the Council of the Federation's veto requires a two-thirds vote of the total number of Duma Deputies.[5] When Duma Deputies overturn a veto or Council Members approve or decide not to deliberate on given legislation within 14 days of receiving it from the Duma, it then proceeds to the President, who must sign or veto it. The Council and President are both constrained by the 14 days they have in which to issue a veto or approve the bill.[6] If the President returns a bill, Duma Deputies can approve it with his amendments by a simple absolute majority or override the President's veto with a two-thirds supermajority vote. After the Duma decides to pursue either of these policy actions the Council of the Federation must resolve to do the same for it to be finalized. The remainder of this chapter will analyze the Duma's, Council of the Federation's, and President's actual use of their constitutional power to veto or overturn vetoes on legislation from 1994 to 1999.

## Veto power from 1994 to 1995

Because Yel'tsin had the power to hire and fire Governors in the Council of Federation from 1994 to 1995, the Council Members' views on legislation were more closely linked with the President's than after December 1995, when they were elected by popular vote.[7] As a result, between 1994 and 1995, 'the Council more frequently rejected laws that the Kremlin opposed'.[8] Because the Duma and Council did not maintain accurate records on the details of all bills vetoed or when vetoes were overturned from 1994 to 1995, it is not possible to accurately calculate data on this.[9] Information about the Council and President's vetoes on the most important bills during this period were published in Russian newspapers and other sources. Thomas Remington found, in an internal report distributed to Duma Deputies in January 1995, that the President rejected 15 of the 116 bills passed by the Duma in 1994.[10] This is a relatively small number of presidential vetoes compared with those of 1996 to 1998 when between 48 and 80 were made each year, as shown in Table 5.2 and discussed later in this chapter. In 1995, 15 vetoes from the President were mentioned or published in Russian newspapers. Even less is written about the Council's vetoes, but at least three were issued in 1994 and seven in 1995. It is possible that there were more, but incomplete data make it difficult to know for sure.

Duma Deputies overturned at least one of the President's vetoes in 1994 and five in 1995 and all of the Council's vetoes except the 1995 bill 'On the Amendments to the Law "On the Prosecutor's Office"'.[11] By manipulating the agenda for plenary sessions, Deputies were able to override most of the vetoes. For the first time, on 12 October 1994, Deputies overrode a veto from the President, on the draft law 'On the Procedures for Considering and Confirming the 1995 Draft Federal Budget of the Russian Federation'. On the same day, they also overcame the Council's veto of the bill 'On the News Media'. Deputies exploited two advantages in that day's agenda: the proposing and scheduling of a no-confidence vote in the Government and the return of Liberal Democratic Party Deputies to plenary meetings. Aleksey Kirpichnikov noted that after the no-confidence motion was initiated:

> the Liberal Democratic Party of Russia, deciding that its boycott was unproductive, returned to the plenary meetings ... As a result, the State Duma again had enough members in attendance to approve a second time, by the necessary majority of 301 votes, draft laws it had adopted earlier that had then been rejected by the President or Council of the Federation. The Deputies made full use of the opportunity and they decided to ignore the President's objections and approved their own version of the law 'On the Procedures for Considering and Confirming the 1995 Draft Federal Budget of the Russian Federation' ... The State Duma was equally successful in dealing with the Council of the Federation's objections to one of the 'Poltoranin' news media laws ... It is clear that the law mainly affects the interests of regional leaders, and the decision of their representative body, the Council of the Federation, which returned the Duma's draft. Now Duma members have taken vengeance on their 'senior comrades'.[12]

To overturn most of the President and Council's vetoes in 1995, Deputies employed a similar technique: they called a special session of

the Duma on 12 August, during a weekend of the Deputies' summer holidays. This, of course, did not create a favorable climate for the President
or Council's vetoes as Deputies were told that the upcoming parliamentary elections and other pertinent issues needed to be resolved and they
would have to sacrifice their holidays as a result. Three of the five presidential vetoes (of the draft laws on the minimum living standard, state
regulation of foreign-trade activity, and banks and banking) and two of
the three vetoes from the Council (of bills on local self-government and
the distribution of single-seat districts for the election of State Duma
Deputies) were overturned during this session.[13] Moreover, in 1995,
the Duma also overcame vetoes from both the Council and President on
the laws 'On the Procedure for the Formation of the Council of the
Federation of the Federal Assembly of the Russian Federation' and 'On
the Elections of Deputies to the State Duma of the Federal Assembly of
the Russian Federation'.[14] Because parliamentary elections were scheduled for December 1995, Deputies had a great incentive in ensuring that
these laws were adopted before then so that the elections would not be
delayed and Yel'tsin could not issue a decree on elections, which would
be contrary to Deputies' interests.[15] Of the two vetoes from the Council
and four from the President on the procedure for electing Council
Members, the Duma overrode three of them (see the discussion below)
before elections were to take place. Similarly, Deputies overturned the
same number of vetoes on the election law for Duma Deputies in April
to June 1995. This was a period of confrontation between the President
and Duma, which culminated in Deputies almost voting no-confidence
in the Government twice in less than two weeks in June 1995,[16] so this
explains why it was not as difficult for Deputies to secure the two-thirds
majority needed to overcome the vetoes.

## Veto power from 1996 to 1999

As Table 5.1 illustrates, the Council of the Federation vetoed more legislation each year from 1996 to 1998 than from 1994 to 1995, although
there were fewer bills in 1994. During this period, Council Members
rejected between 61 and 75 bills each year, comprising 32 percent to
36 percent of all draft laws considered annually. The number of vetoes
issued steadily increased (from 61 in 1996 to 67 in 1997 and 75 in 1998),
while the percentage of legislation vetoed decreased (from 36 percent in
1996 to 32 percent in 1997 and 1998). Vetoes overridden by Duma
Deputies rose from 34 in 1996 to 45 in 1997 and 47 in 1998. Deputies
were successful at overcoming 36 percent of the Council's vetoes in
1996, 67 percent in 1997, and 63 percent in 1998. It is important to note

*Table 5.1* Vetoes issued by the Council of the Federation and overridden by the Duma, 1996–98

| Month/Year | Vetoes issued by the Council of the Federation | Council of the Federation's vetoes overridden by the Duma |
|---|---|---|
| *1996* | | |
| January | 0 | 0 |
| February | 4 | 0 |
| March | 1 | 2 |
| April | 3 | 1 |
| May | 11 | 2 |
| June | 4 | 2 |
| July | 10 | 3 |
| August | 10 | 0 |
| September | 0 | 0 |
| October | 0 | 4 |
| November | 4 | 5 |
| December | 14 | 15 |
| Total | 61 | 34 |
| *1997* | | |
| January | 5 | 3 |
| February | 3 | 3 |
| March | 1 | 3 |
| April | 4 | 3 |
| May | 9 | 2 |
| June | 7 | 14 |
| July | 17 | 0 |
| August | 0 | 0 |
| September | 1 | 2 |
| October | 5 | 3 |
| November | 1 | 3 |
| December | 14 | 9 |
| Total | 67 | 45 |
| *1998* | | |
| January | 6 | 3 |
| February | 5 | 3 |
| March | 8 | 2 |
| April | 8 | 8 |
| May | 3 | 3 |
| June | 5 | 4 |
| July | 20 | 13 |
| August | 0 | 0 |
| September | 4 | 3 |
| October | 12 | 2 |
| November | 4 | 6 |
| Total | 75 | 47 |
| Overall total | 203 | 126 |

*Source*: Calculated by the author from data provided by 'Svedeniya o zakonakh, prinyatykh Gosudarstvennoy Dumoy, napravlennykh v Sovet Federatsii, podpisan-nykh ili otklonennykh prezidentom Rossiyskoy Federatsii' (Internal Document, Moscow: Record Office of the State Duma, December 1998).

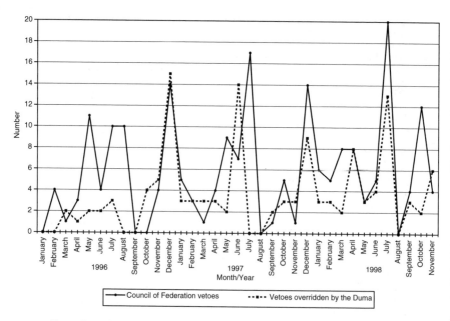

*Figure 5.1*   Council of the Federation vetoes versus veto overrides by the Duma, 1996–98.

that in Table 5.1 the figures for December 1998 were not available so it is likely that there was a higher rate of success for Deputies overriding the Council's vetoes than shown. Once the Duma overturns the Council's veto, the bill is forwarded directly to the President.[17]

It is apparent in Figure 5.1 that most vetoes were issued and overridden during periods of already intense political conflict or for reasons of public opinion. The Council of the Federation approved and the Duma overcame the most vetoes between the appointment of Prime Minister Sergey Kiriyenko in April 1998 and his dismissal in August 1998. From March 1998, when Viktor Chernomyrdin was removed until Kiriyenko was replaced, the Council vetoed 44 bills and the Duma overrode 30 of them. In fact, more vetoes, 20 in all, were issued in the month before Kiriyenko's dismissal than in any other month from 1996 to 1998. Similarly, the third highest number of veto overrides by the Duma, 13 in total, were approved in that month. This was due not so much to the tense relations between the Council and Duma as to those between both of them and the executive.[18] Aleksey Avtonomov asserted that 'the Federation Council rejected quite a few laws to avert presidential vetoes. I know for sure because I talked with some people on the presidential staff who said if the Federation Council had confirmed this law, it would have been rejected by the President.'[19] In fact, Duma Deputy Vladimir Averchev described relations between both chambers as

> satisfactory because the majority of our laws pass through the Council of the Federation. In some cases we have disagreements. This is normal. Sometimes they reject our bill but still we can overcome any weakness with a constitutional majority and in this case they understand the situation. Basically, since the Council of the Federation is not a full-time body, it cannot compete effectively in terms of the legislative process with the Duma.[20]

Similar trends can be seen in the distribution of the President's vetoes and the Duma's and Council's veto overrides in Table 5.2 and Figure 5.2. As with the Council's vetoes, the President issued more vetoes on legislation supported by both chambers and the Council and Duma overrode more of his vetoes during Kiriyenko's Government than at any other time. The next chapter examines the confrontation between the executive and legislature in more detail during this period, but it is striking to note the huge difference in vetoes made by the President and those overturned compared with all other periods from 1994 to 1998. From March to July 1998, the President vetoed 44 bills which the Council of the Federation approved, but he vetoed only seven that were not adopted by the Council. Under Kiriyenko's Government, the Duma and Council overturned more vetoes than in any other five-month time period, with the Duma overriding 30 and the Council 26 of the President's 44 vetoes. In these five months, more vetoes were overridden by both chambers than each had overturned in 1996 and the Council overcame in 1997. This is very significant and shows the intense confrontation between the executive and legislative branch during this period.

There were several other periods with a greater than average number of vetoes. The two more significant ones were the five months between February and July 1997 when the Council vetoed 41 bills, almost as many as during the Kiriyenko period, and between October 1996 and February 1997, when the Duma overrode 30 of the Council's vetoes, as many as while Kiriyenko was Prime Minister. Besides the significant number of vetoes from the Council, the President also rejected more legislation overall from March to July 1997 than in any other time except during Kiriyenko's Government. The main explanation for this was the President's health and public opinion. Following Yel'tsin's heart surgery in Fall 1996, he took some time off to recover and he also contracted double pneumonia at the beginning of 1997, which forced him to restrict his duties for two additional months. The period from October 1996 to February 1997, when Deputies overturned as many of the Council's

*Table 5.2*   Vetoes issued by the President and overridden by the Duma and Council of Federation, 1996–98

| Month/ Year | Vetoes issued by the President | | President's vetoes overridden by the Duma | President's vetoes overridden by the Council of the Federation | Total number of laws | |
|---|---|---|---|---|---|---|
| | Bill was approved by the Council of the Federation | Bill was not passed by the Council of the Federation | | | Total number of bills not signed into law by the President | Total number of bills signed into law by the President |
| **1996** | | | | | | |
| February | 0 | 0 | 0 | 0 | 1 | 3 |
| March | 0 | 4 | 0 | 0 | 4 | 3 |
| April | 2 | 0 | 3 | 1 | 2 | 16 |
| May | 2 | 2 | 1 | 0 | 4 | 21 |
| June | 8 | 2 | 1 | 2 | 1 | 22 |
| July | 5 | 2 | 9 | 1 | 0 | 23 |
| August | 8 | 1 | 0 | 5 | 2 | 22 |
| September | 0 | 0 | 0 | 0 | 0 | 0 |
| October | 0 | 2 | 2 | 0 | 3 | 0 |
| November | 0 | 4 | 2 | 1 | 1 | 20 |
| December | 5 | 1 | 2 | 1 | 5 | 16 |
| Total | 30 | 18 | 20 | 11 | 23 | 146 |
| **1997** | | | | | | |
| January | 5 | 5 | 1 | 1 | 3 | 24 |
| February | 6 | 1 | 6 | 0 | 1 | 21 |
| March | 2 | 5 | 1 | 1 | 1 | 21 |
| April | 4 | 7 | 4 | 1 | 8 | 9 |
| May | 4 | 1 | 1 | 3 | 4 | 12 |
| June | 7 | 1 | 10 | 2 | 6 | 8 |
| July | 12 | 7 | 0 | 3 | 13 | 29 |
| August | 0 | 0 | 0 | 0 | 0 | 0 |
| September | 0 | 0 | 4 | 1 | 1 | 3 |
| October | 2 | 2 | 4 | 0 | 4 | 9 |
| November | 4 | 3 | 2 | 3 | 3 | 9 |
| December | 2 | 0 | 4 | 4 | 6 | 14 |
| Total | 48 | 32 | 37 | 19 | 50 | 159 |
| **1998** | | | | | | |
| January | 5 | 1 | 0 | 1 | 4 | 13 |
| February | 1 | 1 | 1 | 0 | 1 | 16 |
| March | 7 | 0 | 8 | 5 | 2 | 25 |
| April | 2 | 1 | 4 | 5 | 5 | 12 |
| May | 5 | 0 | 5 | 4 | 1 | 16 |
| June | 3 | 2 | 6 | 4 | 7 | 12 |
| July | 20 | 4 | 7 | 8 | 27 | 62 |
| August | 0 | 0 | 0 | 0 | 0 | 0 |
| September | 1 | 1 | 4 | 0 | 4 | 2 |

*Table 5.2   continued*

| Month/ Year | Vetoes issued by the President | | | | Total number of laws | |
|---|---|---|---|---|---|---|
| | Bill was approved by the Council of the Federation | Bill was not passed by the Council of the Federation | President's vetoes overridden by the Duma | President's vetoes overridden by the Council of the Federation | Total number of bills not signed into law by the President | Total number of bills signed into law by the President |
| October | 7 | 0 | 3 | 1 | 15 | 11 |
| November | 1 | 3 | 6 | 7 | 14 | 4 |
| Total | 52 | 13 | 44 | 35 | 80 | 173 |
| Overall total | 130 | 63 | 101 | 65 | 153 | 478 |

*Source*: Calculated by the author from data provided by 'Svedeniya o zakonakh, prinyatykh Gosudarstvennoy Dumoy, napravlennykh v Sovet Federastii, podpisannykh ili otklonennykh prezidentom Rossiyskoy Federatsii' (Internal Document, Moscow: Record Office of the State Duma, December 1998).

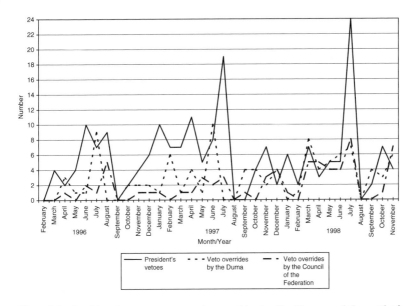

*Figure 5.2*   President's vetoes versus veto overrides by the Duma and Council of Federation, 1996–98.

vetoes as during Kiriyenko's Government, directly corresponds to when Yel'tsin's surgery took place until when he felt well enough to make his first public appearance in 1997 (on 23 February). The Duma took full advantage of this opportunity and overrode many of the Council's and President's vetoes because Yel'tsin was not running the country. During this period the Deputies were undoubtedly able to exert more control over the legislative process.

When Yel'tsin regained his strength and was able to walk on his own in public on 23 February 1997, he chose to reassert his power by vetoing legislation. In an effort to show he was still in control, Yel'tsin said:

> 'I can hit back and I will hit back at the Duma, if that is what it really wants' ... [Kutsyllo explained that] he wanted to show his 'fighting spirit' and refusal to submit to 'Communist intrigues'. Everything was just as it had been before. The only difference was that at that time Boris Yel'tsin was fighting for election to a second term. Now, the President is being forced to fight for the right to be considered a healthy President.[21]

On the same day Yel'tsin explained that he was 'dissatisfied with the Government' and that 'many Russian citizens are dissatisfied with the President. Such people are the majority and that concerns me.'[22] In order to take direct action and get rid of the stagnation in the Government and with reforms, Yel'tsin called for Ministers to be replaced.[23] Besides changing the Government, he also criticized the Duma's passage of laws. During a meeting with Gennadiy Seleznyov, Yel'tsin stated that 'the politicization of the State Duma is lowering the effectiveness of the chamber's legislative activity. Some legislative acts even conflict with the Russian Federation Constitution or law ... I have to return 75 percent of laws to the Duma for further work.'[24] Seleznyov clarified Yel'tsin's remarks by stating that 'according to his data, the President returns somewhat fewer laws to the Duma than that'.[25] Table 5.2 proves that Yel'tsin exaggerated the statistics on the number of vetoes he issued during that time. With his statements, however, Yel'tsin wanted to demonstrate that he was in control again by claiming to veto three-quarters of the legislation submitted to him and to indicate that the Duma was ineffective because most of its bills (supposedly) violated other laws or the Constitution. Further evidence of this is that Yel'tsin vetoed numerous bills during this period citing 'procedural violations' or claiming they did 'not conform conceptually to Russia's Constitution', even when there were no violations in procedure or with existing laws or the Constitution.[26] Another explanation for the number of vetoes is that, besides during Kiriyenko's Government, there were more bills to consider. As an attempt to reinvigorate reforms and the economy, the executive proposed more draft laws to the Duma, which they proceeded to amend, than in any other period under Chernomyrdin or Primakov.[27]

Moreover, as Figure 5.1 illustrates, the most common times to use veto power were at the end of Fall and Spring sessions each year, in June/July (depending on when vacations were scheduled) and December. With the exception of May 1996 and October 1998 when the Council adopted 11 and 12 vetoes, respectively, all of the peaks in Figure 5.1 are in either June/July or December each year. The explanation for this is that Deputies and Council Members wanted to try to finalize legislation debated during the session in the hope that the President might sign it over their vacation.[28] Obviously, the lowest number of vetoes or veto overrides occurred while parliamentarians were on break and at the start of each Fall and Spring session. Also, because there are often gaps between when the Council submits vetoes and when they are considered by the Duma, many of the vetoes that were not overridden in Table 5.1 have not been reconsidered by the Duma or a new bill was drafted in its place.[29] Still, the Duma was successful in overriding most of the Council's vetoes from 1996 to 1998, with an overall rate of overturning about two out of every three vetoes.

Despite the Kiriyenko period, the largest proportion of presidential vetoes issued was in the last month of the Spring session, June, July, or August, depending on the vacation schedule. A similar trend is not seen, as in Figure 5.1, in the last month of the Fall session in relation to presidential vetoes. Because of short delays between when the President decides to veto legislation and when it is reviewed in the Duma, and further delay until it is considered by the Council, the three lines in Figure 5.2 tend to follow similar peaks and declines shortly after each other. An example is the presidential vetoes in June 1996, then Duma overrides in July 1996, and the Council's overrides in August 1996. Moreover, the vetoes and overrides drop to zero during the vacation breaks. In addition, the frequency of vetoes from the Council and President are at relatively the same intervals, as shown in Figure 5.3 when Figures 5.1 and 5.2 are combined. Figure 5.3 illustrates, accounting for a short lag between when the Council debates bills and when they are forwarded to the President, that the Council of the Federation and President tend to issue a similar number of vetoes at similar times. This gives further credence to the argument that there is a correlation between when veto powers are exercised and political, economic, or other events, such as the President's health condition. Indeed, the peaks

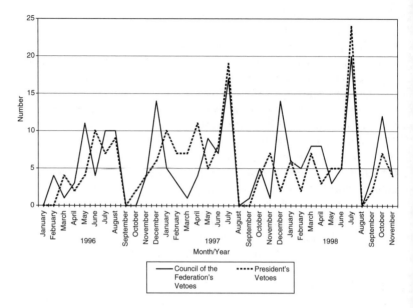

*Figure 5.3*   Council of the Federation's vetoes versus the President's vetoes, 1996–98.

in Figure 5.3 in August 1996, July 1997 and 1998, and October 1998 are congruent. The high and low points between January 1996 and February 1997 and from September 1997 to May 1998 all follow the same pattern, except that the President's vetoes tend to be a month or two behind those from the Council. The discrepancy between the Council's and President's vetoes from January to June 1997 was due to the President's health and desire to reassert control, as described above. Overall, the similarity in Figure 5.3 between the lines for the Council's and the President's vetoes is striking and proves veto power is exercised as a response to external events.

Although the President has the option of returning bills to the Duma with suggested changes, which only requires a simple majority vote in both houses to approve, the President rarely pursued this alternative. In 1996, the President returned four bills and, of these, three were adopted by the legislature with changes.[30] Later years proved to be less successful for the Duma and Council, when the President returned eight bills in 1997 but only one was adopted and of the seven in 1998, three were approved. Overall, the ratio was that more than one in three bills were adopted which the President rejected, but did not veto, from 1996 to 1998. The President has much less of an incentive to return bills with suggestions, unless he supports most of the bill or because of public opinion or time constraints due to economic problems, because it is easier for the legislature to approve them than to override a veto. Doing this also reduces the President's control over the laws in the country because he cannot rule by veto and decree as much. According to Thomas Remington:

> the President's decree power enables him to modify the status quo without action by the Parliament and then to use his veto power under the Constitution to block opposing parliamentary action. The combination of decree and veto power makes the President very powerful in influencing legislation, since he can threaten to veto legislation he dislikes and to govern by decree (except for those areas where the Constitution requires that policy be set by a federal law).[31]

Thus, the President did not choose to relinquish some of his power and return bills to the Duma. Instead, he frequently vetoed legislation, forcing the Duma and Council of the Federation to gather a two-thirds majority vote to override him. As shown in Chapters 6 and 7, because Duma Deputies and Council Members can vote by proxy, it is not as difficult as it might otherwise be to secure two-thirds support to bypass the President's vetoes.

## Conclusions regarding the use of vetoes versus veto overrides

In conclusion, Duma Deputies, Council Members, and the President often exercised their veto and veto override powers from 1996 to 1998. Between 1994 and 1995, both chambers and the President did not use these powers as actively. This was because the legislature, being newly formed and taking the first months of 1994 to establish its own operating procedures, did not debate as many bills in 1994 as in later years. Still, from 1994 to 1995, the Duma challenged the President and Council (when it was basically an extension of the executive branch) on important legislation, including the laws on the rules for Duma and Council elections, as the case studies illustrate. The Duma has become increasingly successful at overturning Council vetoes, with an average of 62 percent. It was demonstrated that during confrontational periods between the legislature and executive, the Council and Duma were able to gather the two-thirds supermajority and override the President's vetoes. Thus, the President is limited in the extent to which he can rule by a combination of decree and vetoes because the Duma and Council restrict his power by overriding his vetoes. If the trend in 1998 continues, when 50 percent of the President's vetoes were bypassed, and the Duma and Council proceed to overcome the President's vetoes on important legislation, the President's power in the legislative process will significantly decrease.

# 6
# Actual Non-legislative Powers of the Russian President and Parliament: Cabinet Formation and Dismissal

Following from the analysis in previous chapters of the Russian President and Parliament's legislative powers, this chapter focuses on their use of non-legislative powers in terms of cabinet formation and dismissal. Determining the composition of the Government is the only non-legislative function, of those considered in Figure 2.1, exercised by the Russian President and Parliament from 1994 to 1999. Although threats were made to dissolve the Duma and impeach the President, they were not fulfilled so this non-legislative power is not considered.

In Russia, the Government is responsible for implementing all laws, decrees, and resolutions in both foreign and domestic policy and eliminating contradictions therein.[1] Constitutionally, the Russian President has the right to form and dismiss the Government, giving him significant powers to influence, via Government officials, how and the extent to which all legislative acts are executed.[2] If an important law, such as the federal budget, is not executed satisfactorily, the Russian President can dissolve the Government and replace it with officials who are more likely to comply with his own objectives. Similarly, although this is a non-legislative responsibility, the lower chamber of the legislature, the Duma, can vote no-confidence in the Government. After two such votes within three months, the President is constitutionally bound to disband either the Duma or the Government.[3] Also, Duma Deputies must approve the President's proposed candidates for Prime Minister, but if they reject his nominations three times, the President must dissolve the Duma and schedule new elections.[4] Since the Council of the Federation does not have a constitutional role in shaping the Government, it will not be considered in this chapter.

The theoretical framework of this chapter is the same as in Chapter 4, when the theory of neo-institutionalism was employed to explain the Russian executive and legislature's incentives and actions in the policy process.

The purpose of this chapter is to ascertain the actual powers of the Russian President and Parliament in the formation and dismissal of the Government from 1994 to 1999. Questions to be addressed include the following: To what extent was the Duma able to exert power in determining the composition of the Government? How and why did the executive and legislature cooperate with or confront each other during the approval of Prime Ministers and votes of no-confidence? Why did the President's removal of Government officials coincide with the Duma's votes of no-confidence? Roll-call analysis of voting on confidence in the Government and the confirmation of the Prime Minister, empirical data on the President's appointments and dismissals of Government officials, and case studies on the dissolution of the entire Government in April and August 1998 offer evidence to answer these questions. I argue that while the President constitutionally has significant powers to compose and dissolve the Government, he was restricted in his ability to fully exercise these powers because of the threat of political and economic crises, a decline in public support, and his own deteriorating health. As a result, Yel'tsin was compelled to bargain with Duma Deputies before their votes of confidence and rejection of his candidates for Prime Minister. Deputies, mostly due to their own interest in self-preservation, also chose not to exercise their powers completely by not rejecting the President's nomination for Prime Minister in the third vote or not passing two votes of no-confidence in the Government within three months. From 1994 to 1999, relations between the executive and legislature on the composition of the Government shifted from confrontational to cooperative, culminating in Yel'tsin's acceptance of the Duma's recommendation of Yevgeniy Primakov for Prime Minister in September 1998. An analysis of this crucial trend is necessary to further understand the nature of executive–legislative relations and power in Russia.

## Constitutional powers of the Russian President, Prime Minister and State Duma in the Government's composition

The Russian President and Duma are mainly responsible for the Government's formation and dismissal, though the Prime Minister has some limited power. While the President must nominate candidates for

Prime Minister to the Duma for confirmation, the Duma can reject the President's choice. As the experience of renominating Prime Minister Sergey Kiriyenko illustrated in April 1998, the President can recommend the same person three times for the Duma's consideration.[5] Once approved, the Prime Minister submits a list of candidates for Deputy Prime Minister and the other ministerial positions. The Prime Minister can also recommend their removal from office to the President. If a candidate for Prime Minister is not supported by a simple majority of Duma Deputies in the third round, the President must dissolve the Duma, except for the circumstances listed in Table 6.1 or once the Duma lays a charge against the President for impeachment.[6]

Due to the constitutional restrictions on dissolving the Duma, the President could only legally disband it in certain periods from January 1994 to December 1998, as shown in Table 6.1. This will be analyzed further when considering the Duma's incentives in voting no-confidence and approving Prime Ministers, although Yel'tsin could have tried unconstitutionally to dismiss the Duma, as he did in September 1993. Of the five-year period considered in this study, for two full years (1994 and 1996) the President could not have dissolved the Duma if it voted no-confidence in the Government twice in three months. The Constitution does not clarify how this would be rectified. In such a situation, since the President must decide whether to replace the Duma or Government, but in 1994 and 1996 the Duma could not have been disbanded, it would seem that the Government, instead, must be dismissed. This was never tested nor has the Constitutional Court ruled on it. In 1994 and 1996, then, if the Duma did not support the Government, it had great incentives to vote no-confidence twice within three months to ensure the Government's dissolution. Although this did not occur, the fact that the Duma could do so makes it, for these two years, equal to the President's power to dissolve the Government. One difference is that the Duma's action would have resulted in the dismissal of the entire Government, while the President had the option of firing the whole Government or just several officials. A federal constitutional law, 'On the Government of the Russian Federation', signed by Yel'tsin on 31 December 1997 as a partial concession to the Duma for approving the 1998 Budget, increased the stakes for the President to replace the Prime Minister because it bound him to dissolve also the entire Government.[7] As a result, the power of the Prime Minister slightly increased since the President had more to lose so he would have to consider his action carefully before replacing the Prime Minister. Duma Deputies can submit recommendations to the President for the removal of specific

*Table 6.1*  Constitutional constraints on the Russian President's ability to dissolve the State Duma, 1994–99

| Month/Year | Constraints on dismissing the Duma constitutionally |
|---|---|
| *Conditions when the Duma could not be dissolved:* | |
| January 1994 to December 1994 | Duma could not be dissolved for voting no-confidence in the Government twice in three months for one year following the Duma elections, in December 1993 (Article 109(3)). |
| December 1995 to June 1996 | Duma could not be dissolved for any reason for six months preceding the presidential elections (June 1996). |
| January 1996 to December 1996 | Duma could not be dissolved for voting no-confidence in the Government twice in three months for one year following the Duma  elections, in December 1995 (Article 109(3)). |
| *Possibilities for dissolving the Duma:* | |
| January 1994 to November 1995 | Duma could be dissolved for rejecting the President's nomination for Prime Minister three times (Article 111). Since Viktor Chernomyrdin was confirmed in the previous legislature and was not dismissed until March 1998, the President could not dissolve the Duma for this reason between January 1994 and March 1998, unless he had decided to replace him. |
| July 1996 to December 1996 | Duma could be dissolved for rejecting the President's nomination for Prime Minister three times (Article 111). |
| January 1997 to December 1998 | Duma could be dissolved for rejecting the President's nomination for Prime Minister three times (Article 111) or for voting no-confidence in the Government twice in three months (Article 109). |

*Source*: Author applied Articles 109, 111, 117 and Section 2 of the 1993 Russian Constitution to the time frame of this study, 1994 to 1999. The Duma can only be disbanded constitutionally if it votes no-confidence in the Government twice within three months or rejects the President's candidate for Prime Minister three times.

Government officials, but they have no authority to dismiss them directly, except with a motion of no-confidence in the Government. Even following a no-confidence vote, the President can choose to disagree with it if it is the first one within a three-month period and no further action is required. Table 2.1 in Chapter 2 scored the powers of cabinet dismissal in Russia as 4 (unlimited) for the President and 1 (Parliament can suggest dismissals to the President) for the Duma, while cabinet formation was 3 (President names the Prime Minister, subject to the Duma's approval, who then chooses the rest of the Government) for the President and 2 for Parliament, illustrating the vast difference in their constitutional authority over the Government. The exact powers which they exercise in determining the Government's composition is the main focus of this chapter.

## The actual powers of the Russian President and Duma in the Government's composition

### Prime Minister Viktor Chernomyrdin's Government, January 1994 to March 1998

Since Viktor Chernomyrdin was appointed Prime Minister on 14 December, 1992 by the Congress of People's Deputies, the 1993 Constitution did not require him to be reconfirmed by the State Duma elected in December 1993.[8] As a result, despite three votes of confidence in his Government from January 1994 to March 1998 by the Duma,[9] Chernomyrdin was first approved by Duma Deputies in August 1996, following Yel'tsin's re-election.[10] Because he was the Prime Minister for more than four of the five years considered in this study, his Government's relations with the Duma and President are worth detailed analysis.

### The Duma's votes of confidence in Chernomyrdin's Government

While Chernomyrdin's Government generally enjoyed the support of Duma Deputies, there were occasional confrontations which led to threats or actual votes of no-confidence. The first vote of no-confidence was held on 27 October, 1994. Deputy Vladimir Nikitin, Chairman of the Foreign and Customs Exchange Regulations and External Debt Sub-Committee and Vice-Chairman of the Duma's Committee on the Budget, Taxes, Banks, and Finance defended the reasons for the motion as a response to economic problems, from 'the Government's failing to carry out the 1994 Budget and the devaluation of the ruble by 30 percent (two weeks prior) to Chernomyrdin's presentation of the unrealistic 1995 (draft) Budget earlier that day'.[11] As will be shown, this is the most common justification for votes of no-confidence because it is the main mechanism that Deputies have for ensuring that the budget is implemented and it places the blame and responsibility on the Government for Russia's economic troubles, which is clearly beneficial to oppositionist Deputies.

*Table 6.2*   Voting behavior of State Duma Deputies on the question of no-confidence in Viktor Chernomyrdin's Government on 27 October 1994

| Political party or faction | Voting on no-confidence in Chenomyrdin's Government 27 October 1994 | | | | |
|---|---|---|---|---|---|
| | *Yes* | *No* | *Abstain* | *Did not vote* | *Total* |
| Russia's Choice | 0 0.0% | 23 31.9% | 10 13.9% | 39* 54.2%* | 72 |
| New Regional Policy | 22 34.4% | 8 12.5% | 7 10.9% | 27* 42.2%* | 64 |
| Liberal Democratic Party | 56* 93.3%* | 0 0.0% | 0 0.0% | 4 6.7% | 60 |
| Communist Party of RF | 45* 97.8%* | 0 0.0% | 0 0.0% | 1 2.2% | 46 |
| Agrarian Party of Russia | 35* 64.8%* | 1 1.9% | 6 11.1% | 12 22.2% | 54 |
| Women of Russia | 1 4.5% | 0 0.0% | 17* 77.3%* | 4 18.2% | 22 |
| Yabloko | 0 0.0% | 0 0.0% | 0 0.0% | 27* 100.0%* | 27 |
| Russian Unity and Accord | 2 6.1% | 17* 51.5%* | 3 9.1% | 11 33.3% | 33 |
| December 12 (1994) | 3 14.3% | 1 4.8% | 7 33.3% | 10* 47.6%* | 21 |
| Democratic Party of Russia | 8* 53.3%* | 2 13.3% | 2 13.3% | 3 20.0% | 15 |
| Independents | 21* 63.6%* | 2 6.1% | 3 9.1% | 7 21.2% | 33 |
| Total | 193* 42.9%* | 54 12.0% | 55 12.2% | 148 32.9% | 450 |

* Indicates the position taken by the highest percentage of Deputies (in a given party or overall).

*Source: Gosudarstvennaya Duma: Stenogramma zasedaniy* (Federal'nogo Sobraniya Rossiyskoy Federatsii, Moscow, Izvestiya, 27 October 1994).

To propose such a motion in a plenary session, 90 Deputies must approve the request. Table 6.2 shows the voting behavior of Deputies by political party on the question of no-confidence in Chernomyrdin's Government. Although this motion failed, it would have passed if only 33 (7 percent) Deputies had changed their position, as a simple majority is required. Party discipline was not particularly strong on this vote.

Only 33 percent of Deputies, those from the Liberal Democratic Party, Communist Party, Yabloko and Women of Russia, were disciplined. The reason was that parties and Deputies were unsure whether to 'abstain', 'not vote', or vote 'yes' to protest against the Government.

It is striking that for such an important issue one-third of all Deputies did not vote. Deputies chose 'not to vote' instead of abstaining when they did not wish to challenge the executive or endorse the party line. According to Vladimir Lukin, one of the founders of the Yabloko Party:

> there are very few instances when we adopt the principle of mandated vote. It is on the budget, the vote of confidence in the Government, and approval of Prime Ministers... In these cases, for members of our political faction (Yabloko), there is a choice between voting (according to party line) and not voting, not participating.[12]

This is the most likely explanation for the significant number of Deputies not voting, especially because Deputies can telephone their party's office in the Duma and have a representative vote for them. Overall, 27 (100 percent) of Yabloko, 39 (54 percent) of Russia's Choice, 27 (42 percent) of New Regional Policy, and 10 (48 percent) of December 12 Deputies could not all have been unable to place a telephone call to announce their vote on that day. Since Yabloko Deputies tend to oppose the Government, they displayed their discontentment by 'not voting'. Similarly, Women of Russia Deputies abstained because Yekaterina Lakhova, the leader of the faction, explained that 'at the moment we cannot express our confidence because we have to call the work of the Government unsatisfactory, but to express no-confidence will only make the situation worse'.[13] The only party with a majority of Deputies who voted 'no', meaning that they endorsed the Government, was Russian Unity and Accord.

Although this motion was not approved, the executive could not claim victory because only 12 percent (54) of Deputies actually rejected it, a very low basis of support on which to maintain relations with the Duma. Moreover, an even worse outcome would have resulted if Yel'tsin had not made concessions to the Agrarian Party several hours before the final result was announced. Yel'tsin fired the Agriculture Minister, Viktor Khlystun, and replaced him with Aleksandr Nazarchuk from the Agrarian Party 'to neutralize the opposition'.[14] This did not have the intended impact as only one Deputy from the Agrarian Party voted for the Government, while 65 percent were against and 33 percent abstained or 'did not vote'. Other concessions were not offered because it appeared even before the debates concluded that the motion would not be successful since Deputies and parties publicly acknowledged their positions beforehand. Most Deputies were not willing to repeat the political crisis of the previous year (September 1993) by voting no-confidence since Yel'tsin could not constitutionally disband the Duma in October 1994, as one year had not transpired since the Duma elections in December 1993 (see Table 6.1).

A further expression of disapproval in the Government came on 21 June, 1995 when Deputies successfully passed a vote of no-confidence.[15] The rationale for this motion was twofold: as a reaction to the more than 114 deaths from the hostage crisis in Budyonnovsk from the war in Chechnya[16] and for oppositionist Deputies to gain an electoral advantage before the parliamentary elections in December 1995 by openly opposing the Chechen War.[17] This was the only vote of no-confidence which Deputies approved between 1994 and 1999.

There was a closed ballot so it is not possible to determine how individual Deputies or parties voted. Overall, 69 percent (241) of Deputies did not support the Government. Only 4 percent more Deputies (16 percent in total) than in the previous vote on 27 October, 1994 (12 percent in all) offered their backing to the Government, as shown in Table 6.3. Similarly, a significant proportion of Deputies (25 percent) chose not to vote. While the exact distribution of ballots is not known, from Deputies' own comments it seems that almost 100 percent of Yabloko, Communist, Agrarian, Liberal Democratic Party, Democratic Party of Russia and New Regional Policy Deputies advocated the

*Table 6.3*    Voting behavior of State Duma Deputies on the question of no-confidence in Viktor Chernomyrdin's Government on 21 June and 1 July 1995 in closed voting

| *Date of the vote of no-confidence* | *Voting on the question of no-confidence in Chernomyrdin's Government (secret vote)* | | | |
|---|---|---|---|---|
| | *Yes* | *No* | *Abstain* | *Not voting* |
| 21 June 1995 (1st: Passed) | 241* | 72 | 20 | 111 |
| | 68.9%* | 16.0% | 4.4% | 24.7% |
| July 1 1995 (2nd: Failed) | 193* | 117 | 48 | 92 |
| | 42.9%* | 26.0% | 10.7% | 20.4% |

* Indicates the position taken by the highest percentage of Deputies (in a given party or overall).

*Source*: *Gosudarstvennaya Duma: Stenogramma zasedaniy* (Federal'nogo Sobraniya Rossiyskoy Federatsii, Moscow, Izvestiya, 21 June, 1 July 1995).

Government's removal. Most Deputies from Stability and Russian Unity and Accord backed the Government, but Women of Russia members either abstained or did not vote. Russia's Choice claimed its position was dependent on the fate of the hostages.[18] The primary goal of this motion for the majority of Deputies was the dismissal of the 'power Ministers', Minister of Internal Affairs Viktor Yerin, Federal Security Service Director Sergey Stepashin, Deputy Prime Minister Nikolay Yegorov, and Minister of Defense Pavel Grachev, who were responsible for the Chechen War. According to Grigory Yavlinskiy, leader of Yabloko, the first vote could have failed because of several technicalities, such as if it had been held after lunch, instead of before, there would have been more time to bargain and fewer Deputies would have attended, and if the question had been raised first to remove only the power-wielding Ministers followed by a vote of no-confidence in the entire Government, instead of the other way around, it is likely that the Government would have had more endorsement.[19] Still, the President might not have replaced the power Ministers if Deputies had only voted no-confidence in them, but the threat of dissolution compelled Yel'tsin to do something.

Because this motion was endorsed by a majority of Deputies and there were no constitutional provisions which restricted the President from disbanding the Duma in June, July and August 1995, one would expect Yel'tsin to have offered the Deputies significant concessions to avert political instability. Publicly Yel'tsin always called for the Duma's dismissal when it encroached on the executive's power, such as with no-confidence votes, but behind the scenes Yel'tsin, Chernomyrdin and other executive officials tried desperately to prevent this.[20] Yel'tsin's Press Service announced, following the Duma's first vote, that 'the President of Russia believes that the Government's dismissal at this time would destabilize the political situation, give rise to negative trends in the economy, and complicate the crime situation'.[21] As a result, Yel'tsin made several important concessions to Deputies before the second vote on 1 July, 1995.[22] Ivan Rybkin, Chairman of the Duma elected in December 1993, suggested that if Yel'tsin removed the 'power Ministers' Deputies would decide on their support for a 'renewed Cabinet', suggesting that the second vote would not be successful.[23] Indeed, Yel'tsin submitted to Deputies' requests and 'presented his plan for getting out of the crisis to Duma leaders', which included the following: the power Ministers, Viktor Yerin, Sergey Stepashin, Nikolay Yegorov, were removed along with Stavropol Territory Governor Yevgeniy Kuznetsov; the Government would cooperate with the Duma to finish the 1996 Budget; Deputies would have an opportunity to participate in the negotiations on Chechnya by being part of

*Table 6.4*   Voting behavior of State Duma Deputies on the approval of Viktor Chernomyrdin as Prime Minister after the August 1996 Presidential Election in closed voting

| Date of Vote | Voting on the approval of Chernomyrdin for Prime Minister (secret vote) | | | |
|---|---|---|---|---|
| | Yes | No | Abstain | Not voting |
| 10 August 1996 (confirmed) | 314* | 85 | 3 | 48 |
| | 69.8%* | 18.9% | 0.7% | 10.7% |

\* Indicates the position taken by the highest percentage of Deputies (in a given party or overall).

*Source*: *Gosudarstvennaya Duma: Stenogramma zasedaniy* (Federal'nogo Sobraniya Rossiyskoy Federatsii, Moscow, Izvestiya, 10 August 1996).

Russia's official delegation in Grozny; and Pavel Grachev's Defense Ministry would be reformed.[24] This experience illustrates that Deputies are able to have their demands met in extreme situations, but the result was very close, as 7 percent more Deputies voting against the Government would have led to the Duma's dissolution.[25]

Since the results of voting within parties and by individuals remained secret, Deputies thought that they would not be as restricted by the party line for the second vote. This is often done when Deputies do not want something to pass but they realize that an open vote risks Deputies following party discipline and the issue being approved.[26] Table 6.3 shows the significant shift from 69 percent of Deputies voting against the Government on 21 June to only 43 percent on 1 July 1995.[27] Even more importantly, 26 percent of Deputies defended the Government, as opposed to 16 percent previously. Again, 20 percent of Deputies did not vote and 11 percent abstained showing that while the Government received backing from only 26 percent, one-third did not overtly disapprove of it. According to Deputy Khamaev, most Deputies had no intention of actually approving the no-confidence motion in the second round 'because to defeat Chernomyrdin's Government implied undoing the whole hierarchy in the executive and extreme confrontation with the executive. That was a high political cost for the Duma'.[28] Moreover, Vil'yam Smirnov, a leading expert on politics in Russia, explained that:

> when the Duma fights against the Government, it is not against the Government, but against the President himself ... The State Duma knows the limits of the Government. It does not want to dismiss Chernomyrdin. Chernomyrdin is a mediator between the liberals/ President's entourage and radical liberalism. There is a 'war of words'

but it is just pressure and there is no intention to dismiss the Government.[29]

While this second vote was not successful, Deputies later decided to use less risky means to gain concessions, such as threatening to hold a confidence vote.

Despite the overwhelming support for Chernomyrdin when 70 percent of Deputies endorsed his reconfirmation as Prime Minister following the 1996 Presidential Elections,[30] as Table 6.4 indicates, the Duma almost held another vote of no-confidence in his Government on 22 October 1997. The political justification for the motion was that Communists and other opposition parties were dissatisfied with the 1998 Budget because they thought that it would unfairly cut subsidies to the regions and further hurt the poor and disadvantaged.[31] The warning that Deputies would hold such a vote was sufficient to convince the President to meet the Deputies' demands. Oppositionists even postponed the debates for one week after Yel'tsin agreed to consider their terms.[32] Yel'tsin appealed to Deputies in a radio address on 17 October 1997 to cancel the vote by stating that:

> I would like the current political crisis to be resolved quickly and happily. It is not doing the country any good. During a week of discussion in the Duma, the value of shares in Russian enterprises fell by 3 trillion rubles. That is an enormous amount of money. We must not keep multiplying these losses and we should not leave the country without a Government. New elections for Deputies must not be undertaken because that would be too heavy a blow to our economy. The executive and legislative branches must sit down at a table and conduct a dialogue, seek compromises, and think first about Russia and the well-being of Russia's people. Therefore, in order to overcome the crisis as soon as possible, I believe it would be useful to hold a roundtable meeting of political parties and movements ... I am once again taking the accommodating step ... This should not be considered a manifestation of weakness. It is an appeal for prudence.[33]

Nikolay Ryzhkov, leader of People's Power in the Duma, confirmed that after two hours of negotiations with Yel'tsin, 'the President took steps to meet practically all of our demands'.[34] Conditions for withdrawing the scheduled vote, which the executive agreed to, were withdrawing the tax code from the 1998 Budget (a major concession by Yel'tsin the evening before the intended vote), postponing housing reform, signing the bill 'On the Government of the Russian Federation' to reduce the President's power over the Government,[35] scheduling regular roundtable meetings, and extending the coverage of Parliament on state-owned television and radio.[36] To ensure the executive fulfilled their bargain, the Deputies refused to approve the 1998 Budget until all conditions were met. Thus, a compromise was reached and the Communists retracted their motion. This was the only other significant threat of a no-confidence vote in Chernomyrdin's Government from 1994 to 1998.

Deputies exploit tactics, such as a vote of no-confidence, for political gain, to obtain concessions and exert some degree of power over the executive. Following three votes of no-confidence in the Government in 1994 to 1995, the experience of October 1997 proved that Deputies could just threaten to hold one and receive favors from the executive. Of course, pursuing this option too frequently would risk it losing significance, but with only five serious warnings or actual votes of no-confidence in five years, Deputies could have achieved greater results with at least a few more. Still, all of the Duma's attempts were successful in that most of their demands were always met. In the next section, I will consider what action Yel'tsin took in response to the Duma's votes of no-confidence in the Government.

### Relations between the Duma's votes of no-confidence in Chernomyrdin's Government and the President's decision to dismiss Government officials

Although the President had no obligation to dismiss Government officials following the Duma's no-confidence votes in the Government, he usually replaced at least several people to avert a political crisis and deter future no-confidence votes in the Government. Besides firing the 'power Ministers' before the vote on 1 July 1995, Yel'tsin also tended to reform the Government after such votes. One week after the vote of no-confidence in the Government failed on 27 October 1994, the Duma adopted a resolution, 'On the Social and Economic Policy of the Russian Government', which recommended personnel changes in the Government in the Duma's favor.[37] In November 1994, Yel'tsin implemented many of the Duma's suggested modifications.

> On the one hand, people whom the Duma dislikes are being removed altogether or pushed into the background: so far, this group includes Shokhin, Vavilov, Burlakov, and Kalmykov. On the other hand, parliamentary protégés are being brought in, or are already there: Aleksandr Nazarchuk (from the Agrarians), Vladimir Panskov (Women of Russia), and Valentin Kovalyov or Vladimir Isakov (the Communists).[38]

In response to the new composition of the Government, Boris Fyodorov, head of the December 12 faction, stated that 'just two or three more people, and the Zhirinovskiyites' and Communists' personnel demands will have been met'.[39] Former Prime Minister Yegor Gaidar was even more severe in his attack on Yel'tsin's cabinet changes by asserting that 'personnel concessions to antimarket forces (oppositionists in the Duma) will add nothing to support for the Government or to the President's authority'.[40] By transforming the Government into one which was more favored by oppositionist Deputies, it was suggested that 'the outcome of this struggle will lead to a further weakening of the Kremlin's power'.[41] Indeed, in the two months following the unsuccessful vote of no-confidence, Yel'tsin submitted to all of the Deputies' suggestions for dismissals and appointments, except for those of Anatoliy Chubais, Andrey Kozyrev, Pavel Grachev and Viktor Yerin,[42] who would be removed in the subsequent two years. As previously mentioned, Yel'tsin replaced the 'power Ministers', which included Yerin[43] and reforming Grachev's department, as a concession to Deputies before the second no-confidence vote in three months, held on 1 July 1995. Chubais was dismissed on 16 January 1996,[44] shortly after Kozyrev, who was elected as a Duma Deputy in December 1995. Grachev also lost his position in Chernomyrdin's new Cabinet by August 1996 to Yevgeniy Primakov. These events were too distant from the July 1995 no-confidence vote to describe them as related, but it is interesting to note that all of the Deputies' demands were met less than two years later.

Because Deputies gave their overwhelming support to Chernomyrdin and reconfirmed him on 10 August 1996, Yel'tsin did not need to make outright concessions to the Duma when the new Government was formed. The threat of the no-confidence vote in October 1997, however, led to several changes in the succeeding month. Although reports claimed that Chubais lost his position as Finance Minister, but remained Deputy Prime Minister, on 19 November 1997 because of a book scandal,[45] Yel'tsin 'in announcing that Chubais had lost one of his posts, said that this was his final concession to the Duma and that he now expects it to adopt the 1998 Budget'.[46] Further dismissals appeared to be more linked with the Duma's pronounced dissatisfaction with the Government in October 1997. Mikhail Zadornov, described by Deputies as the 'best'[47] Chairman of the Duma's Committee on the Budget, Taxes, Banks and Finance and a Yabloko Deputy, assumed Chubais's former role as Finance Minister. Sergey Kiriyenko replaced Boris Nemtsov, who like Chubais was not a favorite among Deputies, as Minister of Fuel and Power.[48] According to Deputy Khamaev:

> it is in the Duma, or in the opposition factions of the Duma, where these personalities grew into sizeable political figures. Examples of such people are, of course, Mikhail Zadornov, who has been a sort of junior leader with Yavlinskiy when he came to the Duma first in 1994. Now, he is the Minister of Finance, and a person of the highest reputation in all segments of the political community. Other Yabloko professionals include Tat'yana Nesterenko, who was Head of the Treasury Department in one of the smallest regions in Russia, in Chukotka, in 1993, and who is now the Director of the Federal Exchequer. She grew into such a professional in the Duma. There are many other examples of this, even Zhirinovskiy's people – Kalashnikov, the Chair of the Committee on Labor and Social Policy. So, if the Duma is capable of breeding such political figures, it means that its weight as an institution is growing.[49]

Because many high-ranking Government positions were offered to Deputies between 1994 and 1999, the perception arose that the Duma was a springboard to greater offices. Moreover, when Deputy Zyuganov was Yel'tsin's challenger in the run-off round of the 1996 Presidential elections, this became even more apparent. The improved identity of the Duma as an institution which bred future political leaders enhanced its prestige and respect.

In addition to these changes in the Government's composition, Yel'tsin utilized his power to replace Ministers and other Government officials rather often between 1994 and 1999. Yel'tsin, constitutionally and in actual practice, definitely had the upper hand in dismissing the Government as he frequently removed those whose actions were not in line with his own objectives and usually did so in response to economic troubles, as examined in the next section.[50]

### A change of Government: the President's nomination and Duma's acceptance and rejection of Prime Minister Sergey Kiriyenko, March to August 1998

While Chernomyrdin's Government survived four years and three months under the State Duma (and six years and three months overall), Sergey Kiriyenko's Government only endured for four months. Yel'tsin nominated Kiriyenko to the position of Prime Minister after he dismissed Chernomyrdin on 23 March 1998. Due to the constitutional law 'On the Government of the Russian Federation',[51] Yel'tsin was compelled to dissolve the entire Government when he removed the Prime Minister. Yel'tsin's reasons for ousting Chernomyrdin were that he did not want him to be the next President in the 2000 elections and Yel'tsin thought he was encroaching on his power by announcing his early candidacy; he thought that the Government needed new approaches because reforms were not being successfully implemented; and reports about his failing health made him want to demonstrate that he was still in control of politics in Russia. Because of the Russian President's immense powers to remove the Government without anyone's approval, he could decide suddenly to disband it without offering any justification. Yel'tsin stated his explanations for replacing Chernomyrdin in a televised address on 23 March 1998:

> Chernomyrdin is stepping down. I have worked with Viktor Chernomyrdin for more than five years, he has done a great deal for the country, and I value his thoroughness and reliability ... The 2000 election is very important to us, one might say to Russia's future. I have instructed Chernomyrdin to concentrate on political preparations for the election ... The current Cabinet of Ministers has, on the whole, accomplished the tasks that were set for it, but has failed to cope with a number of key problems. We have made a certain amount of progress in the economy, but we are still far behind in the social sphere. People do not feel that things are changing for the better. Recently, the Government has obviously been lacking in dynamism and initiative, new views, and fresh approaches.[52]

As far as the reforms and the need for a new approach, Yel'tsin claimed that pay and pension arrears were piling up again but they had been doing so for several months. Moreover, the Government in March 1998 had been significantly revamped on four occasions in a little over a year (in August 1996, January, March and November 1997) so there were many new people and 'fresh approaches'. Yel'tsin could have also made a few personnel changes without firing Chernomyrdin and the entire Government. What seems to be a more likely reason for this action was that 'the President did not see Viktor Chernomyrdin as his successor, and that view was shared by his inner circle – Chief of Staff Valentin Yumashev, Yel'tsin's daughter and advisor Tat'yana Dyachenko, and Press Secretary Sergey Yastrzhembskiy'.[53] As a result, the former Prime Minister seemed to lose popularity rapidly and virtually disappeared from the political scene following the Duma's two rejections of his candidacy for Prime Minister in August 1998.[54] I believe this latter point along with Yel'tsin's desire to re-establish control were the real motivations for the

Government's removal. In an interview with high-ranking Government officials, it was acknowledged that

> 'the state of Boris Yel'tsin's health played a major role here (in Chernomyrdin's dismissal)'...The weaker the prospects of the man in the Prime Minister's chair are, the less independent he will be and the more composed the master of the Kremlin (Yel'tsin) will be. Also, the President will be more confident that no matter what happens with his physical and mental health... nothing (no one) is threatening him.[55]

Lilia Shevtsova, a Senior Associate at the Carnegie Center in Moscow, confirmed that

> power abhors a vacuum. With a chronically weakened leader, it was natural and inevitable for the President's power potential, if not his functions, to start flowing to the Government and the Prime Minister, and for both to begin playing the role of surrogate presidency... In short, everyone (leading Government Ministers and the Prime Ministers) had plunged headlong into politics, an area that the President's team thinks should be the domain only of the President, not of his hired servants... Had Yel'tsin been in better health, he could have quietly put the Prime Minister back in his place, as he had done more than once before.[56]

Thus, Yel'tsin felt more secure with a weak Prime Minister who was much less likely and able to challenge his power.

Yel'tsin chose to nominate the little-known Fuel and Power Minister, Sergey Kiriyenko,[57] who was not part of the oligarchy or involved in politicking with the Duma and therefore, could not threaten his power. Most Deputies were greatly opposed to such a young, inexperienced person becoming Prime Minister. Moreover, they feared that because Yel'tsin's health was declining, Kiriyenko might become the acting President if Yel'tsin was unable to rule.[58] For an official with only one and a half years of experience working in the Government to rule the largest country in the world was an unthinkable prospect for Deputies.[59] This became even more apparent when Deputies overwhelmingly rejected Kiriyenko's candidacy on 10 April 1998. Even though the breakdown of results from the first round was not disclosed, the majority of Deputies did not vote 'no' outright. Table 6.5 shows that he only received 31.8 percent support, while 41.3 percent decided against him, 1.1 percent abstained, and 25.8 percent 'did not vote'. From the wide distribution of votes, it is obvious that Deputies could not decide

*Table 6.5*  Voting behavior of State Duma Deputies on the approval of Sergey Kiriyenko as Prime Minister in the first vote, 10 April 1998

| Date of vote | Voting on the approval of Kiriyenko for Prime Minister (secret vote) | | | |
|---|---|---|---|---|
| | *Yes* | *No* | *Abstain* | *Not voting* |
| 10 April 1998 (1st vote: Failed) | 143 31.8% | 186* 41.3%* | 5 1.1% | 116 25.8% |

* Indicates the position taken by the highest percentage of Deputies (in a given party or overall).

*Source*: *Gosudarstvennaya Duma: Stenogramma zasedaniy* (Federal'nogo Sobraniya Rossiyskoy Federatsii, Moscow, Izvestiya, 10 April 1998).

whether to endorse Kiriyenko or not. Yel'tsin immediately renominated Kiriyenko for confirmation.

The second vote, which constitutionally must not take place more than one week after the previous one, was held on 17 April 1998.[60] Deputies rationally chose to extend the vote to the last possible day, for each round, so they could increase their bargaining time with the executive. This was an open vote so party discipline and voting behavior can be analyzed. Table 6.6 indicates that political parties and even independents tended to vote either for or against Kiriyenko. Compared with the first and third votes, not nearly as many Deputies did not vote (only 11.8 percent). In all, 26 percent decided to endorse and 60 percent to reject Kiriyenko's candidacy, while 2.4 percent abstained. The majority of Deputies from the pro-Government party, Our Home is Russia, Russia's Regions, and independents backed Kiriyenko. Conversely, most Deputies in the oppositionist parties of Yabloko, the Liberal Democratic Party, and the Communist–Agrarian–People's Power coalition chose not to confirm him. Voting behavior within parties was rather disciplined, with very few Deputies in the Communist Party, Liberal Democratic Party, Yabloko, and Agrarian Party diverging from party line. As Vladimir Lukin explained earlier, political parties tend to be the most disciplined when voting on the budget, no-confidence motions, and approving a Prime Minister.[61] The Liberal Democratic Party was the most disciplined with 98 percent not confirming him and only one Deputy not voting. Aleksey Avtonomov, Legal Advisor to the State Duma, explained that:

Liberal Democrats vote according to the decision of Zhirinovskiy. After the vote on Kiriyenko's appointment, a Deputy from the Liberal Democratic Party was interviewed by journalists and he said that no one in his party knew how they would vote during this question

*Table 6.6*   Voting behavior of State Duma Deputies on the approval of Sergey Kiriyenko as Prime Minister in the second vote, 17 April 1998

| Political party or faction | Voting on the approval of Kiriyenko for Prime Minister in the second round 2nd round (17 April 1998) (failed) | | | | |
|---|---|---|---|---|---|
| | Yes | No | Abstain | Did not vote | Total |
| Communist Party of RF | 2 | 121* | 1 | 9 | 133 |
| | 1.5% | 91.0%* | 0.8% | 6.8% | |
| Our Home is Russia | 52* | 0 | 5 | 10 | 67 |
| | 77.6%* | 0.0% | 7.5% | 14.9% | |
| Liberal Democratic Party | 0 | 49* | 0 | 1 | 50 |
| | 0.0% | 98.0%* | 0.0% | 2.0% | |
| Yabloko | 0 | 34* | 0 | 10 | 44 |
| | 0.0% | 77.3%* | 0.0% | 22.7% | |
| Russia's Regions | 34* | 0 | 4 | 4 | 42 |
| | 81.0%* | 0.0% | 9.5% | 9.5% | |
| People's Power | 5 | 33* | 0 | 6 | 44 |
| | 11.4% | 75.0%* | 0.0% | 13.6% | |
| Agrarian Party of Russia | 4 | 29* | 0 | 2 | 35 |
| | 11.4% | 82.9%* | 0.0% | 5.7% | |
| Independents | 18* | 5 | 1 | 7 | 31 |
| | 58.1%* | 16.1% | 3.2% | 22.6% | |
| Total | 115 | 271* | 11 | 53 | 450 |
| | 25.6% | 60.2%* | 2.4% | 11.8% | |

* Indicates the position taken by the highest percentage of Deputies (in a given party or overall).

*Source*: *Gosudarstvennaya Duma: Stenogramma zasedaniy* (Federal'nogo Sobraniya Rossiyskoy Federatsii, Moscow, *Izvestiya*, 17 April 1998).

because they were waiting just for their leader to vote. If he (Zhirinovskiy) shows that he will vote in favor, then they would also vote in favor. All of the members (of the Duma) said there was a special decision of their faction about how to vote. Some factions decided to vote openly and others said it depends on the debates. Only the Liberal Democratic Party Deputies said they did not care and would just wait for a signal from Zhirinovskiy.

The high degree of discipline, with all parties having 75 percent of more Deputies voting in line with the party's decision, meant that it would be more difficult for Yel'tsin to swing the decision in the final round. He would have to make concessions to both political parties and individual Deputies to change the outcome.

*Table 6.7* Voting behavior of State Duma Deputies on the approval of Sergey Kiriyenko as Prime Minister in the third vote, 24 April 1998

| Date of vote | Voting on the approval of Kiriyenko for Prime Minister (secret vote) | | | |
|---|---|---|---|---|
| | *Yes* | *No* | *Abstain* | *Not voting* |
| 24 April 1998 (3rd vote: Approved) | 251* 55.8%* | 25 5.6% | 0 0.0% | 174 38.7% |

\* Indicates the position taken by the highest percentage of Deputies (in a given party or overall).

*Source*: *Gosudarstvennaya Duma: Stenogramma zasedaniy* (Federal'nogo Sobraniya Rossiyskoy Federatsii, Moscow, *Izvestiya*, 24 April 1998).

Although the majority of Deputies did not want to jeopardize their positions by rejecting Kiriyenko three times, the Communists thought they could gain from new elections.[62] As previously mentioned, the problem was that while the leaders of the party would benefit by keeping their positions through the party list, Deputies from single-member constituencies could not be as confident. Their re-election chances were not guaranteed and many were not willing to relinquish the perks of their office for Kiriyenko, who would become Prime Minister even after Yel'tsin disbanded the Duma because Yel'tsin said he had 'no other candidate for Prime Minister'.[63] Opposing the President in a third vote had only the advantage of showing the public that the 'oppositionist parties were truly oppositionists' in that they were willing to risk their jobs to fight the executive.[64] This was too much to offer or concede, as shown by the results of the third round. Instead, Deputies protested Kiriyenko's candidacy in two rounds to gain concessions from Yel'tsin, but retreated in the final stage.

Finally, with 55.8 percent support, Kiriyenko was approved in a third vote by the Duma on 24 April 1998. As in the first round, voting was closed so only the final tally is known. An unusually high number of Deputies, 38.7 percent, did not vote (Table 6.7). Since Deputies can telephone in their votes, it is likely that many of the 174 Deputies were paid to 'stay at home' on that day, though they were not willing to admit to this in interviews. Overall, the results revealed a high degree of discipline with no abstentions and only 5.6 percent (25) casting a 'no' ballot.

It is difficult to judge how concessions from Yel'tsin influenced voting since the first and third rounds were held in secrecy. From the very beginning, negotiations and concessions affected the outcome. Yel'tsin's first major bargain was to delay the initial vote on Kiriyenko by one week to allow more time for talks with (that is, to attempt to persuade) Deputies.

The Constitution stipulates that Deputies must consider the President's nomination one week after he submits it to the Duma.[65] When the week elapsed, the President withdrew the nomination and resubmitted it again. Thus, Deputies should have had until 3 April 1998 to hold the first vote but were instead given until 10 April. The explanation was that 'with a flat rejection looming from a broad majority in the Parliament, Yel'tsin agreed to all-party talks next Tuesday (7 April 1998) to listen to the opposition's suggestions and to put off the vote'.[66] This attempt to bend the Constitution was partially successful as even Kiriyenko was surprised by the amount of support, though it was only from 32 percent of Deputies, that he received in the first round, stating 'honestly, I expected fewer votes'.[67]

Prior to the second round, Yel'tsin met with Seleznyov and 'promised the Speaker that he would not veto some laws that the Duma had recently sent him and would sign the law 'On Restitution [of Cultural Treasures]'.[68] But, Yel'tsin waited until the day the vote was scheduled to offer more significant favors. He told Pavel Borodin, Chief of the President's Administrative Office who is responsible for distributing cars and apartments to state officials:

> 'to deal with any problems' that Deputies might have, provided that Deputies show a 'constructive attitude'...The words 'constructive attitude' should be read as, 'deal with Kiriyenko in the morning, and we will deal with apartments and other benefits in the evening'.[69]

The extent of such gifts was not publicized but as there were no other significant changes in the week between the first and second rounds, one would assume that they had some impact. But, when the actual results of the votes are analyzed, it is apparent that it had the opposite effect. In the second round, 28 Deputies withdrew their support from Kiriyenko and 85 additional Deputies opposed him. The reasons for this were twofold: Deputies knew that Kiriyenko would be proposed again so if they waited for another round, they would receive greater concessions; and they also wanted to express their extreme dissatisfaction in Yel'tsin and his choice of Prime Minister.

Finally, in the third round 55.8 percent of Deputies confirmed Kiriyenko. While 136 Deputies modified their vote to 'yes' between the second and third rounds, they were only partially motivated by concessions. As for the votes of no-confidence, Deputies did not want to jeopardize their positions and knew they had nothing to gain by rejecting Kiriyenko in the last round as he would become Prime Minister anyway, with or without the Duma's approval. On the one hand, Yel'tsin threatened to revise the electoral system by presidential decree if the Duma was dissolved to eliminate party lists and have Deputies elected solely by single seat districts. This removed the Yabloko and Communist Party elite's safe assumption that they would be re-elected if earlier elections were held because their party would secure more than 5 percent of the electorate's support.[70] The Duma countered this by warning that it would hold a vote of confidence in Kiriyenko's Government shortly after it was formed. Furthermore, Deputies began the initial stages for impeaching the President by collecting signatures for the motion to submit it immediately after the third vote, if Kiriyenko was not approved. The Constitution states that the Duma cannot be dissolved from the moment it begins impeachment proceedings against the President until a final decision is reached by the Council of the Federation. In this case, most Deputies thought that it was too risky to cause such a crisis because of the instability it would cause in the political system and for their own positions,[71] so they endorsed Kiriyenko. In fact, oppositionists could 'explain a vote for Kiriyenko by citing the need not only to save the Duma but also to preserve the present political system',[72] so Yel'tsin would be seen as the person responsible both for threatening such a crisis and for Kiriyenko's actions, and oppositionists could still be viewed as opponents of the executive. Thus, due to the risk of having to surrender their positions, Deputies had more to lose than the President in the Government's formation and dismissal, although a political and economic crisis resulting from dismissing the Duma could be politically costly for the President.

### The President's dismissal of officials in Kiriyenko's Government

Because Kiriyenko was Prime Minister for only four months (or three months, from when the Government was completely formed on 5 May 1998) there was not really an opportunity to hold a vote of confidence or for the President to dismiss many officials. There was great continuity between the composition of Chernomyrdin's and Kiriyenko's Governments.[73] The problem was that 'Yel'tsin was approving for ministerial posts the people who held those posts before or people whom the Duma factions emphatically did not want to see in the Government'.[74] In only one and a half months after its formation the State Duma was calling for Yel'tsin and the Government to resign. These demands were initiated in the province of Ryazan' on 27 May 1998 but within a month other regional Dumas supported their cause.[75] Then, in early July, State Duma Deputies appealed for Yel'tsin's removal and changes in the

Government by threatening to schedule a no-confidence vote.[76] The severe economic problems in August 1998 proved that Kiriyenko's Government did not have control over the financial situation in Russia. According to Tat'yana Koshkaryova and Rustam Narzikulov,

> there is no economic solution to the current financial crisis [of August 1998]: It can be resolved only by political means...The Kiriyenko Cabinet is incapable even of adequately assessing the situation in the market, let alone coping with the crisis. But the market's only part of it. It is unheard of to have a Prime Minister who does not exercise some control over the economic departments...It is clear that the main cause of the 'hysteria' [Kiriyenko's own description] in the market is a weak and incompetent Government.[77]

Because Kiriyenko's office was short-lived and he did not exert much control or cause significant change, he has been described as a 'pocket Prime Minister'.[78] Yel'tsin removed Kiriyenko on 23 August 1998, just two days after the Duma approved a resolution which asked the President to step down voluntarily and one day before the Duma was scheduled to hold a vote of no-confidence in the Government, which was bound to pass.[79] Thus, a combination of the economic crisis and pressure from the Duma caused Yel'tsin to dissolve the Government.

## A new Government: the President's nominations and Duma's acceptance and rejection of Viktor Chernomyrdin and Yevgeniy Primakov for Prime Minister, August and September 1998

Following Kiriyenko's dismissal, Yel'tsin nominated Viktor Chernomyrdin as Prime Minister. In a televised address on 24 August 1998, Yel'tsin explained:

> I made a difficult decision yesterday. I asked Viktor Chernomyrdin to lead the Government. Five months ago, no one anticipated that the world financial crisis would hit Russia so hard and that the country's economic situation would become so difficult. Under these circumstances, the main priority is to prevent any backsliding and to maintain stability. What we need today are the kind of people commonly known as 'heavyweights'. In my judgement, we need the experience and 'weight' of Chernomyrdin...I ask the Deputies, regional leaders

and all Russian citizens to understand me and to support my decision. In the current situation, there is no time for lengthy discussions for what is most important to all of us is the fate of Russia, stability, and decent living conditions for Russia's people.[80]

It is apparent from Yel'tsin's speech that he thought Chernomyrdin would bring 'stability' by ending the financial crisis because of his 'experience'. Also, since he had been Prime Minister for over five and a half years and seemed to have had good relations with the Duma previously, Yel'tsin thought he would be quickly approved by Deputies and that 'lengthy discussions' and concessions would not be necessary to convince them. In August 1998, the political and economic conditions were different from April 1998 when Kiriyenko was being confirmed. Deputies realized that Yel'tsin, despite threats, would not disband the Duma because with the economic collapse at the time, such action would plunge Russia into a completely volatile situation. This was too risky for Yel'tsin's own survival, financial markets, and democratic stability in Russia.

First, Yel'tsin thought Chernomyrdin would win approval in the Duma since he had previously enjoyed its support. Table 6.8 shows the voting behavior of Deputies on the nomination of Chernomyrdin for Prime Minister. On 31 August 1998 when the Deputies first rejected his candidacy, 21 percent voted in favor, while 56 percent voted 'no', 23 percent 'did not vote', and no one abstained. There are several explanations why Deputies rejected Chernomyrdin. Oppositionists blamed Chernomyrdin for many of the economic troubles in August 1998. Gennadiy Zyuganov issued a statement on 26 August 1998 that 'most of the blame for the tragedy that has befallen Russia rests, first and foremost, with Yel'tsin, Chernomyrdin, and their Government, which, under the West's directions, are pursuing a policy that is deadly for our state'.[81] Another reason was that Yel'tsin supported Chernomyrdin's candidacy for the 2000 Presidential elections when he recommended him for Prime Minister. Thus, the entire rules of the game changed as Deputies believed they were choosing not only a Prime Minister but a possible President. According to Yelena Dikun and Sergey Gavrilov, when

the President was prepared to replace Sergey Kiriyenko with Viktor Chernomyrdin, that turn of events suited most of the parliamentarians just fine – the leftist opposition had always been able to get along with the former Prime Minister. While Kiriyenko was still in office, the divvying up of portfolios in the future Government began behind closed

**Table 6.8** Voting behavior of State Duma Deputies on nominations of Viktor Chernomyrdin and Yevgeniy Primakov for Prime Minister in August/September 1998

*Voting on the nominations of Viktor Chernomyrdin and Yevgeniy Primakov for Prime Minister*

| Political party or faction | 1st round (Chernomyrdin, 31 August 1988) | | | | | 2nd round (Chernomyrdin, 7 September 1998) | | | | | 3rd round (Primakov, 11 September 1998) | | | | |
|---|---|---|---|---|---|---|---|---|---|---|---|---|---|---|---|
| | Yes | No | Abstain | Did not vote | Total | Yes | No | Abstain | Did not vote | Total | Yes | No | Abstain | Did not vote | Total |
| Communist Party of RF | 0 (0.0%) | 122* (93.1%*) | 0 (0.0%) | 9 (6.9%) | 131 | 2 (1.5%) | 127* (96.9%*) | 0 (0.0%) | 2 (1.5%) | 131 | 121* (92.4%*) | 1 (0.8%) | 2 (1.5%) | 7 (5.3%) | 131 |
| Our Home is Russia | 63* (94.0%*) | 1 (1.5%) | 0 (0.0%) | 3 (4.5%) | 67 | 64* (97.0%*) | 0 (0.0%) | 0 (0.0%) | 2 (3.0%) | 66 | 32* (48.5%*) | 1 (1.5%) | 5 (7.6%) | 28 (42.4%) | 66 |
| Liberal Democratic Party | 0 (0.0%) | 1 (2.0%) | 0 (0.0%) | 49* (98.0%*) | 50 | 48* (96.0%*) | 0 (0.0%) | 0 (0.0%) | 2 (4.0%) | 50 | 0 (0.0%) | 49* (98.0%*) | 1 (2.0%) | 0 (0.0%) | 50 |
| Yabloko | 0 (0.0%) | 42* (95.5%*) | 0 (0.0%) | 2 (4.5%) | 44 | 0 (0.0%) | 43* (97.7%*) | 0 (0.0%) | 1 (2.3%) | 44 | 43* (97.7%*) | 0 (0.0%) | 0 (0.0%) | 1 (2.3%) | 44 |
| Russia's Regions | 24* (54.5%*) | 11 (25.0%) | 0 (0.0%) | 9 (20.5%) | 44 | 14 (32.6%) | 12 (27.9%) | 0 (0.0%) | 17* (39.5%*) | 43 | 34* (79.1%*) | 1 (2.3%) | 3 (7.0%) | 5 (11.6%) | 43 |
| People's Power | 2 (4.4%) | 30* (66.7%*) | 0 (0.0%) | 13 (28.9%) | 45 | 2 (4.4%) | 41* (91.1%*) | 0 (0.0%) | 2 (4.4%) | 45 | 36* (80.0%*) | 3 (6.7%) | 2 (4.4%) | 4 (8.9%) | 45 |
| Agrarian Party of Russia | 1 (2.8%) | 34* (94.4%*) | 0 (0.0%) | 1 (2.8%) | 36 | 1 (2.8%) | 33* (91.7%*) | 0 (0.0%) | 2 (5.6%) | 36 | 36* (100.0%*) | 0 (0.0%) | 0 (0.0%) | 0 (0.0%) | 36 |
| Independents | 4 (14.8%) | 10 (37.0%) | 0 (0.0%) | 13* (48.1%*) | 27 | 7 (25.0%) | 17* (60.7%*) | 1 (3.6%) | 3 (10.7%) | 28 | 13* (46.4%*) | 8 (28.6%) | 2 (7.1%) | 5 (17.9%) | 28 |
| Total | 94 (20.9%) | 251* (55.8%*) | 0 (0.0%) | 105 (23.3%) | 450 | 138 (30.7%) | 273* (60.7%*) | 1 (0.2%) | 38 (8.4%) | 450 | 315* (70.0%*) | 63 (14.0%) | 15 (3.3%) | 57 (12.7%) | 450 |

* Indicates the position taken by the highest percentage of Deputies in a given party.

*Source: Gosudarstvennaya Duma: Stenogramma zasedaniy (Federal'nogo Sobraniya Rossiyskoy Federatsii; Moscow, Izvestiya, 31 August and 7, 11 September 1998).*

doors ... On Monday, August 24, 1998, the President announced that he regarded Chernomyrdin as his successor. 'Those were fatal words for Viktor Chernomyrdin', a prominent member of the Duma's opposition said. 'It is one thing to have Chernomyrdin as a candidate for Prime Minister, but for President – that is another matter entirely. Besides, we are not talking about 2000, but about the next few months [assuming that Yel'tsin would leave office]' ... Meanwhile, the distribution of portfolios in the Duma stopped and bargaining took a new turn.[82]

The executive's other mistake occurred during negotiations with Communists when it was openly admitted that Yel'tsin was weak. Although

> the regime's weakness was no secret before that, of course, the admission made it far worse. Zyuganov is very well aware that the Yel'tsin of 1998 is not the Yel'tsin of 1993. He knows what it cost the President back then to bring tanks onto the streets of Moscow. He is certain that the President could not repeat that episode today.[83]

This gave Communists further resolve to challenge Yel'tsin. Deputies ordered an impeachment commission to draft two articles against the President to be submitted for a vote if he presented Chernomyrdin as a candidate in a third round.[84] Moreover, with an unstable economy and only an acting Government, the markets continued to lose confidence and Yel'tsin's popularity declined. Yel'tsin, therefore, had a great incentive to concede to the Duma's wishes and ensure that the Prime Minister was accepted promptly. While Yel'tsin agreed to all of the Deputies' demands, the Communists backed out of their agreements for the above reasons and rejected Chernomyrin in two rounds.[85]

In the second round, Chernomyrdin gained 10 percent support, with 31 percent of Deputies voting 'yes', but 5 percent more Deputies voted 'no', 61 percent in total. The number of Deputies not voting decreased from 105 (23 percent) to 38 (8 percent). Predictably, Chernomyrdin's party, Our Home is Russia overwhelmingly voted for him in both rounds, with 94 percent doing so in the first vote and 97 percent in the second. As a result of concessions, the Liberal Democratic Party shifted from 98 percent of its Deputies not voting in the first instance to 96 percent voting in favor of Chernomyrdin on 7 September 1998. There is no other explanation for such a significant shift within one week. The only other major movement was with Russia's Regions where 55 percent cast their ballots for Chernomyrdin in the first round and then he lost

10 votes when 40 percent 'did not vote' in the next round. As in the first round, Deputies tended to reject concessions from Yel'tsin,[86] as shown by the decline in support between rounds, for the previously mentioned reasons.

When Yelt'sin realized after the second round that even more Deputies had voted against Chernomyrdin than before, he modified his tactics and considered the Deputies' suggestions for Prime Minister. The recommendation of Grigory Yavlinskiy, leader of the Yabloko Party, of Yevgeniy Primakov for Prime Minister won Yel'tsin's approval. Primakov was nominated and a vote was held on 11 September 1998. This was a significant turning point in executive–legislative relations in Russia as Yel'tsin recognized that he had to concede to the oppositionists and accept their candidate for Prime Minister, otherwise Russia would suffer an even more severe political and economic crisis, possibly leading to Yel'tsin's own removal. Primakov received the support of 315 (70 percent) Deputies, just one vote more than Chernomyrdin won in August 1996. In fact, comparing Tables 6.8 and 6.4 it is apparent that the voting was also similar as 11 percent did not vote for Chernomyrdin in August 1996 and 13 percent for Primakov in September 1998, 1 percent and 3 percent, respectively, abstained, and 19 percent and 14 percent of Deputies voted against them. This symmetry in voting patterns tends to suggest that when a candidate is well regarded, Deputies openly support him and are less indecisive, as shown by the low percentage of abstentions and those not voting. The Liberal Democratic Party was the only group where the majority of Deputies did not vote for Primakov. Yabloko Deputies, although they usually oppose the executive, rallied behind Primakov (with 98 percent support) but this was because he was Yavlinskiy's recommendation.

Comparing voting results by party in Table 6.8 shows that overall there was very strong party discipline. The Communist Party, Liberal Democratic Party, Yabloko, People's Power, and Agrarian Party all displayed this. The independents by their very nature were not disciplined since they are not affiliated with a party and have diverse views. Similarly, Russia's Regions, while being a political party, tends to have weak party discipline. For all three rounds, the ballots of the Deputies of Russia's Regions were dispersed and in the second round independents voted more congruently than they did. Our Home is Russia Deputies were disciplined when voting on Chernomyrdin but they were more undecided on Primakov where positions were widely divided.

Most Deputies endorsed Primakov and his officials so they had little incentive to remove him from 11 September 1998 to May 1999.

Yel'tsin dismissed Primakov and his Government on 12 May 1999 and he was replaced by Sergey Stepashin. There are several explanations for Primakov's dismissal. The most plausible reason is that it was a reactive measure against the Duma's impeachment proceedings against the President. Although the Duma did not actually succeed in passing any of the impeachment issues, as previously mentioned, this was not necessarily the goal. Deputies wanted to exert power and intimidate the President who was losing power and popularity to Primakov. Yel'tsin knew how popular Primakov was among Duma Deputies and removing him was his response to the Duma's attempts to impeach him. The Russian President and Parliament play a political game – one side makes a move which challenges the other side and the other side responds accordingly.

It was apparent in the first months of 1999 that Primakov was usurping Yel'tsin's power and his dismissal was also a reaction to put an end to this and to show everyone that Yel'tsin was still in charge. Examples of Primakov's efforts include negotiating limits to the President's constitutional powers while Yel'tsin was sick in January 1999. Primakov met with Duma Deputies to discuss a law preventing the President from dismissing the Government or dissolving Parliament. Newspaper headlines read 'Primakov Acts to Curb Yel'tsin's Powers'. Thus, although Primakov's removal was a reaction to the Duma's impeachment debates, Yel'tsin's decision was also influenced by the following: his illness and personal need to show he was still in control; Primakov's increasing power; rumors that Primakov was conspiring with the Communists to overthrow the President which were fueled by oligarchs and 'the Family's' fears; and the declining economy. For Primakov, the advantage of his timely dismissal was twofold: he avoided having to face responsibility for an unrealistic budget because budget reports were not due until June, and he regained his popularity, making him a viable candidate for the 2000 presidential elections. As examined in other chapters, Primakov helped to bridge the gap between the executive and legislature which created a less confrontational environment from September 1998 to April 1999.

## Conclusions: confrontation or cooperation in the formation and dismissal of the Government

In conclusion, the nature of executive–legislative relations in the sphere of Government formation and dismissal fluctuated between cooperative and confrontational from 1994 to 1999. The greatest conflicts arose between 21 June and 1 July 1995, when there was a possibility that the second vote of no-confidence in the Government in less than three months might pass; between 23 March and 24 April 1998, when Chernomyrdin was removed and during Kiriyenko's three rounds of approval by the Duma; between 23 August and 10 September 1998, when Yel'tsin nominated Chernomyrdin for Prime Minister and backed his candidacy for the 2000 Presidential elections until Yel'tsin accepted the recommendation of Primakov; and in May 1999 when Yel'tsin dismissed Primakov and the Duma attempted to impeach Yel'tsin. Periods with slightly less confrontation between branches were from 20 to 27 October 1994, when the Duma initiated but failed to approve a motion of no-confidence; from 7 to 22 October 1997, when the Duma threatened and almost held a vote on its confidence in the Government; and from 24 April to 23 August 1998, when Kiriyenko's Government was in power. The most cooperative times were during Chernomyrdin's, excluding the dates mentioned, and Primakov's Governments, reaching their high point on 10 September 1998, when Yel'tsin nominated Primakov and the Duma endorsed him the following day. Comparing the Governments of Chernomyrdin and Primakov, relations between the Duma and executive were better in the latter than in the former. Overall, executive–legislative relations shifted from cooperative (with Chernomyrdin) to confrontational (with Kiriyenko) and back to cooperative again (with Primakov).

Moreover, many of the predictions about the outcome of no-confidence votes and the approval of Prime Ministers in Russia tended to be incorrect from 1994 to 1999 because people underestimated Duma Deputies and the President as rational political actors throughout much of this period. As shown, both Deputies and the President had very little or no incentives, depending on the situation, to vote no-confidence in the Government twice in three months or dissolve the Government or Duma, respectively. They made these threats to intimidate, gain concessions, and deter certain actions of the other body, but they even admitted that these were threats which they did not intend to carry out. As for all rational actors in the game of politics, it is important to make such warnings as believable as possible. But, since the political chaos that could result from the Duma's or Government's dissolution threatened both the President's and Deputies' positions, they had few incentives to actually fulfill such statements. For example, in October 1997, 'Yel'tsin declared, contrary to his previous threats to "deal with" the Duma, that he had never had any thought of dissolving it'.[87] Such threats are just part of the political games and intrigue used by Russian politicians and should be considered as a component of the policy process in Russia.

Thus, while the President has unlimited power to dismiss the Government, the Duma can threaten or actually hold votes of no-confidence, which depending on the political and economic conditions at the time, tended to persuade Yel'tsin to either replace officials (in October 1994, June 1995, and October 1997) or remove the Government (in August 1998). In composing the Government, the President's powers are more restricted because the Prime Minister must be confirmed by the Duma. For the two instances when Yel'tsin replaced the Prime Minister, he was compelled to consider the Duma's interests, especially in August 1998. Although Yel'tsin could appoint whoever he chooses to the Government, from 1994 to April 1999 he often offered portfolios to Duma Deputies as concessions. In conclusion, even though the Duma's powers are not as extensive as the President's in forming and dissolving the Government, between 1994 and May 1999 the Duma successfully challenged the President's ability to exert his power in this sphere on several significant occasions.

# 7
# Budgetary Powers: the Power Struggle between the Executive and Legislature

Approving and implementing the annual federal budget are the most important responsibilities the State Duma and Government, respectively, have in the policy process. The federal budget determines which federal laws, resolutions, and presidential decrees will be funded and thus implemented. As a result, the body which has the power to draft, amend, and execute the budget has considerable influence. The focus of this chapter is on the actual budget powers that the President, Government, Duma, and Council of the Federation exercised in the negotiations, approval and implementation of the annual federal budgets from 1994 to 1999. Because the federal budgets are considered in the year prior to their scheduled implementation, proceedings for the 1994 to 1999 Budget legislation are analyzed. This chapter uses roll-call voting in the Duma and Council of the Federation to examine trends in voting behavior for and against budget legislation among political factions and the strength of majorities and the opposition in Parliament. The theoretical literature for this chapter is the same as in Chapter 4 when these issues were discussed in broader terms of policy-making in Russia. Incentives for the Government, President, Duma and Council to make different budgetary decisions will be considered, along with the outcomes of these actions. Conclusions will then be drawn about the roles of the legislature and executive in the budgetary process as they relate to the broader context of executive–legislative relations and parliamentary/presidential power in the policy process in Russia. Through this analysis I will show that Parliament has the ability to exert some degree of power over the Government and President in adopting and amending the federal budget, though the Government has great power in implementing the budget law.

## Constitutional powers of the Russian Executive and Legislature in the budgetary process

Because the Constitution stipulates that the Government first submits a draft budget to the Duma and the Duma then must liaise with the Government to pass the budget legislation in four readings, the Duma and Government are the principal participants in the budget proceedings.[1] The President and Council of the Federation also have some powers in the budgetary process. After the Duma approves the budget, the Council of the Federation must vote to reject or pass it.[2] If the Council vetoes the budget, the Duma can either override the veto with a two-thirds vote of the total number of Deputies, although they do not need to be present to vote, or establish a conciliatory committee, the exact composition of which is not set by law, with representatives from the Council, Duma and Government, to reach an agreement on the contested issues.[3] Once an arrangement is reached or the veto is overridden, the President must either sign or veto the budget legislation. If he signs it, it becomes law within 14 days.[4] But, if the President vetoes the bill, it is returned to the Duma which either votes with a two-thirds majority of all members to override the veto or calls for the formation of a conciliatory commission to reach a compromise on the disputed areas. Then, the entire process is repeated all over again with the submission of the revised draft to the Duma for a vote.[5]

After the budget is approved, the Government, Duma and Council of the Federation work to implement it, with the Government being primarily responsible for its execution. Although the Government is constitutionally liable for ensuring the realization of the budget's objectives, the Duma and Council of the Federation monitor its progress.[6] The Government must submit quarterly reports to the Duma on the budget's status.[7] Moreover, the Duma and Council assume a more active role by forming an Accounting Office to oversee the execution of the budget. One-half of the Office's auditors are appointed and removed by the Council and the other half by the Duma. The Duma selects the Chairperson, while the Council chooses the Vice-Chairperson of the Office.[8] This Office only has a monitoring function so it cannot enforce the budget, but it can conduct audits on the fulfillment of the budget's goals and offer amendments. It also recommends the dismissal of Ministers or other Government officials to the President when the budget is inadequate or officials are not performing their duties. If a budget becomes unrealistic and cannot be implemented, the Government must submit amendments and revisions of the budget law to the Duma for consideration and approval, as for the 1997 Budget law. Procedures for amending the budget are established each year as separate provisions in the law and they must be approved by Parliament.[9] This chapter will focus on how and the extent to which the Russian legislature and executive exercised their constitutional powers in regard to the 1994 to 1999 Budgets.

## The Russian Government's role in the budgetary process

The Russian Government has a much more significant role in the budgetary process than the President, as it must draft and implement the budget. According to the Chairman of the Duma's Budget Committee, Aleksandr Zhukov, 'the Minister of Finance drafts something in June [each year] and then presents it to the Duma'.[10] Because the Duma must pass the budget before it can be implemented, the Government has an incentive to cooperate and negotiate with the Duma. Archie Brown suggests, in reference to Anders Aslund's statement that 'Parliament has felt excluded' when it was not consulted on economic policy, that 'that particular mistake, at least, has not been made by Primakov'.[11] Indeed, the Government increasingly, from 1994 to 1999, worked more closely with the Duma, although this was partly because of Yel'tsin's poor health and, latterly, Primakov's favor among Duma Deputies. Still, Primakov was not above using threats to garner support for the budget: he 'warned: if the Duma does not sign the [1999] Budget, the Government will resign'.[12] Overall, Aleksey Golovkov, Vice-Chairman of the Duma's Budget Committee and Former Head of President Yel'tsin's Staff, explained that budget negotiations

> did not help relations between the Duma and Yel'tsin, but they did help those between the Duma and Government. Yel'tsin took no part in these … the relations between the Duma and Government are always moving towards bettering themselves. The members of these two bodies are getting more professional, and the experience and know how of the Deputies grows. In one way or another, the Government continues to work in a more peaceful and normal manner with the Duma. The procedure is normal, and everything is built around compromise.[13]

Furthermore, Zhukov stated that even though there were problems with the 1997 Budget, for example,

> the experience of cooperation between the Government and the Duma was very good ... We formed a special commission that consisted of four parts: the Duma, Council of the Federation, the Government, and the President's representatives. We went through a lot of discussions and after that we made a lot of changes to the budget.[14]

Moreover, the Government must be cautious in its negotiations with the Duma, but must also act in ways which do not displease the President, as its survival is dependent on the confidence of both bodies. For example, when the Government introduced sharp spending cuts in the 1998 Budget, and the Duma subsequently rejected it, some thought that 'the Government may also find itself taken to task for its failure to secure the passage of the 1998 draft Budget', meaning a dismissal or vote of no-confidence.[15] This, in fact, almost occurred in the debates on the 1995 Budget, when the Duma, unsatisfied with the drafts, offered a no-confidence motion in the Government on 27 October 1994 which failed by 32 votes.[16]

In addition to considering the Duma and President's views, the Government must also account for those of foreign lenders. According to Sergey Nikiforov, Member of the Duma's Budget Committee:

> the Government is very dependent on the opinions of the IMF. The IMF demands that the Government, to get money from them, pass certain laws concerning the budget. A 'proper' country needs to have a law on the budget, they think. So, the Government is stuck between arguing with the Duma and satisfying the IMF.[17]

In fact, the IMF has even resorted to 'punishing' the Government, by withholding funds, because of the Duma's reluctance to cooperate with the Government. For example, in July 1998 before the political and economic crisis in August,

> the International Monetary Fund's Board of Executive Directors had approved the disbursement of the first part of the stabilization credit to Russia. But, the amount, $4.8 billion, was $800 million less than what had been promised a week ago. Thus, the Fund has punished the Government for the Duma's failure to pass the anti-crisis package.[18]

Furthermore, the Duma has the power, indeed the responsibility, to confirm all of the loan agreements that are reached by the Russian President and Government with international organizations. From a statement by the State Duma, 'On the Russian Federation Government's Negotiations with Respect to a Stabilization Loan', the Duma clarified that

> all of the Government's loan-related accords with international organizations are invalid unless they are ratified by the Duma ... Under the law 'On International Treaties of the Russian Federation', the Duma is supposed to ratify such treaties. In addition, each year the Duma separately confirms, in the budget, the foreign borrowing program.[19]

This is a very significant power. The Duma began investigations in 1998 to determine whether several agreements with international financial organizations were illegal because they violated this law. With such dependence on the Duma both to approve the annual budget and all loan packages before receiving funding for reforms, the Government and President often make considerable concessions to the Duma to secure its passage. Either through appearances by the President and Prime Minister in the Duma or round-table discussions with parliamentary leaders, the executive makes an effort to appease Parliament.[20] All of these constraints limit the Government's power in drafting and ensuring the approval of budget legislation. The Government, however, has immense, and at times unchecked, powers in implementing the budget, as will be examined throughout this chapter.

## The Duma's power to influence the annual federal Budget

The two main ways of assessing the Duma's power in the budgetary process are to analyze the roll-call voting for each budget from 1994 to 1999, including the preliminary readings of the legislation, and by studying the amendments to and negotiations on the budget before and after it is signed by the President. An examination of roll-call voting during the four required readings of each budget is important because it shows the following: the political parties that support or reject the budget each year, those which bargain with the executive and change their votes between readings, the strength of the opposition, and the executive's ability to command a majority in the Duma. As previously mentioned, the Duma can insert amendments in budget legislation before it is forwarded to the Council of the Federation. This is a powerful tool because it enables the Duma to alter the budget without the approval of the Government or another body. Moreover, once the President signs the budget, the Duma can amend and revise it following

Table 7.1  Voting behavior on the 1994 to 1996 Federal Budgets in the State Duma elected in December 1993

| Political party of faction | 1994 Budget | | | | | 1995 Budget | | | | | 1996 Budget | | | | |
|---|---|---|---|---|---|---|---|---|---|---|---|---|---|---|---|
| *Voting on federal budget legislation as a number and percentage of Duma Deputies* | Yes | No | Abstain | Did not vote | Total | Yes | No | Abstain | Did not vote | Total | Yes | No | Abstain | Did not vote | Total |
| Russia's Choice | 45* 62.5%* | 3 4.2% | 0 0.0% | 24 33.3% | 72 | 48* 81.4%* | 1 1.7% | 0 0.0% | 10 16.9% | 59 | 41* 83.7%* | 0 0.0% | 0 0.0% | 8 16.3% | 49 |
| New Regional Policy | 49* 76.6%* | 3 4.7% | 4 6.3% | 8 12.5% | 64 | 45* 88.2%* | 4 7.8% | 0 0.0% | 2 3.9% | 51 | 27* 75.0%* | 1 2.8% | 0 0.0% | 8 22.2% | 36 |
| Liberal Democratic Party | 2 3.3% | 50* 83.3%* | 0 0.0% | 8 13.3% | 60 | 51* 91.1%* | 1 1.8% | 0 9.0% | 4 7.1% | 56 | 45* 81.8%* | 0 0.0% | 2 3.6% | 8 14.5% | 55 |
| Communist Party | 41* 89.1%* | 1 2.2% | 0 0.0% | 4 8.7% | 46 | 0 0.0% | 35* 76.1%* | 0 0.0% | 11 23.9% | 46 | 0 0.0% | 44* 95.7%* | 0 0.0% | 2 4.3% | 46 |
| Agrarian Party | 44* 81.5%* | 1 1.9% | 0 0.0% | 9 16.7% | 54 | 48* 88.9%* | 1 1.9% | 0 0.0% | 5 9.3% | 54 | 44* 86.3%* | 1 2.0% | 1 2.0% | 5 9.8% | 51 |
| Women of Russia | 20* 87.0%* | 0 0.0% | 0 0.0% | 3 13.0% | 23 | 20* 90.9%* | 0 0.0% | 0 0.0% | 2 9.1% | 22 | 19* 95.0%* | 0 0.0% | 0 0.0% | 1 5.0% | 20 |
| Yabloko | 0 0.0% | 15* 53.6%* | 2 7.1% | 11 39.3% | 28 | 0 0.0% | 17* 63.0%* | 0 0.0% | 10 37.0% | 27 | 0 0.0% | 19* 70.4%* | 0 0.0% | 8 29.6% | 27 |

Table 7.1  *continued*

**Voting on federal budget legislation as a number and percentage of Duma Deputies**

| Political party or faction | 1994 Budget | | | | | 1995 Budget | | | | | 1996 Budget | | | | |
|---|---|---|---|---|---|---|---|---|---|---|---|---|---|---|---|
| | Yes | No | Abstain | Did not vote | Total | Yes | No | Abstain | Did not vote | Total | Yes | No | Abstain | Did not vote | Total |
| Russian Unity and Accord | 26* 78.8%* | 0 0.0% | 0 0.0% | 7 21.2% | 33 | 22* 78.6%* | 0 0.0% | 0 0.0% | 6 21.4% | 28 | 8* 66.7%* | 0 0.0% | 0 0.0% | 4 33.3% | 12 |
| December 12 (1994 Budget) | 18* 72.0%* | 1 4.0% | 1 4.0% | 5 20.0% | 25 | | | | | | | | | | |
| Stability (1995, 1996 Budget) | | | | | | 20* 57.1%* | 1 2.9% | 0 0.0% | 14 40.0% | 35 | 18* 51.4%* | 0 0.0% | 1 2.9% | 16 45.7% | 35 |
| Russia (1996 Budget) | | | | | | | | | | | 24* 66.7%* | 0 0.0% | 0 0.0% | 12 33.3% | 36 |
| Democratic Party of Russia | 11* 73.3%* | 1 6.7% | 1 6.7% | 2 13.3% | 15 | 2 22.2% | 6* 66.7%* | 0 0.0% | 1 11.1% | 9 | 4 40.0% | 0 0.0% | 1 10.0% | 5* 50.0%* | 10 |
| Independents | 16* 57.1%* | 5 17.9% | 0 0.0% | 7 25.0% | 28 | 26* 44.1%* | 15 25.4% | 0 0.0% | 18 30.5% | 59 | 20 31.7% | 6 9.5% | 1 1.6% | 36* 57.1%* | 63 |
| Total | 272* 60.4%* | 80 17.8% | 8 1.8% | 90 20.0% | 450 | 282* 62.7%* | 81 18.0% | 0 0.0% | 87 19.3% | 450 | 250* 55.6%* | 71 15.8% | 6 1.3% | 123 27.3% | 450 |

* Indicates the position taken by the highest number of Deputies in a party.

** The Deputies Group of December 12 dissolved in Fall 1994 and two new groups were subsequently formed, 'Stability' and 'Russia' in Summer 1995.

*Source: Gosudarstvennaya Duma: Stenogramma zasedaniy* (Federal'nogo Sobraniya Rossiyskoy Federatsii, Moscow, *Izvestiya*, 24 June and 23 December 1994 and 6 December 1995).

the same procedure as for adopting a parliamentary law. The Duma can also, in certain years determined by the budget law, vote for or against the Government's amendments to the budget. As a result, the Duma can postpone deliberations on such changes to delay the implementation of certain laws or decrees, due to a lack of sufficient funds. These factors will be considered in relation to the 1994 to 1999 Budget laws.

## Debates on the 1994 to 1996 Budget legislation in the State Duma

Voting on the 1994 to 1996 Budgets in the Duma will be considered separately from the 1997 to 1999 Budgets because the December 1995 Duma elections resulted in different parties holding power when the 1997 and later Budgets were debated. Table 7.1 shows that the 1994 to 1996 Budget laws encountered little opposition in the Duma in the final round of voting, as only between 16 percent and 18 percent of the Deputies voted against them in each of these three years. The highlighted areas in the Table represent the position of the majority of Deputies in a given party on the budget for that year. More Deputies chose not to vote rather than to abstain or vote against the legislation. This is similar to what was shown in Chapter 6 regarding the decision of not voting, which is different from abstaining, as a means of protesting the legislation less blatantly than voting 'no'. It is occasionally true that Deputies are away from Moscow and are unable to vote on the budget legislation. But, since the budget is the most important legislation the Duma votes on each year and because it was proven in Chapter 6 that Deputies tend to use it to oppose legislation, the high percentage, between 20 percent and 30 percent of Deputies not voting is not completely due to unavoidable absences from the Duma. As previously mentioned, a Deputy could intentionally choose not to vote, instead of abstaining, if their views differed from the party line but they did not want to draw attention to this or if they wanted to oppose the executive branch. It is striking that in the final round of voting on the 1994 to 1996 Budgets, at most, 1.8 percent of Deputies abstained from voting; whereas, in 11 instances, 30 percent or more Deputies in a given party did not vote, instead of abstaining. For the 1994 to 1996 Budgets these groups included Russia's Choice and Yabloko Deputies on the 1994 Budget; Yabloko, Stability, and Independent Deputies on the 1995 Budget; and Yabloko, Russian Unity and Accord, Stability, Russia, Democratic Party of Russia, and Independent Deputies on the 1996 Budget. Besides Russia's Choice in 1994 and Russian Unity and Accord in 1996, all of these parties are oppositionist, centrist or comprised of independents. Yabloko is a democratic party, but as shown in Chapter 3, tends to oppose the Government and President on legislative matters. Indeed, the vast majority of Yabloko Deputies voted against the budget legislation from 1994 to 1996. Moreover, on the 1995 and 1996 Budget legislation all Yabloko Deputies either voted against it or did not vote. The factions composed of independents, the parties of December 12, Stability, and Russia, and the independents not belonging to factions had at least 20 percent of Deputies not voting. On the 1996 Budget, the majority of the independents did not vote in the final round and one-half of all parties had 30 percent or more Deputies not voting. With the exception of at most three votes in a different category and excluding independents not belonging to factions, all Deputies in a given party voted in at most two different positions, usually for or against and not voting. Also, the majority of Deputies in each party or faction across years, from the 1994 to 1996 Budgets, supported the same position, with the exception of the Independents and Democratic Party of Russia where the majority of Deputies alternated between voting in favor of the legislation or not voting, and the Liberal Democratic Party and Communist Party where the majority of Deputies changed their positions to vote in favor or against the legislation between these years.

Furthermore, the parties with the majority of Deputies voting against the budget are oppositionist parties. Even though soon after the passage of the 1994 Budget, the Liberal-Democratic party proved to be less confrontational with the Government and was usually the first or second party to accept bribes for votes on legislation, they were an oppositionist party in 1994. (See Chapters 3 and 4 for more detailed analysis.) Conversely, the Communist Party grew more confrontational with 76 percent of Deputies rejecting the 1995 Budget and 96 percent refusing to accept the 1996 Budget.[21] Yabloko is the only party which consistently, from the 1994 to 1996 Budgets, had a majority of its Deputies voting against the legislation. Because Yabloko doubled in size and the Communist Party more than tripled in the number of seats it held in the Duma after the 1995 elections, these parties will be seen to be more important when Table 7.2 is examined. Democratic Party of Russia had a majority of its Deputies opposing the 1995 Budget but even though it is a centrist party, this is not very significant as the composition of the party decreased by 40 percent from 1994 to 1995 and because, with only nine Deputies in 1995, if two Deputies changed their vote a different result would have occurred.

Changes in the votes of the majority of party members between readings of the legislation indicate that amendments were made to the legislation or negotiations took place between the party or Duma as a whole

*Table 7.2* Voting behavior on the 1997 to 1999 Federal Budgets in the State Duma elected in December 1995

| Political party or faction | Voting on federal budget legislation as a number and percentage of Duma Deputies | | | | | | | | | | | | | | |
|---|---|---|---|---|---|---|---|---|---|---|---|---|---|---|---|
| | 1994 Budget | | | | | 1995 Budget | | | | | 1996 Budget | | | | |
| | Yes | No | Abstain | Did not vote | Total | Yes | No | Abstain | Did not vote | Total | Yes | No | Abstain | Did not vote | Total |
| Communist Party of RF | 71* (49.3%*) | 32 (22.2%) | 13 (9.0%) | 28 (19.4%) | 144 | 52 (38.5%) | 63* (46.7%*) | 2 (1.5%) | 18 (13.3%) | 135 | 118* (91.5%*) | 5 (3.9%) | 0 (0.0%) | 6 (4.7%) | 129 |
| Our Home is Russia | 58* (90.6%*) | 0 (0.0%) | 0 (0.0%) | 6 (9.4%) | 64 | 63* (95.5%*) | 0 (0.0%) | 0 (0.0%) | 3 (4.5%) | 66 | 54* (91.5%*) | 0 (0.0%) | 1 (1.7%) | 4 (6.8%) | 59 |
| Liberal Democratic Party | 50* (98.0%*) | 0 (0.0%) | 0 (0.0%) | 1 (2.0%) | 51 | 49* (98.0%*) | 0 (0.0%) | 0 (0.0%) | 1 (2.0%) | 50 | 47* (94.0%*) | 0 (0.0%) | 1 (2.0%) | 2 (4.0%) | 50 |
| Yabloko | 0 (0.0%) | 38* (82.6%*) | 0 (0.0%) | 8 (17.4%) | 46 | 0 (0.0%) | 40* (90.9%*) | 0 (0.0%) | 4 (9.1%) | 44 | 0 (0.0%) | 40* (88.9%*) | 0 (0.0%) | 5 (11.1%) | 45 |
| Russia's Regions | 30* (71.4%*) | 3 (7.1%) | 0 (0.0%) | 9 (21.4%) | 42 | 36* (85.7%*) | 2 (4.8%) | 0 (0.0%) | 4 (9.5%) | 42 | 23* (51.1%*) | 6 (13.3%) | 3 (6.7%) | 13 (28.9%) | 45 |
| People's Power | 11* (33.3%*) | 10 (30.3%) | 1 (3.0%) | 11* (33.3%*) | 33 | 16 (37.2%) | 17* (39.5%*) | 0 (0.0%) | 10 (23.3%) | 43 | 30* (65.2%*) | 4 (8.7%) | 1 (2.2%) | 11 (23.9%) | 46 |
| Agrarian Party of Russia | 15* (41.7%*) | 5 (13.9%) | 3 (8.3%) | 13 (36.1%) | 36 | 28* (80.0%*) | 4 (11.4%) | 0 (0.0%) | 3 (8.6%) | 35 | 30* (83.3%*) | 0 (0.0%) | 0 (0.0%) | 6 (16.7%) | 36 |
| Independents | 10 (40.0%) | 2 (8.0%) | 0 (0.0%) | 13* (52.0%*) | 25 | 8 (30.8%) | 3 (11.5%) | 0 (0.0%) | 15* (57.7%*) | 26 | 6 (19.4%) | 3 (9.7%) | 0 (0.0%) | 22* (71.0%*) | 31 |
| Total | 245* (54.4%*) | 90 (20.0%) | 17 (3.8%) | 98 (21.8%) | 450 | 252* (56.0%*) | 129 (28.7%) | 2 (0.4%) | 67 (14.9%) | 450 | 308* (68.4%*) | 58 (12.9%) | 6 (1.3%) | 78 (17.3%) | 450 |

* Indicates the position taken by the highest percentage of Deputies in a party.

*Source:* *Gosudarstvennaya Duma: Stenogramma zasedaniy* (Federal'nogo Sobraniya Rossiyskoy Federatsii, Moscow, *Izvestiya*, 24 January 1997, 4 March 1998 and 5 February 1999, respectively).

and the executive. According to Dvorkovitch speaking on behalf of the Government's policy, 'when entire political parties shift their votes between readings on budget legislation, it means that some concessions have been made by the executive'.[22] Examples of concessions are an approval to amend the budget (usually meaning that the President would not veto it on the basis of the new amendments), money, and the executive's support for the passage of other legislation. Because most negotiations with the Government or President occur behind closed doors and are not made public, it is difficult to determine to what degree bribes or negotiations took place. In interviews on the 1997 to 1999 Budgets several Deputies admitted to this, but little evidence exists. It is also problematic to prove that amendments to the budget legislation caused some Deputies to change their votes between readings because during the interviews I found that most would not divulge this. Since negotiations or bribes are not usually publicized it is not possible to ascertain accurately whether they changed their votes for these reasons. An analysis of changes in the voting behavior of the majority of Deputies between budget readings will illustrate Deputies' attempts to assert their power, either in negotiations or amendments to the law.

During the 1994 Budget readings, a majority of party members in six of the 11 parties, comprising 59 percent of all Deputies, changed their votes between the first or second and third readings.[23] Most shifts tend to occur between the first and second or second and third readings because the second and third readings concern the allotment of revenue. The first reading is to set the major parameters for the budget, while the second is for the allocation of expenditure and the third, to determine the distribution of expenditure by specific monetary organizations. The fourth reading is merely for editorial purposes.[24] The majority of Deputies from the Russia's Choice faction changed their votes from 'no' in the first round, not voting in the second round, and 'yes' in the third (final) round, indicating that an amendment to the budget or other concession was, most likely, made to the Party. Liberal-Democratic Deputies mostly voted 'yes' in the first two rounds and 'no' in the final round, to show their opposition to the Government and/or because their demands for bribes were not met, even after four rounds. Since Yel'tsin and the Government only need to obtain the support of 50 percent of Deputies for the budget to proceed, they have no incentive to secure backing from all Deputies, and thus, they offer concessions to those most willing to negotiate or to Deputies whose votes they need to achieve the 50 percent threshold. Yabloko, the Democratic Party of Russia, New Regional Policy, and December 12 each had a majority of

Deputies who shifted their votes from not voting in the first two rounds to a vote of 'yes' or 'no' in the final round.[25]

During the 1995 Budget debates, only four of the 11 factions, totalling 33 percent of Deputies, had a majority of Deputies who changed votes between rounds.[26] With 59 percent of Deputies not voting in favor of the 1994 Budget, the executive had more reason to bargain with Deputies than with only 33 percent of Deputies not voting in favor of the budget in the initial rounds. Most of the Yabloko Deputies, similarly to the 1994 Budget, did not vote in the second round but modified their vote to 'no' for the third and final rounds. Deputies from the Democratic Party of Russia chose to split their votes, with one-third voting 'yes', 'no', and not voting in the first round, while most Deputies voted 'yes' in the second and 'no' in the third and fourth rounds. The Agrarian Party and Independents tended to vote 'no' in the first round and later supported the legislation by the third round because they received concessions, as discussed later in this chapter.[27]

There was significantly less fluctuation in the voting on the 1996 Budget, by only 11 percent of Deputies in parties, because elections for the new Duma took place in December 1995 and Deputies wanted to approve the budget before a new Duma was elected.[28] This is also apparent since it was the earliest and quickest budget passed by the Duma under Chernomyrdin's Government, with the second and final readings on the same day, 6 December 1995.[29] Elections to the Duma were held just 11 days later, on 17 December 1995. Russian Unity and Accord and Russia were the only parties to alter their vote from a majority of Deputies not voting in the first round to supporting the legislation in the second and third rounds. Moreover, many Deputies did not attempt to negotiate agreements with the executive on the 1996 Budget because it was unclear whether their factions would obtain at least 5 percent of the vote in the new elections. Their main goal was to push forward the legislation before elections. These figures show that due to fluctuations in voting behavior for entire parties between readings, as Dvorkovitch agreed, the executive made concessions to the Duma. With negotiations and bribes (as proven later), the executive was able to command a majority in the Duma, sufficient enough to approve the 1994 to 1996 Budgets.

## Debates on the 1997 to 1999 Budget legislation in the State Duma

There are some similarities in the overall voting behavior of Deputies on the 1994 to 1999 Budgets. Comparing Tables 7.1 and 7.2, the percentage

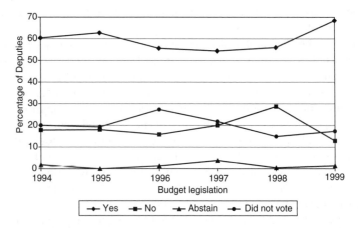

*Figure 7.1*   Voting behavior on the 1994 to 1999 Federal Budgets as a percentage of the total number of Duma Deputies.

of Deputies who abstained from voting remained very low, peaking at 3.8 percent on the 1997 Budget, but remaining at less than 2 percent in all other final readings of the 1994 to 1999 Budgets. Figure 7.1 illustrates that the percentage of Deputies supporting the budget in the final reading peaked for the 1999 Budget, at 68.4 percent which is enough to override any veto from the Council of the Federation or President, but which was always between 54 percent and 68 percent for all six budgets. Regarding the unusual level of support for the 1999 Budget, Dvorkovitch explains that

> the 1999 Budget was adopted in a record number of days, usually it takes three to five months. There are two reasons for this. The first is political, as an indication of trust in the new Government and Primakov. The second reason is that the Duma before elections [in December 1999] understands that whatever they adopt now is probably going to influence the election campaign.[30]

Deputies are motivated by political interests and as the discussion in the previous chapter illustrated, most were eager to show their support for Primakov by voting in favor of the 1999 Budget in record time and with the highest percentage of 'yes' votes to indicate this. Their own re-election campaigns also gave reason to show backing for Primakov, who in late 1998 had a high level of public support. The percentage of Deputies voting 'no' on the budget legislation reached its lowest point on the 1999 Budget, with 12.9 percent, and peaked at 28.7 percent for the 1998 Budget. Between 15 percent and 27 percent of Deputies did not vote on each of the 1997 to 1999 Budgets in the final round.

There are differences between the roll-call voting of individual parties on the 1994 to 1996 Budgets in the Duma and on the 1997 to 1999 Budgets due to the change in the political composition of the Duma after the 1995 elections. Among the parties that maintained seats in the Duma after the 1995 elections, the one similarity is that the voting of the majority of Deputies in the parties remained the same. Most Agrarian Party Deputies supported all of the Budgets, Yabloko and Liberal-Democratic Party Deputies (with the exception of the 1994 Budget for reasons explained above) voted against all of them, while Communist Party Deputies tended to shift between 'yes' and 'no' voting on the budgets.

One of the main differences with the voting behavior for the 1997 to 1999 Budgets was that the voting of half of the Deputies belonging to parties was more fragmented than for the 1994 to 1996 Budgets. Unlike the 1994 to 1996 Budget votes where no party (except for the New Regional Policy party on the 1994 Budget, but only by one vote) had its votes split in more than two different ways on a given budget (excluding a less than three-vote deviation which was deemed insignificant), parties tended to vote in at least three different ways for the 1997 to 1999 Budgets. Fragmented parties were from the coalition of the Communist–Agrarian–People's Power, which accounts for slightly more than half of Deputies in parties. The Communist Party went from being very disciplined on earlier budgets, with between 76 percent and 96 percent of Deputies voting for the same position to as low as 47 percent for the 1997 to 1999 Budgets. More significantly, the rest of the Deputies, who voted against the party line, did not just abstain or not vote, but voted for the opposing position of the party. On the 1998 Budget, 39 percent of Communist Party Deputies voted to support the budget, although the party line was against the budget, though less than half of the Deputies voted accordingly. Gennadiy Zyuganov freed Deputies of the Communist Party from having to vote in line with the party's position on the 1998 Budget, according to a Deputy from the Communist Party, Aleksandr Ponomarev.[31] This was a tactical measure which aided the passage of the budget in the final reading. In addition, less than half of the Deputies in People's Power adopted the party line and of those who did not, the votes were dispersed between not voting and the opposite of the party's line. The Agrarian Party which was highly disciplined on prior budget legislation,

with at most two Deputies voting against the party line, had only 42 percent of its Deputies supporting the party line on the 1997 Budget, though
in later budget votes it was more unified, with 80 percent or more following the party's choice. One explanation for the increased fragmentation
within the Communist Party, as suggested in Chapter 3, is that because the
number of seats held by the party more than tripled after the 1995 election, there was a greater possibility for division within the party. Some
members of the Communist Party elected in 1995 were more oppositionist and extremist than the party leader, Zyuganov.[32] Conversely, People's
Power was formed after the 1995 elections and was comprised of independents and others from different parties. This, coupled with the fact that
it is part of a coalition with the Communist Party and Agrarian Party,
although not all Deputies in the party support this coalition for all votes,
explains the fragmentation within the party.

There was much less variation in the voting preferences of the majority of Deputies in a given party during the readings for the 1997 to 1999
Budgets than for previous budgets. In four rounds of voting on the 1999
Budget, there were no fluctuations due to Primakov's closer relations
with Deputies than other Prime Ministers have enjoyed, as shown
above.[33] Primakov also took time to consult Deputies while drafting the
1999 Budget, negotiate revisions and amendments, and visit the Duma
on several occasions to elicit support for it. The position which the
majority of Deputies in a party held for the four readings of the 1997
and 1998 Budgets remained constant, except for a four-vote change after
the first round of the 1998 Budget by Deputies in People's Power and a
change of one vote on the 1997 Budget.[34] Although the party vote did
not oscillate, the number of Deputies endorsing a given position
changed throughout the readings. Even with limited fluctuation in the
voting, the Duma did not approve realistic budgets.

Indeed, most of the budgets, especially the 1997 Budget, were partially
unimplementable. But, as explained above, this is the best policy option
for the Duma because it provided Deputies with an opportunity to negotiate with and/or criticize the Government. As a result of the problems with
the 1997 Budget, the Duma had more chances to bargain with the
Government. According to Golovkov, 'there was a compromise that
showed our power, in the sense that the Government moved in the direction of the Duma, after the Duma voted for a fourth time that
the [1997] Budget was sufficiently lacking and unsatisfactory'.[35] Aleksandr
Shokhin, former leader of the pro-Government party, Our Home
is Russia, Former First Deputy Chairman of the Duma, and Former

First Deputy Prime Minister and Minister of Finance, stated that the Duma's

> instrument for control [of the executive] is the budget. After adopting the budget, the Duma has the opportunity to criticize the Government. Even in this year [1997], when the Government presented the first draft of the budget, this budget was very unrealistic but after meeting [in the special commission] we increased [budget] income by 30 billion rubles ... Yavlinskiy criticized the Government just for this compromise with Leftist factions. In the Spring [1997], when the Government reports to the Duma, in the first quarter of the year, if it cannot meet the budget [objectives], the Leftist wing will have the opportunity to raise a no-confidence vote in the Government. It is a real problem for the Government.[36]

In 'Russian Economy: Trends and Perspectives', the authors explain that

> the State Duma, in its turn, is not at all interested in a realistic budget because the perspectives of gaining more political capital at the expense of criticism of an inefficient performance of the Government seems more real than prospects of economic growth and expansion of possibilities of the 1998 Budget.[37]

Thus, the Duma was more politically motivated to pass unrealistic budgets from 1994 to 1998 than to back down on some disagreements with the executive and cooperate to adopt a realistic budget.

During budget readings, the Duma, as a whole or through individual factions, usually negotiates concessions from the Government and President. While many of these are secret and not publicized, some of the most significant ones are made public. It is often difficult, even when negotiations appear in the media, to find out about them. The 1995 Budget, the only budget under Chernomyrdin's Government to pass in the Duma before the start of the year in which it was to be implemented, was approved with detrimental concessions from the Government. Budget revenues were already limited, but

> seeking to please the parliamentary factions, the Government agreed to grant an additional 550 billion rubles to farms so they could pay for fuel and machine parts during the spring planting ... The Agrarian Party was the most successful lobby during the budget debate, more than doubling the initial allocation to agriculture to 12.8 trillion rubles.[38]

Each year the Government, according to the Deputy Minister of Finance Oleg V'yugin's Assistant, 'allocates a part of the budget expenditure for concessions to the Duma. From the view of fiscal efficiency this is bad but it usually happens. The budget is not good from an economic point of view but only from a political point of view.'[39] In the debates for the 1996 Budget, the Agrarian Party, one of the strongest lobbies in budget proceedings because the party itself is centred around special interests (of Agrarians), gained concessions from the Government. According to Svetlana Lolayeva, 'the [1996] Budget's fate was decided through traditional bargaining with the Agrarians – a half-hour pause during which the Deputies feverishly adopted various draft laws one after the other, while Government representatives, from all indicators, consulted with the Prime Minister by telephone [about the concessions]'.[40] It is possible that other parties did as well, but closed door meetings are kept private, unless a member publicizes their contents. Following a secret meeting between oppositionist factions in the Duma and Chernomyrdin while the first reading of the 1997 Budget was debated in the Duma, Gennadiy Zyuganov said before the vote was taken that 'the Cabinet had accepted two-thirds of the Communists' demands, and therefore the Communists were willing to support the Budget'.[41] Thus, Communist Deputies modified their votes on the 1997 Budget by bargaining with the executive. Duma Deputies received, according to what is publicized, more concessions overall on the 1998 Budget. David McHugh found that the Duma

> won limited control over spending priorities by requiring cuts to be made proportionally across the board, preventing the Government from cutting some programs more deeply than others. That would spread the pain of cuts over the entire budget, instead of axing the raft of pork-barrel spending items to which the opposition won agreement in November (1997)...[The Government also] agreed to inform the legislature and mass media within three days that it is making cuts. The Government must also give the Duma proposals for improving tax collection and Government efficiency within three months of the budget taking effect. Ministers won support of the leftist-nationalist People's Power faction by agreeing to favored budget treatment for closed areas where military and nuclear installations are located.[42]

Moreover, the President conceded to signing a major law which would give the Duma greater power over the Government and reduce the President's power, the law 'On the Government', to compel the Duma to support the 1998 Budget. Yel'tsin had opposed this law only a week earlier but 'was forced to make this most unexpected decision and accede to the opposition's wishes by the real threat hanging over the 1998 Budget'.[43] Among other things, this law meant that if the President dismissed the Prime Minister, he must also disband the Government, as discussed in the previous chapter. Even for the 1999 Budget, although Primakov enjoyed favor with the majority of Deputies, he had to make concessions to the Duma. While the 1999 Budget passed in its first reading:

> Primakov still had to do a bit of work to persuade the Deputies. Besides meeting with the faction leaders, he had to personally make the rounds of the Deputies' factions; in short, he had to go through the required political budget ritual. On this basis, one could say that the Prime Minister is no longer politically sacrosanct. He may be liked, respected and feared, but in public he has to show a degree of political dependence on the legislative branch and be willing to compromise with it. This produced another important result: both branches showed willingness to compromise, and this is unquestionably something that can only be welcomed.[44]

In the second reading of the 1999 Budget, the Duma more directly challenged the executive's power by reducing the budget of the President's Administration.

> On expenditures for state funds, the Duma reduced the expenditure of the President's spending and increased its (the Duma's) expenditure. The Government proposed a proportional reduction. The Duma, then, in the final reading reduced the President's administrative funds proportionally much more than the Duma's own.[45]

While the executive did not command a majority on the 1994 to 1998 Budgets, it was able to secure it by conceding to some of the Deputies' conditions. Concessions during the budgetary process are an important way for Deputies to try to attain greater influence and/or advantages than they might otherwise be given in negotiations on other types of legislation. The extent to which it employs tricks, delays debates, and demands concessions from the executive serve to help it exert power in the budgetary process.

## The Council of the Federation's power in the budgetary process

The Council of the Federation's incentives and actions in the budgetary process are determined by the votes of Duma Deputies and Council

Members' own preferences. When the Duma approves a budget with a two-thirds vote of the total number of Deputies, the Council has no incentive to reject the budget because the Duma could override the veto. The only reason would be if Council Members greatly disapprove of the budget and want to demonstrate this, but the drawbacks would outweigh the benefits of doing so, as explained earlier in this chapter. Since most Council Members do not belong to a political party it is not possible to analyze the voting behavior of Members except in overall terms. Council Members all have an interest in securing as much money as possible for their region, although they do not possess much bargaining power when Duma Deputies can override a veto by the Council with a two-thirds vote (and Deputies need not be present to vote). Zhukov acknowledges that the main source of problems between the Duma and Council is funding 'problems of regions, in connection with the budget'.[46] According to Oleg Bocharov, Deputy of the Moscow City Duma (1994–99) and Chairman of the Commission on Legislation and Security:

> the Moscow budget is part of the federal budget. Russia consists of 89 subjects. Only six of them finance the budget, the rest (83) just receive money from the federal budget. Moscow is a city, but at the same time a subject of the Russian Federation and we help to finance the federal budget.[47]

Because of the extreme disproportion between the number of regions paying in to the federal budget and those receiving subsidies, a former Moscow City Duma Deputy explained that:

> those regions which receive subsidies, which are in fact financially bankrupt, are interested in getting as much money as they can, and those regions which are donors, which fill the federal budget, are interested in giving as little as possible and keeping as much as possible for themselves.[48]

Even though Moscow is only a city, it is one of Russia's largest donors to the federal budget but, in the 1998 Budget for example, it did not receive any subsidies in return.[49] It is obvious, then, why regional interests prevail in the Council's budget debates: the wealthiest regions fight to get some money back from their contributions to the budget, while poorer regions try to negotiate greater subsidies. Moreover, the Council also lobbies for concessions in the budget each year. It agreed to pass the 1999 Budget, for example, only after Primakov agreed to comply with

*Table 7.3* Voting Behavior on the 1994 to 1999 federal budgets in the Council of the Federation

| Budget legislation | Voting on federal budget legislation as a number and percentage of Members of the Council of the Federation | | | |
|---|---|---|---|---|
| | *Yes* | *No* | *Abstain* | *Did not vote* |
| 1994 Budget | 100 | 19 | 0 | 59 |
| | 56.2% | 10.7% | 0.0% | 33.1% |
| 1995 Budget | 99 | 24 | 6 | 49 |
| | 55.6% | 13.5% | 3.4% | 27.5% |
| 1996 Budget | 95 | 14 | 3 | 66 |
| | 53.4% | 7.9% | 1.7% | 37.1% |
| 1997 Budget | 120 | 25 | 9 | 24 |
| | 67.4% | 14.0% | 5.1% | 13.5% |
| 1998 Budget | 115 | 22 | 4 | 37 |
| | 64.6% | 12.4% | 2.2% | 20.8% |
| 1999 Budget | 130 | 18 | 3 | 27 |
| | 73.0% | 10.1% | 1.7% | 15.2% |
| Total | 659 | 122 | 25 | 262 |
| | 61.7% | 11.4% | 2.3% | 24.5% |

*Source*: *Sovet Federatsii: Stenogramma zasedaniy* (Federal'nogo Sobraniya Rossiykoy Federatsii, Moscow, *Izvestiya*, 1994 to 1999).

one (the main one) of its six demands: to restore equity and divide the revenues of the consolidated budget 50–50 between the Government and the Federation members, rather than 54–46.[50] This is just one of many examples of negotiations which are believed to occur to bolster Council Members' support for the budget.

Although the Council approved the 1994 to 1999 Budgets in the first round without vetoing them, they had varying levels of endorsement. As shown in Table 7.3, votes in favor of the budgets fluctuated between 53 percent on the 1996 Budget to 73 percent on the 1999 Budget. Council Members had no incentive to veto the 1999 or 1995 Budgets because the Duma most likely would have overturned any veto, as the final vote in the Duma was 68 percent and 63 percent, respectively. Similar to the overall voting results in the Duma, Council Members tended to rarely abstain from voting, only 2.3 percent on average. Moreover, as in the Duma, the second most common position on the budget by Council Members was not to vote, 24.5 percent on average chose to do so, followed by a vote against the legislation, which 11.4 percent of Members on average took.[51]

Relations between the Duma and Council have improved with successive budgets. Vladimir Shumeyko, Chairman of the Council of the Federation from 1994 to 1996, stated after the first session of the Duma in January 1994

> that if everything in the Duma keeps happening in as disorderly a way as it did on the first day, it will be necessary to decide on the question of transferring the right to confirm the budget to the Council of the Federation ... if a legal way to bypass the Duma regarding implementation of the law on the budget is found, it will be easy to extend this method to all other laws of any significance.[52]

Of course, Shumeyko's suggestion of the possibility of transferring budget power to the Council is not only unconstitutional, but would require approval by the Duma. The Duma would not relinquish its most powerful tool in the policy process. Comments like Shumeyko's and Yel'tsin's, which we will discuss later, add to the misconception about the power of the Duma in the budgetary process. If one did not realize that Shumeyko's statement was unconstitutional, one would tend to believe that it could possibly happen or that Yel'tsin's demands for the Duma to pass the budget really encourage the Duma to adopt it, rather than what actually occurs, that it incites oppositionists to oppose it further.[53] As shown in previous chapters, the Duma, Council, Government, and President, but mostly the Duma and President, are not pleased when another body attempts or threatens to usurp their power. Still, the Council did not reject the six budgets, from 1994 to 1999, though it tends to approve them unenthusiastically. For example, Council Members used the discussion time of the 1997 Budget to complain about the Government's shortcomings. Various Members protested that the budget was unrealistic and that their regions did not receive enough money from the 1996 Budget because the Government cut spending to cover shortages in tax collection.[54] Even with hours of complaints, the Council reluctantly passed the 1997 Budget, because they claimed, as for other budgets, that they had no choice since a veto would mean further delays of funds to their, mostly, cash-strapped regions, and more economic troubles.

## The Russian President's power in the budgetary process

Although the President did not veto the 1994 to 1999 Budgets,[55] he often blamed the Duma, Council and/or Government for 'giving him no choice but to sign the legislation'.[56] Even though the Duma could have, most likely, overridden a veto from the President on the 1995 or 1999 Budgets, the President signed the bills into law just as for the other budgets where there was less of a possibility that Parliament could override a veto. Some of the oppositionist Deputies, however, might have modified their votes from 'no' to 'yes' to overturn a veto from the President. For the 1998 Budget, Yel'tsin threatened to dissolve the Duma, which would be unconstitutional if they refused to adopt a budget sequestration plan, but the Duma's Chairman, Gennadiy Seleznyov responded 'there are no weak-willed members left in the Duma. The President should realize that any yelling draws a reciprocal reaction, and the Deputies will consider the laws presented to them with prejudice and irritation.'[57] Regarding the 1997 Budget which was unimplementable, but was signed by the President, and for which the Government had to submit extensive revisions to the Duma after it became law, Zhukov maintains that the President knew the budget was flawed but blamed the Duma anyway. Zhukov stated in September 1997 that 'Yel'tsin thinks, knows, that the Government made a lot of mistakes when it tried to create the [1997] Budget last year. It is not the fault of the Duma, but that of the Government.'[58] Yel'tsin confirmed in a message to the Council of the Federation that:

> it was clear back at the beginning of the year [1997] that the law [1997 Budget] was unrealistic in many major respects. Yet it was defended by the Government, adopted by the Duma, and approved by the Council of the Federation. It was even signed by the President (himself). I state once again that I will no longer allow such things to happen.[59]

Unfortunately, true to Yel'tsin's style, he did not keep his promise and for the 1998 Budget Yel'tsin

> moved with surprising speed to accommodate the largest faction in the Duma that has protested Kiriyenko's appointment, the Communists, fulfilling one of Zyuganov's two demands (the more important one) by signing the 1998 Budget. The President has, in effect, put his signature on an unrealistic budget with expenditure numbers that are obviously too high and very skimpy revenues.[60]

The 1998 Budget did, indeed, prove to be unrealistic. Yel'tsin often publicly blames the Duma, and rarely the Government, for such problems.

When Yel'tsin really wanted the budget passed to fund his decrees, obtain more money from Western financial institutions (for example, the IMF and World Bank), or for public reasons, he sent his representatives to bargain with the Duma. Unusually, Yel'tsin appeared before Duma Deputies and Council Members on 18 February 1998. He spoke for 30 minutes to encourage the prompt passage of the 1998 Budget legislation. According to Shokhin, 'Yel'tsin uses compromises to reach agreement with Parliament. After adopting the [1998] Budget [by the Duma], Yel'tsin agreed to sign the law "On Government." '[61] For public opinion, to show that he was still in control even after numerous hospital stays, Yel'tsin often publicly demanded that the Duma approve the budget and he followed this with a reassurance that the 'Duma would soon be won over'.[62] Vladimir Nikitin, Vice-Chairman of the Duma's Budget Committee, stated that 'when the budget is not passed this reflects poorly on the President, because people suffer and the country is put in danger'.[63] In fact, Yel'tsin confirmed this after signing the 1997 Budget by stating, 'I signed it, gritting my teeth, because rejecting the budget now would mean exacerbating the political situation in Russia to its breaking point. A new wave of instability would strike our most unprotected citizens, this would be the most painful blow of all.'[64] In fact, Bekker argues that the Duma is the cause of the economic crises in Russia because by

> actively pushing through laws that keep constricting the Government's budget possibilities, the Deputies are just as zealously preventing the executive branch from breaking through on another front – untangling the knots that slow the investment process. Year after year the Duma sinks the Land Code and the Law on Mortgages, and the Law on Production-Sharing Agreements, which promised an influx of tens of billions of dollars into Russia, is still effectively blocked… Because of the budget crisis that has been thrust upon them, the Kremlin and White House are forced to continually make excuses to society. The Communists, on the other hand, are using the Government's defensive position to repeatedly hammer into the public consciousness the idea that the reform policy is bankrupt.[65]

If this is true, then, along with the IMF's demands to the executive to secure Parliament's approval of the budget for loans, it provided Yel'tsin and the Government with significant reason to concede to at least some of the Duma's and Council's requests. Also, although Yel'tsin did not have much direct influence in the budgetary process except via the

Government and in concessions to Parliament, he still used the budget as a means of publicly displaying that he was in control, though this was not actually true, at least, in the budgetary proceedings.

## The case of the 1997 Budget

The 1997 Budget was certainly the most problematic budget, in that after a lengthy process of adopting it, it could not be implemented and needed to be significantly revised later in 1997. Since it was the only budget which had to be resubmitted to the Duma for drastic revisions even after the President's approval, an analysis of the 1997 Budget will provide a more detailed examination of the interaction between the executive and legislature in the budgetary process. From the first meeting of the new Government (following the June–July 1996 Presidential elections) on 22 August 1996 until 25 February 1997, when Yel'tsin signed the final version into law, the debate over the 1997 Budget was a source of great conflict between the President, Government, Duma and Council. They all disagreed over what should be cut and how to restructure the economy for 1997, since severe economic problems abounded and the 1997 Budget was intended to stabilize the economy. Viktor Chernomyrdin linked the 1997 Budget to economic revival in a meeting with the Government on 22 August 1997. He warned 'that if these knots [in reference to the draft budget] are not untied by the end of the year, it would be unrealistic to expect economic revival in 1997'.[66] This shows, once again, the importance of a realistic budget to the economic situation in Russia. As all bodies realize that this is one of the most powerful pawns in the policy process because of its wide-ranging consequences, it is in the Duma's interest to extend the debate as long as possible to use it to gain concessions. This is not economically wise, but politically, it is very powerful. Viktor Chernomyrdin, Prime Minister from January 1994 to March 1998, addressed the executive branch in August 1996 and stressed the need for improving executive–legislative relations by adopting and coordinating a budget for 1997. He called also for 'a new culture of interrelations with Parliament',[67] because the budget was so important as to require full cooperation from the Government.

On 11 October 1996, the Government submitted its first draft of the 1997 Budget to the State Duma, which promptly rejected it and sent it back to the Government on 16 October. The first draft

envisages revenues in the amount of 422.6 trillion rubles and expenditures of 511.7 trillion rubles. This means that the planned budget deficit is 89.1 trillion rubles, an amount that, according to calculations by Government experts, should not exceed 3.3% of gross domestic product, which is forecast at a level of 2.8 quadrillion rubles.[68]

A revised draft was presented by the Government on 24 October, in which the total spending and revenue were cut by 0.25 percent but a 6.5 trillion ruble addition was made to finance cuts in the military.[69] Since it did not receive favorable support by Duma Deputies, a trilateral Budget Conciliation Commission, between the Council, Duma and Government, was established to facilitate redrafting the budget. This joint commission agreed to a new revised budget on 14 November 1996.

When the new draft was passed on to the State Duma for debate, the 'battle began'.[70] Between 14 November and 15 December the debate intensified and attempts were made by the Duma to impeach Yel'tsin and raise a vote of no-confidence in the Government, while the President threatened to dissolve the Duma. The Duma had a constitutional right to do so, but Yel'tsin's threats of disbanding the Duma were unconstitutional, given the situation. Viktor Chernomyrdin met with the leaders of Yabloko, the Communists, LDPR, and Agrarian Party, all of whom opposed the revised budget, to persuade them to adopt the budget on 5 December.[71] Irina Savvateyeva stated that:

> many participants in the budgetary process feel that there is a rather high likelihood that the country's basic financial document will not be adopted. And the real reason, it seems, is quite banal: It hasn't been bargained over… It is no secret that the budget has been an object of outright bargaining between the executive and legislative branches for several years now… the executive branch has made no moves toward accommodation, thereby greatly perplexing the Duma opposition, which has become accustomed to the traditional procedure for bargaining over the budget.[72]

At this point, the debate on the budget was at an impasse because the Government and Yel'tsin wanted the Duma to consent to its side without negotiating any 'middle ground'. Both sides were unwilling to compromise, lest the executive might appear to be 'giving in' to the demands of a 'Communist' Parliament. Chernomyrdin finally accepted most of the Communist Party's 11 demands and negotiated with the other parties. Sergey Belyayev, leader, at the time, of the pro-Government party, Our Home is Russia, maintained that the budget was 'used as a card in a political game in both houses', though the Government needed the Duma's approval and had no choice but to make some concessions to Deputies.[73] The Duma met on 6 December to discuss the budget but decided to postpone voting on the issue until 15 December, when it passed in the first reading mostly because the Government submitted to the Duma's demands. Second and third readings were scheduled for 28 December, when these drafts passed with only People's Power and Yabloko against them.[74] Because the budget passed after negotiations between the Government, Yel'tsin and the Duma, it was hailed as a turning point for cooperation between the branches.[75] On 24 January 1997 the fourth reading of the budget took place in the Duma, and the budget was approved. But, immediately Yel'tsin's Ministers and the Government, trying to distance themselves from the bill, opposed the budget. Yevgeniy Yasin, the Minister of the Economy, described the 1997 Budget as 'unrealistic' and said 'it contains too many new obligations'.[76] The legislation was forwarded to the Council where it was approved on 12 February 1997 after some heated debates because the Council could only accept or reject it in its entirety.[77] Council Members disagreed with it but felt that they had no choice but to vote in favor of it. In addition, Yel'tsin, in a radio address on 28 February, announced that he had signed the budget into law, but had

> considerable doubts on many key items. There are very great doubts as to whether the budget can be implemented. First, the Government did not fully cope with its task: it included a number of unrealistic provisions in the budget. The Duma, where populism and lobbyists' interests prevailed, really 'knocked itself out'. After the Deputies' amendments, the budget was even worse.[78]

Distancing themselves from the budget was a wise political move, as the budget soon proved to be unimplementable. In the case of the 1997 Budget, the Government, Duma, Council and President exercised the best policy options in the given circumstances, as discussed earlier in this chapter. The result, however, was a budget that could not be implemented and which was not fulfilled until half-way through the year it was intended to cover.

## Budget implementation: is it actually enacted?

After lengthy debates, negotiations, drafting and redrafting, and resubmission, can budget laws actually be implemented or are they unrealistic?

According to Oksana Dmitriyeva, Chairwoman of the Duma's Subcommittee on the Budget:

> even when the budget is fulfilled overall, as happened in 1995, some line items (for example, loans from the budget) are overfilled by 500%, while others (such as science and culture) are underfinanced by 50%. Budget fulfilment is carried out in accordance with unwritten rules and mysterious customs.[79]

Thomas Remington maintains, referring to the 1994 to 1996 Budgets, that:

> budget practices unfortunately encourage the exercise of unaccountable influence over the allocation of resources. Particularly vulnerable to abuse is the practice of creating special-purpose off-budget funds in order to shelter state revenues from legislative scrutiny ... At the federal level the two major categories of protected funds are those for social support, and those under ministry control ... they are not subject to regular audits by Parliament or the Government's own controllers, [and this] renders them susceptible to misallocation. Recently a rare audit of the Pension Fund by the Parliament's Budget Committee discovered three billion rubles that had not been accounted for.[80]

A presidential decree, however, signed in November 1997, banned the Government's use of these off-budget resources.[81] On 4 March 1998, Finance Minister, Mikhail Zadornov said that 'the Government will abide by the presidential decree and ignore the budget provision'.[82] From 1994 to 1996, Robert Orttung and Scott Parrish also note that budget implementation was often subject to corruption and mismanagement. Orttung and Parrish found that 'while the budget passed by the assembly specifies expenditures in various areas, Yel'tsin and Chernomyrdin have used the Finance Ministry effectively to control federal expenditures, often ignoring targets and priorities set in the budget'.[83] This is unconstitutional and illegal. Yel'tsin even admitted, in a message to the Council of the Federation on 5 May 1997, that the budget is, at times, illegally executed: 'Many laws are impossible to enforce because of a lack of financial guarantees. There have been cases in which laws that are in direct conflict with the current [1997] federal budget have been adopted (meaning signed by the President).'[84] One specific example of the failure to implement the budget fully was given in the Ministry of Finance's report to the Duma's Budget Committee on the 1996 Budget. For 'the first quarter of 1996, the revenue side of the Budget was fulfilled by 68 percent and the expenditure side by 75 percent, leaving the deficit 50 percent greater than planned'.[85] Parliament's Accounting Office which monitors the budget's execution said that there were large discrepancies between this report and their figures, resulting in the Government's report not being accepted by the Duma.[86] Audits by the Accounting Office are the Duma's only check on the accuracy of the Government's statements on the budget.

Numerous laws, decrees, resolutions and treaties are not implemented every year because of inadequate funding provided in the budget. There are no statistics on this available in the public domain, but most Deputies and executive officials whom I interviewed believed it was substantial. According to Igor Mal'kov, Duma Deputy and Member of the Duma's Committee on International Affairs, 'many laws in the field of social policy [are not implemented], almost half of the population are entitled to social benefits, but to implement these benefits half of the budget is required which is adopted by the Duma. These laws are not implemented at the moment because of economic reasons.'[87] Aleksandr Kozyrev, Vice-Chairman of the Duma's Committee on International Affairs, similarly stated that:

> we think that laws must be implemented. Now, for example, we received this draft budget (1998 Budget) and it includes suggestions by the Government to halt implementation of 19 federal laws because there is no money in the budget to finance them therefore these laws should be rescinded. We are against this because it is easier to change bad bureaucrats who cannot implement laws than to rescind the laws. This is the essence of the struggle between the Duma and executive.[88]

Despite what Kozyrev asserts about removing inadequate Government officials, it is very difficult for the Government to implement the budget in Russia's cash-strapped economy. Unfortunately, as has been the case, often more important laws and decrees are funded at the expense of others. This has detrimental consequences on the entire legal system in Russia. According to Aleksey Andreev, Vice-Chairman of the Duma's Committee on International Affairs:

> there are some laws which are not backed up financially. These are the laws which stipulate some benefits for a certain social group, but there is no money available to implement these laws, for example

the law 'On Veterans'. It is a very good law, but there is not enough money to implement it to its full extent. As a result, the arrears on the law are accumulating and it is implemented only partially. This, by the way, brings harm to the legislative process as such, and to the politics of respect for the law.[89]

Therefore, incomplete execution of budget laws affects all aspects of the process of democratic transition and market reforms in Russia, because without sufficient funds for these laws and decrees, they cannot be fully implemented.

The Duma approved amendments on the budgets after the President signed them into law. Although the Government must submit these amendments to the Duma for approval, the Duma's support is necessary for these revisions which are intended to make the budget more realistic and implementable.[90] The 1994 Budget was amended once on 23 December 1994.[91] The 1995 Budget was amended three times on 24 April, 22 August and 27 December 1995.[92] More substantial amendments and additions were made to the 1996 and 1997 Budgets, with eight and four separate changes, respectively.[93] The 1998 Budget could not be amended in this way because a separate provision was not included in the drafts, although the Government could alter it without the Duma's permission. Amendments are only useful, however, if new funds are found or can be redistributed to finance underfunded laws, decrees, resolutions and treaties. Another problem is that due to the length of time it takes to pass amendments to the budget, which follow the same procedures as parliamentary laws, the budget is often close to expiry by the time they are approved.[94] For example, the 23 December 1994 amendment to the 1994 Budget and the 27 December 1995 amendment to the 1995 Budget were adopted one week prior to the respective budget's expiry date. These late amendments are only significant if the previous year's budget is used for the first quarter of the next year, which almost always happens.

## Conclusions

In conclusion, the Duma, Council, Government and President tend to exercise their best policy options, as determined at the beginning of this chapter, each year in the budgetary process. Unfortunately, the result is often that unrealistic budgets are passed which cannot be fully implemented, causing economic problems in Russia to be further exacerbated. Vyacheslav Kuznetsov, Vice-Chairman of the Duma's Budget Committee and Vice-Chairman of Our Home is Russia, acknowledged that the Duma, Government, Council and President tend to agree that 'even if a budget is unimplementable but adopted as a document it is better for the country's well-being than the absence of any budget'.[95] Still, the Duma does skillfully wield power by delaying consideration of the budget, demanding concessions often with Deputies choosing not to vote to show that their position is negotiable, and securing a two-thirds majority to override a possible veto from the Council or President. In fact, the OECD concluded that 'Parliament is behaving much more like a "normal" legislative body than the previous Parliament, having introduced a number of new or modified laws in the economic area ... and having collaborated closely with the Government in detailed revisions to the (1995) Budget'.[96] The Council has some, but limited, power, in that it voices its disdain for the Government on economic issues when the annual budget is discussed at a plenary session. It can also veto the budget, but never chose to do so for the 1994 to 1999 Budgets, similar to the President. When the Government can manipulate how funds are spent and distributed, it has considerable power in the budgetary process. As I have shown, the Government can decide when drafting the legislation and implementing it if certain laws, decrees, resolutions or treaties should not be financed, and therefore, they are postponed or become void. The Duma is really the only check on the Government's power, through the Accounting Office, though the Council partially controls this also, deciding whether to approve amendments to the budget, and demanding that the Government is more fiscally responsible by voicing its opinion in the next year's budget debates, or holding a vote of no-confidence in the Government. For a time, at least, there were improved relations between the executive and legislature following Primakov's appointment but it remains to be seen what will happen under his successor. Thus, because the Duma and Council's passage of the federal budget can affect the amount of loans given by international financial institutions and can lead to economic chaos (if it is not accepted or if Parliament adopts amendments to it which are not in the interests of market reforms), the Government and President have significant interests in gaining Parliament's support. Boris Makarenko, one of Yel'tsin's campaign advisors, stated that:

> Yel'tsin often realizes that there is no other alternative than to conciliate the Duma and key players in the Duma because you need a budget to be a legal document which you can show to the IMF or to any other sponsor, and a legal document means it has to have the seal

of the Duma on it. If the Duma is dominated by Communists, well, too bad, you have to talk to the Communists. You have to sit over a cup of tea with Zyuganov or Zhirinovskiy even if you do not like them. That is a rule of thumb explanation for why Yel'tsin appeared in the Duma and agrees to reconciliation.[97]

This means that Parliament, especially the Duma, has great power in the budget proceedings, though the Government has immense powers in its implementation. Still, a budget cannot be implemented until its passage is secured in Parliament.

# 8
# Conclusions: Parliamentary Power and the Democratic Transition and Consolidation Process in Russia

> When legislative power is united with executive power in a single person or in a single body of the magistracy, there is no liberty, because one can fear that the same ruler or senate that makes tyrannical laws will execute them tyrannically ... The representative body should not be chosen in order to make some resolution for action, a thing it would not do well, but in order to make laws or in order to see if those they have made have been well executed; these are things it can do very well and that only it can do well ... The two (chambers of the legislature) should be bound by the executive power, which should itself be bound by the legislative power.
>
> Montesquieu, *The Spirit of the Laws*

The purpose of this chapter is to draw conclusions about the power of the Russian Parliament and President in the legislative process from 1994 to 1999. Conclusions about the type of political system in Russia will be discussed along with trends in executive–legislative relations. These findings will be applied to theories of democratic transition and consolidation to determine whether favorable conditions and institutions exist for democratic stability in Russia. Suggestions are, then, provided for further work in this subject area.

## Parliamentary and Presidential powers: results and trends

From 1994 to May 1999, the power of the Russian Parliament, especially the State Duma, gradually increased. The sources and nature of this crucial trend are the legislators' heightened ability and desire to exercise their constitutional powers to a greater extent and to challenge the executive's powers. In Chapter 2, on the basis of the Troxel–Skach model, the 1993 Russian Constitution was described as semi-presidential, because the President has slightly more powers than the legislature. The introductory chapter, however, explained the problem with classifying political systems is that models and definitions in the existing literature tend to focus only on the constitutional powers to assess regime type. When these were applied to the 1993 Russian Constitution, the result was that three possible regime types described the same system. I argued that the reason for this disparity was that the models did not consider the actual constitutional powers used by these bodies. The Troxel–Skach model introduced in Chapter 2 was meant as a starting point for the classification of regime type. Its advantage is also that it can be utilized for comparative analysis of the powers of presidents and parliaments across countries. While this demonstrated that Russia constitutionally has a semi-presidential system, Chapter 3 found that structurally it does also. Because of the ability of Duma Deputies to organize coalitions to oppose the executive and the strict party discipline within parties during the voting on the important issues of the federal budget, no-confidence in the Government, and the approval of the Prime Minister for example, they can challenge the executive's power. As the President did not join a political party and the pro-Government parties (until September 1998) had a very small percentage of the seats in the Duma, the President and Government were forced to negotiate with and offer concessions to Deputies on key issues. Moreover, the parallel structure and composition of the Duma's and Council's committees with those in the executive facilitated cooperation between the branches. As a result of the full-time nature of the Duma and its capacity to employ agenda-setting techniques as powerful tools to pass legislation or override vetoes, the lower house gained credibility as an effective institution which could exert influence in the policy process.

The four chapters on the actual powers of the President and Parliament also led me to characterize the political system in Russia as semi-presidential. Of the powers analyzed in the Troxel–Skach model, those which were exercised in Russia between 1994 and 1999 formed the basis of separate chapters. The first of these, on parliamentary laws versus presidential decrees, proved that Yel'tsin was increasingly, from 1996 to 1999, restricted in his ability to use his decree power by Parliament overriding his vetoes and approving federal and constitutional laws. Although occasionally he would not sign laws which were adopted by the Duma and Council of the Federation, the Constitutional

Court issued rulings which compelled him to do so. Further evidence that the President sometimes resorted to unconstitutional means was given in Chapter 5 on veto and veto override powers. Even though it was unconstitutional, the President occasionally decided to veto legislation twice even after both chambers overturned his first veto. They were, however, able to force him to sign draft laws in return for passing an executive bill or other concessions. Additionally, because Deputies and Council Members could vote by proxy, this was a powerful tool which made it easier to secure the simple majority to approve legislation or the two-thirds supermajority to override vetoes. While for budget debates and in approving and vetoing legislation, the trend in executive–legislative relations was *from* confrontational *to* cooperative, Chapter 6 found that in the area of cabinet formation and dismissal the nature of executive–legislative relations tended to *fluctuate between* confrontational and cooperative. Moreover, although the President has unlimited power to dismiss the Government, the Duma was able on several occasions to threaten or actually vote no-confidence in the Government. As a response, Yel'tsin tended to replace Government officials or remove the entire Government, as shown in Chapter 6. I argued that the President's power was more restricted in forming the Government as the Prime Minister must be confirmed by the Duma. Deputies challenged Yel'tsin during the first two rounds of voting to gain concessions, and in the case of September 1998, to have their candidate nominated for Prime Minister. Finally, in the deliberations on the annual federal budget discussed in Chapter 7, I demonstrated that the Duma and Council have great powers because the executive needs the legislature's approval before the budget can be implemented. This was also a precondition for receiving most of the loans from Western international financial organizations, such as the IMF. Parliament also has some capacity to check the Government's implementation of the budget through the Accounting Office, which can recommend the removal of Government officials and dispute the Government's quarterly reports on the budget. Thus, because the Russian Parliament and President challenged each other's power in all aspects of the policy process, although the President had greater powers than Parliament, I characterize the political system in Russia from 1994 to May 1999 as semi-presidential. Overall, during this period, relations between the executive and legislature shifted from confrontational to cooperative. An analysis of the effect of the regime type and nature of executive–legislative relations on democratic transition and consolidation in Russia follows.

## Neo-institutionalism and democratic transition and consolidation

The final aim of this study is to relate regime type, determined on the basis of actual, structural and written powers, to democratic transition and consolidation. Both 'new' and 'old' institutionalists argue that institutions affect democracy but political scientists debate whether parliamentary institutions should have much power during a nation's transition to and consolidation of democracy. I accept Juan Linz and Alfred Stepan's definition of democratic transition and consolidation in their seminal work, *Problems of Democratic Transition and Consolidation*. They write:

> ... A democratic transition is complete when sufficient agreement has been reached about political procedures to produce an elected government, when a government comes to power that is the direct result of a free and popular vote, when this government *de facto* has the authority to generate new policies, and when the executive, legislative and judicial power generated by the new democracy does not have to share power with other bodies *de jure* ...
>
> No modern polity can become democratically consolidated unless it is first a state ... If a functioning state exists, five other interconnected and mutually reinforcing conditions must also exist or be crafted for a democracy to be consolidated. First, the conditions must exist for the development of a free and lively civil society. Second, there must be a relatively autonomous and valued political society. Third, there must be a rule of law to ensure legal guarantees for citizens' freedoms and independent associational life. Fourth, there must be a state bureaucracy that is usable by the new democratic government. Fifth, there must be an institutionalized economic society.[1]

On the basis of this classification, Russia is currently at the stage of democratic transition because there has been agreement about electoral rules and constitutional powers for six years but they have yet to be fully ingrained in the system. This is because there has not been a non-violent transfer of power to a new leader and Yel'tsin threatened to change the electoral laws for the Duma and institute new ones by decree if it was prematurely dissolved. Of the conditions necessary for democratic consolidation, political society was the one considered in this study. The others are equally important, but are only indirectly linked to executive–legislative relations and powers. In Linz's and Stepan's analysis, the formation of a political society is dependent on the 'development of a normatively positive appreciation of those core institutions of a democratic political society – political parties, elections, electoral rules, political leadership, interparty alliances, and legislatures'.[2] Since all of these 'core institutions' were examined, it is an appropriate definition to employ. Also, it relates neo-institutionalism to democracy by using institutions to define democratic transition and consolidation.

While some would argue that Russia is already a democracy,[3] most political scientists would agree that Russia is still in the democratic transition phase, but that it is on the way to democratic consolidation, in several respects, though democracy is not yet guaranteed for the long term. Some academics, such as Peter Reddaway, go further and argue that the 1993 Parliamentary elections and Constitution 'were a further step in Russia's transition from a fragile, embryonic democracy to a condition of chronic instability and at least partial disintegration'.[4] By examining how established the above institutions are in Russia, through an analysis of executive–legislative relations and powers, I intended to clarify the issue and assess the level of democratic consolidation with regard to political society in Russia. It is important to note that as only one of the five factors for democratic consolidation is discussed here, I am not arguing that democratic consolidation has occurred, but that within the political sphere one can find several of the preconditions for it to take place in Russia. In relation to political society, this study underlined the fact that political parties were able to compete in elections and in the policy-making process from 1994 to 1999. As discussed, the President was sometimes able to command majorities on legislation and on the formation of the Government, but often only after negotiations and concessions. The opposition was successful in securing majorities to override vetoes from the Council and President, oppose Prime Ministerial candidates in the first two rounds of voting, and delay the executive's bills while adopting legislation not always favored by the executive, which served as a check on executive power. Despite threats to delay elections if electoral laws were not approved on time, the 1995 Parliamentary and 1996 Presidential elections were held according to schedule. The electoral rules were determined in a process of bargaining and discussions which truly tested the two-year provisional legislature. Vetoes were overridden, threats were made to pursue unconstitutional methods, and concessions were offered but in the end, the electoral procedure was determined constitutionally by a federal law approved by Parliament. As previously mentioned, without a transfer of power to a new leader, it is difficult to determine the likelihood for democratic success in Russia. It is, however, significant that the political leadership, although occasionally adopting unconstitutional practices, tends to abide by the laws and work within the established institutions. Moreover, interparty alliances were strong in some cases. The Communist Party formed a coalition with the Agrarian and People's Power, which was disciplined in its voting and constituted just under 50 percent of the Duma's seats. Yabloko was usually even more oppositionist than this faction, while the nationalist Liberal-Democratic Party was often the second party to support the executive, after Chernomyrdin's party, Our Home is Russia. Bargaining between factions was characterized as normal. As demonstrated in Chapters 6 and 7 in the analysis of roll-call data on the budget, no-confidence votes, and the confirmation of Prime Ministerial candidates, Duma factions tended to vote together, although Yabloko frequently refused to side with the Communist–Agrarian–People's Power bloc in pro-Government decisions, such as budget approval. For Linz and Stepan's last criterion for democratic consolidation in political society, the Russian legislature was the focus of this study and it has been proven that it is able to check and even restrict the executive's power in several different policy areas. Thus, the political institutions exist to make democratic consolidation possible, but there is still a lack of development of the other four factors needed for consolidation and at least two successive, non-violent transfers of executive and legislative power have yet to occur. As a result, Russia remains in the democratic transition phase.

## Regime type and democratic consolidation

'New institutionalists' disagree as to whether a presidential, semi-presidential, or parliamentary system is best for democratic consolidation. Since I maintain that a 'weak' parliament combined with a 'strong' president hinders the consolidation of democracy, it follows that a semi-presidential or parliamentary system is better suited for democratic consolidation. There is substantial evidence to prove that parliamentary systems are best for democratic consolidation and stability. According to Thomas Remington:

> The consensus in the past was that the cause of stability in fragile democratic systems was best served by institutional arrangements that reward representativeness over effectiveness; therefore parliamentarism, and electoral systems facilitating a sense of inclusion by

all organized sections of the population through proportionalism, were thought more likely to survive than systems that allow the electoral victors to win all the stakes, as is the case with presidencies and majoritarian legislatures. The crises in Russia, Georgia, Ukraine, and several other former Soviet republics seem to support this view ... Parliamentary elections, it seems, can achieve a peaceful transition to democracy in systems where the old ruling elites are willing to share or surrender power and challengers are sufficiently organized, powerful and self-disciplined to assume responsibility for government.[5]

Similarly, Alfred Stepan and Cindy Skach, Adam Przeworski and Mike Alvarez found that strong presidential systems are more vulnerable to collapse than parliamentary ones in times of transition.[6] Juan Linz stated that a presidential system leads to policy-making inefficiency and political instability. This is because both the president and parliament are popularly elected, they have 'democratic legitimacy', making it difficult to resolve conflicts between them. Also, presidential systems are 'rigid' because if political views shift or the system is confronted with new challenges, it is not possible to change the government before the next election.[7] I agree with Stepan, Skach, Linz and others who argue that parliamentarism is the most conducive to democratic consolidation. Since Russia does not have a parliamentary system, the question for this study is whether a semi-presidential or a presidential system is more conducive to democracy in Russia.

Some academics argue that presidentialism is best for democratic consolidation. According to Shugart and Carey and Donald Horowitz, if a nation is deeply divided, then an elected president (especially if the election system favors the election of a centrist) may actually improve stability.[8] In Scott Mainwaring's view, presidentialism in a two-party system discourages extremism and creates incentives for the president's party in the assembly to increase support for the president. He asserts that it is not 'the coexistence of a president and a representative legislature in itself that creates dangerous crises, but the presence of multiple parties in parliament, since it is both difficult and unrewarding to cobble together majorities to pass the president's bills'.[9] Mainwaring's argument that presidentialism provides incentives for the president's party in the legislature to back him/her does not hold true for Russia because the president sees himself as being above parties (later analysis of 'delegative democracy' will show the negative effect of this on democratic consolidation). What is dangerous in the case of Russia is for presidentialism to become superpresidentialism[10] or even authoritarianism. Due to the history of 'strong' leaders in Russia who disband 'weaker' parliaments when they challenge the leader's rule, a presidential system with a 'strong' president is not the best system for democratic consolidation in Russia. The likelihood is too great that a president who is constitutionally extremely powerful or who could exert control unconstitutionally without repercussions (for example, Yel'tsin in September to December 1993) would become an authoritarian leader. Indeed, Shugart and Carey themselves argue that a system where the president has great powers over the legislative branch is unstable.[11]

Linz and Stepan found that the Russian Parliament and the President in 1991 were crisis-prone because of dual legitimacy. Their powers were not clearly defined and demarcated, which led to the 1993 coup when Parliament attempted to take over the Government.[12] A strong parliament and strong president are not necessarily the ideal structure for government either, because they have dual legitimacy. As a result of the 1993 Constitution, the Parliament and President's powers are now more clearly defined and separated, although the Constitution has been called the 'President's Constitution'.[13] Scholars, such as David Lane, state that:

> a new executive presidency was created which had effectively diminished the role of the Parliament and allowed Yel'tsin to rule by decree... The resulting presidential power created by the December 1993 elections and the ratification of a new Russian Constitution turned into a major victory for Yel'tsin. Presidential power, in some ways not unlike Soviet power before it, triumphed – at least constitutionally.[14]

I believe that such characterizations of the constitutional powers of the Russian President and Parliament following the December 1993 elections are greatly exaggerated because as shown in Chapter 2 and throughout this study, Parliament's role was far from meaningless after the 1993 elections. Of course, everyone would agree that Parliament from 1991 to 1993 was relatively more powerful than from 1994 to 1999. Still, the legislature between 1994 and 1999 successfully challenged the power of the executive in all of the four areas of the policy process considered in this study.

Thus far it has been argued that a presidential system and a system of 'dual powers' (with a 'strong' president and 'strong' parliament) are not the most conducive systems for democratic consolidation in Russia. While a system of semi-presidentialism is best for democratic consolidation in

Russia, the author is not arguing or considering whether semi-presidentialism is *always* best.[15] The concept of semi-presidentialism referred to is one in between presidentialism and a system of dual-legitimacy, where the president has slightly more power than parliament, as defined in Figure 1.1 in Chapter 1. Semi-presidentialism is best suited for democratic consolidation in Russia because of the dangers an elective president can create for parliamentary institutions. The debate on this subject is centred around Guillermo O'Donnell's concept of 'delegative democracy', the opposite of representative democracy.[16] Delegative democracy is defined as systems where the president sees himself/herself as being above parties, sees legislative institutions as nuisances which he/she should not be required to account to, and concentrates power in his/her own offices.[17] O'Donnell believes that delegative democracy, more than representative democracy, is a destabilizing system which threatens parliamentary autonomy.[18] Although Yel'tsin has always seen himself as 'above parties', the other two characterizations do not apply to Russia from 1994 to 1999. A Constitution which granted the President even more powers would increase the likelihood of such a situation in Russia. Yel'tsin on numerous occasions had to account to the legislature, for example to encourage it to approve the annual federal budget or his candidate for Prime Minister. While he did try to concentrate power in the Presidential Administration, as shown in Chapter 3, he was limited in the extent to which he could do so by the Constitution and the legislature. Moreover, delegative democracy hinders one of the key characteristics of democracy: cooperation between branches. According to John Lowenhardt, 'the actors in a democratic system "must cooperate in order to compete" ... a government bureaucracy lacking cooperative motivation and skills will undermine the democratic system' and democratic consolidation.[19] As demonstrated, this conceptualization described Russian politics from 1994 to May 1999, that the executive and legislature were compelled to 'cooperate in order to compete'. In Chapters 4 through 7, on the President's and Parliament's actual use of their constitutional powers, it was shown that during this period relations between branches gradually shifted from confrontational to cooperative. As Lowenhardt notes, this is very favorable for democratic consolidation in Russia.

## Further work

Because this is the first comprehensive study on the power of the Russian Parliament from 1994 to 1999, there are many opportunities for future study and examination. I considered four spheres in which the

President and Parliament exercise their constitutional powers, but additional areas for further work could include their influence over the judiciary, especially the Constitutional Court, the threats and failed attempts to impeach the President or dissolve the Duma, and the unsuccessful efforts to amend the Constitution to redistribute powers between the executive and legislature. Additional factors to consider are the effect of lobbying in the Duma and the influence of oligarchs on the President. These both, most likely, significantly affect the decisions and actions of President and Parliament. Moreover, it would be interesting to examine further the use and effect of concessions and bribes between the Duma, Council of the Federation, President and Government. As previously mentioned, limited details are known about these deals but it is obvious that they greatly impacted relations and decisions that were made. Another very important area is on the implementation of laws and decrees. This study examined that issue briefly but a comprehensive analysis of this would greatly contribute to the literature as numerous decrees and laws are adopted but some of them in their entirety and many to some degree are not, and in certain cases cannot be, executed. In Chapter 7, I explained that this was mostly due to a lack of funding for these laws but there are other factors as well, including contradictions between regional and federal law and a lack of structures to enforce their implementation throughout Russia. The subjects of executive–legislative relations and the power of both bodies in Russia are only just beginning to receive the attention they deserve. A great deal has been written about President Yel'tsin, but a study of executive–legislative relations cannot be complete or accurate without considering the power of the Parliament. Because the Duma elected in 1993 is the *only* parliament in the history of Russia to survive past its first term, hold regular sessions, and come to power in open elections with competing political parties, its survival is of particular importance to democracy in Russia and demands extensive study.

## Conclusions

In conclusion, Russia had a semi-presidential system in terms of the constitutional, structural, and actual powers of the President and Parliament from 1994 to 1999. Relations between the executive and legislature gradually shifted from confrontational to more cooperative in nature up to May 1999. However, the powers exercised by the Russian President and Parliament fluctuated between January 1994 and May 1999: the Russian Parliament gained greater power, while the President's authority slightly declined as Parliament continued to challenge his power. Explanations for this crucial trend were President Boris Yel'tsin's failing health, the appointment of the Parliament's choice of Prime Minister Yevgeniy Primakov, economic crises which made the executive more dependent on Parliament's swift approval of the budget, Yel'tsin's diminished public support, Parliament's greater ability to form coalitions to override the President's vetoes, and the ever-shrinking areas where the President could issue decrees because they were already covered by parliamentary laws. As a result, democratic transition was occurring, at least in the political sphere. Although the political institutions existed to make democratic consolidation possible, without two non-violent handovers of power to a new President and a Parliament which endures for more than two full terms, the future of democracy in Russia is not guaranteed. Parliament's ability to assert more power and challenge the executive's authority in all aspects of the policy process, however, meant that political power in Russia, between 1994 to 1999, was not completely controlled by an authoritarian President who ruled by decree, but that significant checks and balances existed between the branches to create possible conditions for democracy.

# 9
## Postscript: Parliamentary Power in Russia from May 1999 to January 2001

'We underestimated the importance of the opposition of institutions like the Duma during the Yel'tsin years',[1] Michael McFaul has admitted, and many people continue to do so. Although the focus of this book is on parliamentary power during the Yel'tsin era from 1994 to 1999, analysis of executive–legislative relations in Russia following Primakov's dismissal by Yel'tsin is necessary. Contrary to reports since May 1999 that the Duma is weak, I demonstrate how the Duma's power continued to grow. These events after May 1999 are not unimportant or outside my argument, but they occurred after this book was accepted for publication. The purpose of the postscript is to refute claims that events such as the dismissal of Primakov, the appointment of Stepashin and Putin as prime ministers, and Putin's election to the presidency are counter to my argument that parliamentary power is increasing in Russia. Following a brief research trip at the beginning of 2001 I gained access to material and data enabling me to update the book up to 2001. In this postscript I will examine parliamentary power in Russia from May 1999 to January 2001 and explain how events during this time relate to my argument of parliamentary power in Russia.

This book employed three methods to assess parliamentary and presidential power in a given country: through written, structural, and actual powers. The written, or constitutional, powers of the Russian president and parliament have changed little since May 1999, still being based on the 1993 Constitution. As a result, I focus on the structural and actual powers, meaning the *exercise* of their written powers. I will discuss how parliamentary and presidential elections affected the composition of the Duma and relations with the new executive. For actual powers, the period since May 1999 saw an increase in parliamentary laws, three new cabinets, the passage of two federal budgets, and a number of vetoes and

176

overrides. Both Yel'tsin's and Putin's use of their presidential powers will be examined and compared to the Duma's exercise of their powers pre- and post- the December 1999 elections.

## Structural powers

The December 1999 elections for the Duma and the March 2000 presidential elections were further evidence of the continuing progress towards democratic consolidation in Russia as they were non-violent, legal, and democratic transfers of power.[2] Despite fears that Yel'tsin might use the problems in Dagestan or Chechnya to call a state of emergency and postpone the parliamentary and presidential elections, they went ahead. The presidential elections actually took place three months early as Yel'tsin resigned on 31 December 1999, forcing new presidential elections to be held within three months, as per the Constitution. In this section I examine the impact of the parliamentary and presidential elections on executive–legislative relations, in addition to the forthcoming structural changes to the Council of the Federation and political parties.

### The 1999 Parliamentary Elections

The Duma saw a nonviolent, democratic transfer of power following the December 1999 elections. This was only the second of such transfers of parliamentary power in Russia's history, as Yel'tsin dissolved the 1992 parliament and the 1993 Duma had only a two-year trial period.[3] On 19 December 1999, 60.5 percent of registered voters voted on the composition of the new Duma. As described in Chapter 3, parliamentary seats are allocated with half going to the winners of the proportional representation party list ballots and half to winners of single-member constituencies. In the 1999 election, the Communist Party won 24.3 percent of the vote, entitling them to 67 seats, as shown by Table 9.1. This is actually 30 percent of the Duma seats from the party list vote because for the party list, a party or faction must earn at least 5 percent of the vote in order to receive at least one Duma seat. Party list seats are divided proportionally among the parties or blocs which pass the 5 percent barrier, so those that obtain seats tend to hold a greater percentage of them than the percentage of the PR vote they won. The Unity Party, endorsed by, at that time, Prime Minister Vladimir Putin, came in a close second with 23 percent of the vote and 64 seats. Fatherland – All Russia, former Prime Minister Yevgeniy Primakov's party, won 13 percent of the vote and 37 seats. The Union of Right Forces which was expected to fare

Table 9.1  Results of the December 1999 Russian State Duma elections

| Political parties and factions | PR party list | | | Single-member constituencies | | Total on 19 Dec. 1999 | | Total on 19 Jan. 2000 | | Total on 1 Feb. 2001 | |
|---|---|---|---|---|---|---|---|---|---|---|---|
| | vote % | seats | % seats | seats | % seats | seats | % seats | seats | % seats | seats | % seats |
| Communist Party of the Russian Federation | 24.3 | 67 | 29.8 | 47 | 20.9 | 114 | 25.3 | 95 | 21.0 | 87 | 19.3 |
| Unity Party | 23.3 | 64 | 28.4 | 9 | 4.0 | 73 | 16.2 | 81 | 18.0 | 84* | 18.7 |
| People's Deputy Group | 0.0 | 0 | 0.0 | 0 | 0.0 | 0 | 0.0 | 58 | 12.8 | 62* | 13.8 |
| Fatherland – All Russia | 13.3 | 37 | 16.4 | 29 | 12.9 | 66 | 14.7 | 43 | 9.6 | 45 | 10.0 |
| Russia's Regions | 0.0 | 0 | 0.0 | 0 | 0.0 | 0 | 0.0 | 40 | 8.8 | 44* | 9.8 |
| Agro-industrial Group | 0.0 | 0 | 0.0 | 0 | 0.0 | 0 | 0.0 | 36 | 8.0 | 42* | 9.3 |
| Union of Right Forces | 8.5 | 24 | 10.7 | 5 | 2.2 | 29 | 6.4 | 33 | 7.3 | 33* | 7.3 |
| Yabloko | 5.9 | 16 | 7.1 | 4 | 1.8 | 20 | 4.4 | 21 | 4.7 | 19 | 4.2 |
| Liberal Democratic Party (Zhirinovskiy Bloc) | 5.9 | 17 | 7.6 | 0 | 0.0 | 17 | 3.8 | 17 | 3.7 | 14 | 3.1 |
| Our Home is Russia | 1.2 | 0 | 0.0 | 8 | 3.6 | 8 | 1.8 | 0 | 0.0 | 0 | 0.0 |
| Independents | 0.0 | 0 | 0.0 | 114 | 50.7 | 114 | 25.3 | 26 | 3.5 | 20 | 4.4 |
| Other parties[1] | 15.7 | 0 | 0.0 | 9 | 4.0 | 9 | 2.0 | 0 | 0.0 | 0 | 0.0 |
| Total | | 225 | | 225 | | 450 | | 450 | | 450 | |

[1] Other parties include: Movement in Support of the Army (DPA) with 2 seats, Block of General Andrey Nikolaev and Academician Svyatoslav Fyodorov with 1 seat, Russian National Union (ROS) with 2 seats, Congress of Russian Communities–Yuri Boldyrev Movement (KRO–DYB) with 1 seat, Party of Pensioners (PP) with 1 seat, Spiritual Heritage (DN) with 1 seat, and the Russian Socialist Party (RSP) with 1 seat.

*Sources:* 'Statement of Results (Decision No. 65/764–3)', Central Electoral Commission, Moscow, Russia, 29 December 1999.
Data on the number of Duma Deputies in Parties in January 2000 is from *Rossiyskaya Gazeta*, 19 January 2000 and *RFE/FL Newsline*, 19 January 2000.
Data on the number of Duma Deputies in Parties in February 2001 is from the Records Department at the State Duma on 1 February 2001 and is used with permission.

* Indicate parties or factions which gained members following the election from Deputies changing party affiliation.

better only received 8.5 percent of the vote, but this still ensured them 24 seats. Yabloko and Zhirinovskiy's party both garnered 6 percent of the vote, resulting in 16 and 17 seats, respectively. Parties and movements, such as Our Home is Russia, the Agrarian Party, Russia's Regions, People's Power, Russia's Choice, Women of Russia, and the Party of Russian Unity and Accord, all of which won seats in the 1995 Duma election did not win any seats from the party list vote. Sixteen percent of the vote went to other parties which did not pass the 5 percent barrier.

For the single-member constituencies, the biggest winners were independents with 51 percent of the vote. Table 3.1 in Chapter 3 illustrates that independents historically have been successful in the single-member districts, winning 64 percent of such seats in 1993 and 35 percent in 1995. In fact, since independents by their very nature cannot participate in the party list vote, all of their seats come from the single mandate district vote. Of the political parties, the Communist Party had the greatest success in the single districts with 47 seats, or 21 percent of the 225 seats allotted. Fatherland was the only other party to receive double-digit seats with 29 seats, or 13 percent of the total. The rest of the parties ranged from receiving one to nine seats, as Table 9.1 indicates.

The overall results for the election showed that the Communist Party was the greatest winner with 25.3 percent of the 450 Duma seats, or 114. Independents also won 114 seats but their challenge would be to form parties or blocs to maintain a significant presence. The Unity Party won 73 seats which surpassed some expectations. Fatherland came in third for the political groups with 66 seats, or 14.7 percent. Parties with less than 10 percent of the seats included the Union of Right Forces with 6.4 percent, Yabloko with 4.4 percent, Zhirinovskiy's Bloc with 3.8 percent, Our Home is Russia with 2 percent, and seven other parties with less than 1 percent which are listed on Table 9.1.

There were several structural changes even before the Duma elections. First, the Liberal Democratic Party of Russia, headed by Zhirinovskiy, was disqualified for improper income declarations to the Central Election Committee. For the 1999 elections, Zhirinovskiy formed a coalition with Russia's Spiritual Revival and the Russian Union of Free Youth called the Zhirinovskiy Bloc.[4] This probably contributed to its loss of 34 seats, more than 50 percent of those won in the 1995 elections. Also, the Duma introduced changes in the law 'On the Election of State Duma Deputies'. Nikolai Petrov indicates that:

the Duma did, however, introduce a number of significant changes in the Duma election law. Their purpose is to make the election mechanisms more precise and useful, reduce subjectivity, eliminate opportunities for state authorities to interfere with the electoral process, and fill in the gaps identified during the previous election campaign. The most important changes include the following: the new law is more specific about registration procedures ... the scope of personal information a candidate has to present to the CEC to register has been significantly expanded ... [and] a new and very important element of the forthcoming elections is the more independent role played by the Central Election Commission.[5]

Such changes are positive indications for democracy as they strengthen existing mechanisms in place which validate the elections and help to reduce corruption. They, arguably, contribute to making the system fairer by placing additional checks on voting. Of course laws and what happens in practice can be different, but this law, in theory, helps to ensure one person equals one vote and that everyone who wishes to vote can do so.

Further structural changes occurred following the elections. Within one month of the elections, parties and factions began reorganizing themselves so as to wield more influence. Votes in the Duma for everything from Duma committee appointments to passing legislation requires at least a simple majority, if not more. Forming coalitions and parties with a large number of Deputies helps Deputies gain power and support for their beliefs. This is evidenced by the significant number of Deputies, especially independents and those from small parties, who joined groups other than the one they were elected to. By 19 January 2000, three new groups formed and one dissolved. Our Home is Russia, after receiving less than 2 percent of the total seats, found its eight Deputies joining other parties. The People's Deputy Group, Russia's Regions, and the Agro-industrial Group were formed as a result of changing alliances. The People's Deputy Group functioned like a satellite of Unity and the Agro-Industrial Group as a satellite of the Communists. Russia's Regions was formed by some of the 'All Russia' Deputies after they broke with Fatherland, as well as many independents. The People's Group secured 58 Deputies within a month, resulting in 13 percent of all seats, while Russia's Regions and the Agro-industrial Group held 8 percent each of the seats. Because of these new groups, Independents shrank from 114 Deputies to only 26, or 3.5 percent. The small parties which won one or two seats lost their members to other parties by 19 January 2000. Yabloko Party membership gained a Deputy, but it was one of the biggest losers in the election, losing more than 50 percent of its seats from the 1995 elections, when it won 46 seats. Zhirinovskiy's Bloc stayed the same, while the Union of Right Forces gained four and Unity gained eight Deputies. The parties which lost the largest number of Deputies were the Communist Party, reducing its size by 19 Deputies, and Fatherland, which lost 23 Deputies. Another important structural change was the law 'On Political Parties' passed in the Summer of 2001, which 'provides incentives for party amalgamations and *could* lead not only to fewer but also to stronger parties'.[6] Steven Fish explains that:

> the law has been widely portrayed as a naked bid to eliminate most parties and assert full state control over the few that survive. But the actual effects of the law are unpredictable. Most of the parties that the new rules will eliminate are insignificant groups that create more noise than choice during elections... the new regulations may spur the overdue emergence of several substantial parties that cover the breadth of the political spectrum and that are more disciplined, internally coherent, and deeply rooted in society.[7]

Thus, the law, in theory, will lead to even greater party consolidation.

In reality, even before the law was approved, there was increasing consolidation of parties, from January 2000 to February 2001. Independents continued to lose and by February 2001 only 20 Deputies considered themselves not affiliated with any party or bloc. Membership in the Union of Right Forces did not change. Yabloko and Zhirinovskiy's Bloc lost members – two and three, respectively. The Communist Party lost the most with its membership decreasing by eight Deputies to 87 in total. They remained, however, the largest party with 19.3 percent of all seats. Unity's membership grew by three to 84 and it remained a close second in total membership to the Communist Party. Other winners included the new groups with the People's Group adding four seats, making it the third largest political group with 14 percent of all seats; Russia's Regions with four more seats; the Agro-industrial Group adding six Deputies; and, Fatherland managed to add two Deputies.

Despite the changes in party affiliation, there was a good degree of consistency between the 1995 and 1999 elections as far as parliament's composition was concerned. Four out of seven of the parties which won seats in the 1999 election also had seats in the previous Duma: the Communist Party, Yabloko, Liberal-Democratic Party, and Our Home is Russia. Of the three groups established following the 1999 election, two of the three were similar to those in the 1996–99 Duma: Russia's Regions and the Agrarian Party. In fact, the volatility index, used in Chapter 3 and developed by Przeworski and Sprague, shows that the public tended to support many of the same candidates as in the 1995 election.[8] Volatility is calculated by taking the absolute value of the sum of the percentage of votes added or lost by each party in the current election, as compared to the previous election, and dividing by two. Russia's parliamentary election volatility decreased from 47.1 between 1993 and 1995 to 19.6 after the 1999 elections. This is a large decrease, which is very good for democratic consolidation, and it shows an increased stability in parties. The score of 19.6 is closer to the West, which is around 10 and not in the high forties which was greater than any other democracy calculated by Dalton, Flanagan, Alt and Beck.[9] Richard Rose argues the opposite, that there has been discontinuity in parties:

> there is a big turnover in the number of parties on the ballot from one election to the next. In the 1993 Duma election, there were 13 parties on the proportional representation ballot; in 1995, there were 43; and in 1999, the number was down to 26. In a new democracy, party formation invariably involves a certain amount of trial and error, but in Russia party turnover has been so abnormal.[10]

One of the main reasons for the difference in conclusions between Rose and myself is that Rose looks at the number of parties on the ballot. As I have argued and as Fish has cited above, many parties on the election ballot are insignificant and irrelevant.[11] Looking at parties on the ballot does not offer much insight into party continuity or discontinuity if most of those parties never make it into the Duma.

There was greater party consolidation as a result of the 1999 elections than previously existed in post-Soviet Russia. Using the Laakso–Taagepera Index, from Chapter 3,[12] on the effective number of parties after the 1999 Duma election, we find that the effective number of parties has continually decreased from 9.09 after the 1993 elections to 5.66 after the 1995 elections and 5.44 after the December 1999 Duma elections. With the number of effective parties continuing to decline, this is a great sign for democratic consolidation and a positive trend for democracy. Also, within a month after the elections the six parties with two seats each or less joined other parties. Our Home is Russia also dissolved, even though it won eight seats, and its members joined other parties.

Also, the percentage of disproportionality significantly decreased from the 1995 to 1999 elections. Disproportionality is a calculation of the share of votes to the share of seats a party obtains. Taagepera and Shugart's formula for this was outlined in Chapter 3.[13] The percentage after the 1995 elections was 49 percent which was the highest of any country holding democratic, PR elections. But, in the 1999 elections, the percentage was only 17.85 percent, a significant decrease. This is the percentage of disproportionality in Britain and is similar to most Western countries. As Duverger noted, disproportionality is what induces under-represented parties to dissolve.[14] A lower disproportionality percentage means there is greater party consolidation, especially as compared to the 1995 elections.

How does this increase in party consolidation play out in the Duma? First, the establishment of Unity as a political party illustrates the consolidation of pro-Kremlin forces. The Unity party in only eight months became a major player, indeed the second most powerful party in the Duma. As a pro-Putin party, on face value it seemed just to be the result of Putin's efforts as it is made up of Putin supporters. But the effort to establish Unity as a fully fledged party meant that it was serious about consolidating power and trying to establish itself as a long-term party capable of competing at all levels of government, unlike 'Our Home is Russia' which was a movement, not a party. Second, there is serious talk among the top party leaders and efforts are being made to reduce the number of parties, such as by the law 'On Political Parties' passed in 2001. Putin, and others, talk about a three-party system in Russia, with Unity, the Communists, and a combination of Yabloko and the Union of Right forces. Sergey Stepashin on 14 March 2000 said 'I believe that the next four years will allow us to form a solid two or three-party system, which will bring us to the point where during the next elections we will be able to offer candidates from the parties in a civilized way.'[15]

Within the first year of the Duma elected in 1999, Yabloko and the Union of Right Forces have begun to form a union, as predicted by Putin. Regarding the union between Yabloko and the Union of Right Forces, Valeriy Airapteov, the Chief of Staff of the Yabloko Party in the Duma, indicated in September 2000 that:

> there are not many differences between the two political organizations. The two blocs will try to work together to find common ground and democratic candidates in the upcoming regional elections … But, there are some in Yabloko who are not happy about such a union, though 99% of the Union of Right Forces are glad about the coalition.[16]

The leaders of the Union of Right Forces clearly do support this union, as Airapetov suggests. Boris Mints, Chairman of the Union of Right

Forces Executive Committee and Head of the party's Party-Building Committee, acknowledged that 'one of the Union of Right Forces key new objectives is to come to an agreement with Yabloko to form a joint political organization. After six months of working together, it has become apparent that we hold almost identical positions.'[17] And seven months after Mints' statement, Yegor Gaidar, the co-chairman of the Union of Right Forces, stated that 'on our relations with Yabloko, they are better than they were during all the period of transition. We are intensively cooperating in the Duma; we are working as a single parliamentary group, with a joint position on most of the important issues.'[18] But, there are still some differences between the two parties which impede a formal union. According to Yulia Malysheva, a Union of Right Forces member and a Moscow Council Representative, differences between the parties include the following: that the Union of Right Forces tends to support big business, while Yabloko focuses on developing small to medium-sized businesses; the former has tried to cooperate with the ruling party, but Yabloko defines itself as the party of the opposition; and, the former believes in lowering taxes so that average citizens can improve their economic condition, but Yabloko supports higher taxes.[19] If these two parties join forces, they will have 52 Deputies (based on the party totals as of 1 February 2001), making them the fourth most powerful group. Such a union seems extremely likely. Irina Kuzmina, the Press Secretary of Yabloko's St Petersburg branch, acknowledged that 'in recent appearances, both Khakamada and Nemtsov have publicly supported Yavlinskiy'.[20] As I discussed in detail in Chapter 3, fewer political parties tends to result in a stronger parliament which is more capable of challenging the executive by overriding vetoes, rejecting executive-backed legislation, and bartering for concessions. It provides a greater check on the power of the executive and is important for the consolidation of democracy.

### Committee structure

Although there was the same number of committees as for the 1996–99 Duma, a total of 28, with the Duma elections in 1999 there were bound to be some changes in the organization of committees. This is because not all of the same parties remained in power so Deputies would have to fight again for seats on the most important committees. As far as the actual focus of the committees is concerned, there were some structural changes. There were no additional overarching topics which necessitated the forming of new committees, but existing committees shifted their focus. The 1996–99 Duma Committee on Tourism and Sport split and the sport portion combined with the Health Care Committee to form a new joint committee. And the remaining tourism part of the committee and the Culture Committee joined to form a new committee. The, arguably, most powerful committee of 1996–99 of Banks, Taxes, Finance and the Budget split into two committees: with the budget and taxes comprising one and finance and credit organizations forming a second.[21] There had been discussion about breaking up this Committee for several years, even before the 1999 elections, because it was so powerful and covered so many important areas. The intention was to divide up the balance of power slightly more evenly between the committees.

Because committee appointments and chairmanships are an important way of exercising power in the Duma, the fight over these following the 1999 elections was intense. The committee you sit on as a Deputy can affect your ability to influence politics and power-brokering in the Duma and with the executive. Since the committees discuss whether legislation should be debated on the Duma floor, the more powerful committees, such as the Budget and Tax Committee, have greater bargaining power with other organs of the state as they discuss the most important issues. Also, committee chairmanships can lead to higher positions of power, as was shown in the 1996–99 Duma when chairman and vice-chairman were often offered positions as Government Ministers.

The fight over committee appointments in the Duma following the 1999 elections was, in part, a fight for the presidency. It even prompted Putin's direct involvement. It is difficult for one to imagine Yel'tsin visiting the Duma to negotiate committee distribution. Nikolai Petrov wrote that 'the main struggle in the upcoming (1999) parliamentary elections is between Yevgeniy Primakov and the Kremlin (Putin)'.[22] But, the struggle over committee appointments was a play-out of this fight between Primakov and Putin for the presidency. On 18 January 2000, Unity (pro-Putin) announced a deal with the Communist Party which resulted in them holding a majority of the committee chairmanships in the Duma. According to Roy Medvedev, 'the surprise parliamentary alliance between the Unity bloc and the CPRF called into question the characterization of Unity as part of the right wing. It suggested either that Putin had made a shift to the left – or that most of the political parties in Russia were lining up loyally behind the Putin regime.'[23] Contrary to the view that parties cooperated with Unity to be loyal to Putin, 'Unity's alliance with the Communists turned out to be beneficial for both parties.'[24] The purpose of the deal was to vote themselves into almost all of the key committees in the Duma and to ensure that the

Communists maintained their member, Gennadiy Selezynov, as Speaker.[25] Other factions stormed out of the Duma claiming that it was unfair, but it was legal and a part of coalition-building. It shows how weak parties will continue to have difficulty influencing politics and may force a Yabloko–Union of Right Forces coalition. Putin even became involved in a 'peacemaker' role. Rumors in Moscow were that the purpose was to deal a 'death blow' to Primakov before the presidential elections by denying him the one platform that could have given him a strong basis from which to campaign against Putin. This also hurt Primakov's relation with the Communist Party as they abandoned him and joined forces with Unity. Moreover, Primakov's own party, Fatherland, did not acquire any meaningful party assignments. This appears to be a temporary arrangement to benefit both parties, as the Communist Party does not always vote with Unity. Unity benefited from this alliance because otherwise it would have been dependent on Russia's Regions and the People's Deputy Group for support and they would have probably exploited that to the fullest extent.

This coalition, which would have been unthinkable in the Yel'tsin era on an issue such as committee assignments, is also due to a change in party cleavages. Regina Smyth notes that 'rather than old system versus new system, we are seeing divisions along the lines of the amount of state intervention in social, political, and economic life. So, there are divisions on how strong the state should be.'[26] This is particularly evident in the presidential elections and in the leadership style of the new executive following the 2000 presidential elections. Moreover, we continue to see Duma elections becoming a dry run for the presidential elections and the Duma growing as a professional organization which trains people to assume higher office.

## Forthcoming changes to the Council of the Federation

The Council of the Federation did not see any significant changes in its composition as its Members tend not to be affiliated with political parties and are elected at the regional level and not on a set day. Between May 1999 and this book's completion in 2001, Yegor Stroyev remained head of the Council of the Federation. Although there was some turnover in the membership with regional elections, it did not fundamentally alter the nature or composition of the Council of the Federation. The significant change would come in December 2001, when governors and legislative heads who up to that point comprised the CF would no longer be allowed to remain Members. The new CF in

2002 is made up of two representatives from each of Russia's 89 regions, one of whom is appointed by the governor while the other is selected by the region's legislature, but neither can be the head of these organizations. The specifics of the new law and controversy surrounding it are as follows.

On 19 July 2000, the Duma overrode the CF's veto on the bill which allows the president to dismiss governors and disband local parliaments if governors or legislative heads violate federal laws. A court ruling and confirmation from the General Prosecutor's office are necessary to confirm that the leader is subject to criminal charges. On 26 July 2000, the Council of the Federation approved legislation on restructuring its organization. Although Putin proposed the legislation, it was revised during a conciliatory commission with Duma Deputies and CF Members. The new law states that CF Members must relinquish their seats on 31 December 2001. After that date governors must appoint a representative and the regional legislatures will elect a delegate instead of having the speaker automatically gain membership to the CF. When CF Members were questioned as to why they approved a law which ensures their own demise from the Federal Assembly, Alexander Surikov, the Altay Governor and a CF Member, claimed that 'the law will be in force, whether we reject it or approve it'.[27] This is because Duma Deputies would try to gather enough support to override the Council of Federation's veto.

There was a mixed reaction to this restructuring. The positive effect will be that governors will have more time to work in their regions and they can send a representative who voices the governor's opinions (and the same is true for each region's legislature). The disadvantage is that governors will not have a direct voice in Moscow. But, as the governor selects his/her representative, that person is likely to be an envoy rather than an independent self-promoter. Also, this representative is just a surrogate for the real person and it does not mean they are any less corruptible. Michael McFaul expressed concern over the structural changes to the CF in September 2000 by stating that 'Putin has gained the power to remove governors and dissolve regional legislators … This change has been the biggest setback for what little fragile democratic institutions were alive before Putin.'[28] I think this is an exaggeration. As I explain below, a strong president does not necessarily mean a weak legislature. 'Putin has the power to remove governors who are corrupt only after a court ruling and confirmation of the crime by a federal court. I see this more as a necessary evil of trying to reduce corruption than as a symbol of the weakness of the institution. Others, in addition to McFaul, see this change as an example of Putin consolidating his power, but I think this restructuring helps the Duma. Most Duma Deputies did not like the CF under Yel'tsin because they described it as an 'arm' of the executive. While I have demonstrated that this is an exaggeration, the CF did tend to be much more pro-Kremlin than the Duma under Yel'tsin. With Putin's suggested changes, this will ensure that executive leaders and legislative heads of regions are not members of the CF; instead they must appoint a representative. A representative will no longer have the right to immunity, but must be held accountable for criminal acts. Corruption is such a problem in Russia that it threatens the continuing development of a stable, legitimate legal system. Sergey Stepashin stated, prior to the March 2000 presidential elections, that Putin was, in fact, one of the best people to reduce corruption.

> Because Putin is less reliant on the oligarchs for money and since he has expressed initial support for the anti-corruption plan, Stepashin remains positive about his (own) anti-corruption measures being passed ... (Stepashin said) 'Putin is not engaged with any of the financial groups, known as oligarchs (as Yel'tsin was known to rely on]. Yel'tsin won the elections of 1996, when he was already considerably ill, because of those groups. After Putin's election, he will not have to pay such debts [to oligarchs as Yel'tsin did).'[29]

This is not a symbol of the all-powerful Putin, but the legislation was passed both by the Duma and Council of the Federation. CF Members also realized that if they did not pass it, the Duma could have, most likely, gathered the support to override the CF's veto.

I view this as more of a regional versus federal struggle than a president–parliamentary struggle as Duma Deputies supported it and a core of Deputies had been calling for changes to the structure of the CF for years. In fact, the structure of the Council of the Federation was revised prior to the 1996 elections also. In response to the concern expressed about this bill regarding Putin's ability to remove governors if they violate the Constitution, since the governors would no longer sit in the CF, there is no reason why they should not be held accountable for their actions. Over the past seven years, there have been numerous reports on how regional governors have stolen large sums of money from their constituents through taxes, requiring pay-offs, and embezzlement. The CF had, especially under Yel'tsin, functioned more like the House of Lords in Britain than the Senate in the United States. This is not to say that it is any less democratic than the lower house of the Russian legislature, only that the Duma has more legislative power than the CF, as the Duma can override the CF's vetoes, CF approval is not needed for many laws (as detailed in Chapter 2), and all laws must be approved by the Duma (the CF cannot override the Duma's 'veto' or non-passage of legislation).

Throughout the 1999–2001 period, the Council of the Federation committees stayed the same in number, structure, and topic; no further discussion of them is required here as they have already been described in Chapter 3.

## Putin becomes President

This was the first time in Russia's thousand-year history that there was a democratic, nonviolent, legal transfer of power for the leader of the nation.[30] To minimize this would be to overlook the events leading up to the elections which could have resulted in a coup, political upheaval, or violent protests. This is because Yel'tsin resigned on 31 December 1999, six months early, and Vladimir Putin was in power for three months, as is constitutional, before the presidential elections. Not only during this three-month period could attempts have been made to oust him, but also during and shortly after the March 2000 elections. This did not occur.

Putin was Yel'tsin's presidential favorite from even before the parliamentary elections. I believe Putin and Yel'tsin even agreed on this in August 1999, shortly after his confirmation as Prime Minister. This is because both Stepashin and Primakov made their presidential aspirations public and Yel'tsin reacted negatively against them, eventually sacking them both within a few months. Putin made his presidential hopes public the day after his confirmation and Yel'tsin continued to support him vehemently. Once Putin was confirmed as Prime Minister on 16 August 1999 (see details in the next section), he faced several threats to his electoral victory: decreased voter turnout, catastrophe in his Chechen military campaign and escalating problems with Dagestan, a possible connection between Putin and the apartment bombings in September, and Primakov. In the section above on the 1999 Duma elections and committee appointments, I explain how the 'Primakov threat' was diminished. The Chechen campaign actually proved to be an advantage in some respects for Putin as his strong, unyielding character with the Chechens typified what Russians tend to like in a leader. Voter turnout was even higher than for the parliamentary elections with 68.4 percent of registered voters casting votes. Plus, Putin was helped by his three-month trial run as president, that is the interim between Yel'tsin's resignation and the presidential election. This gave Putin an opportunity to present himself as a capable, strong leader and it also gave him access to resources to support his campaign, including visibility through the media.

Putin was the clear winner in the presidential election with 52.9 percent of the vote, as shown in Table 9.2.[31] The only other candidate that presented a challenge for a possible run-off had Putin received less than 50 percent of the vote was Gennadiy Zyuganov, who lost the run-off round with Yel'tsin in 1996. Zyuganov won 29.2 percent of the vote. In the 1996 elections Zyuganov had 32 percent of the vote in the first round, compared to Yel'tsin's 35 percent, and he received 40 percent support in the second round. Other candidates who ran in both 1996 and 2000 were Grigory Yavlinskiy, with 6 percent of the vote in 2000, and Vladimir Zhirinovskiy, with 3 percent. Aman-Geldy Tuleev also won 3 percent but the remaining six candidates all received less than 1.5 percent of the vote each. It was, however, the first time that a woman ran, Ella Pamfilova of the For Citizen's Worth Party, gathering 1 percent of the vote. Yuri Skuratov, the disgraced Prosecutor General, protested the scandal against him with the sexual videotapes and ran on an anti-Kremlin platform. Two percent of the voting population voted against all candidates, which was similar to the 1996 elections.

Using the Laasko–Taagepera Index, as was done for the parliamentary elections and in Chapter 3, we find that there has been a consolidation of parties/candidates in the presidential elections. For the presidential

*Table 9.2*   Results of the March 2000 Presidential Elections in Russia

| Candidates | Percentage vote (%) |
| --- | --- |
| Vladimir Putin | 52.9 |
| Gennadiy Zyuganov, Communist Party | 29.2 |
| Grigory Yavlinskiy, Yabloko | 5.8 |
| Aman-Geldy Tuleev | 3.0 |
| Vladimir Zhirinovskiy, Liberal-Democratic Party | 2.7 |
| Konstantin Titov, Union of Right Forces | 1.5 |
| Ella Pamfilova, For Citizen's Worth | 1.0 |
| Stanislav Govorukhin | 0.4 |
| Yuri Skuratov | 0.4 |
| Aleksei Podberezhin, Spiritual Heritage | 0.1 |
| Umar Dzhabrailov | 0.1 |
| Against All | 1.9 |
| Invalid votes | 0.6 |
| Total valid votes (of registered voters) | 68.0 |
| Total votes cast (of registered voters) | 68.4 |

*Source*: 'Statement of Official 2000 Russian Presidential Election Results', published by the Central Electoral Commission, Moscow, Russia, 6 April 2000.

elections there is a similar positive decrease in the effective number of parties as we saw in the parliamentary elections. The reduction is from 3.89 in 1996 Round 1 of the elections to 2.67 in the first round of the 2000 presidential elections. In fact, there was not even a need for a second round as Putin was accorded 53 percent of the vote (less than 50 percent demands a second round run-off between the top two candidates). As in the parliamentary elections, this is a positive sign for democracy as fewer parties/candidates permits more serious campaigning focusing on two or three realistic people, instead of 11 candidates where only two are likely winners.

Putin's strong character has caused fear that he will be an authoritarian president.[32] He is even made out, at times, to be more authoritarian and dictatorial than Yel'tsin. Just because he is the former head of the FSB and was an officer of the KGB does not necessarily mean he is authoritarian and undemocratic. Former President George Bush was head of the CIA and he was not an authoritarian or undemocratic president of the United States. For example, the *Financial Times* ran an article stating 'Mr. Putin's election is no triumph of liberal politics. Russia's new president is a former KGB officer and head of the internal intelligence service. He was schooled in an organization that can best be described as secretive and vicious.'[33] Politics in any country is secretive and vicious, so he will be well skilled. Sergey Stepashin insists Putin is not an authoritarian leader. Stepashin said in January 2000 that 'I really do know Putin very well, perhaps better than anyone in Moscow. With the exception, probably, of Anatoliy Chubais. I frequently talk with Putin. And, I can tell you that this man is not authoritarian.'[34]

Putin's mantra focuses around strengthening the state. This does not mean solely strengthening the executive branch, but it means making federal bodies more powerful than local government and holding people accountable.[35] Although Putin wants to strengthen the state, it is not at the expense of the Duma. Putin said during his State of the Nation address on 8 July 2000 that 'it is advantageous for a weak power to have weak parties ... But a strong power is interested in having strong rivals'.[36] Thus, contrary to many Western fears about a strong leader, there is no reason why this means a weak parliament. As I suggested in Chapter 2's discussion of regime types, this is a system of dual powers where both are very strong in written and actual powers. Russia has not reached that level yet, but it is essential to realize that a strong president is not, in itself, undemocratic as long as there are checks and balances on his power and strong opponents (whether an institution such as the Duma or political parties, or both) to do this. Putin's philosophy is that only a powerful state based on the rule of law can guarantee and monitor Russia's economic and political development, meaning civil society, free press, strong political parties, private property rights, and fair competition. Regardless of how selective Putin is in his application of this, the fact remains that there are checks on his power. A 'depiction (of the arbitrary rule of a president) also tends to exaggerate the power of the president and the marginality of the State Duma and Federation Council ... Both placed significant checks on presidential power.'[37]

Regarding the regime type characterization with a strong president, Martha Olcott and Marina Ottaway developed a term called semi-authoritarianism. They define this as 'the existence and persistence of mechanisms that effectively prevent the transfer of power through elections from the hands of the incumbent leaders or party to a new political elite or political organization'.[38] In their paper on this concept they do not include Russia in their analysis, but instead use the characterization for such countries as Kazakhstan, Azerbaijan, Peru and Venezuela, among others. To describe Russia as semi-authoritarian in this context would be an exaggeration. We have now seen three legitimate, nonviolent transfers of power with the presidential and parliamentary elections. Of course, only successive transfers of power will ensure democratic consolidation, but democratic transition has occurred in the political sphere. Russia remains a semi-presidential regime as it has been since 1994, although the exercise of constitutional powers has fluctuated between 1994 and 2001.

Regarding the, arguably, authoritarian tendencies of Putin, Michael McFaul notes that present-day Russia cannot be compared to its past. 'Princes were not removed from power by the ballot box as were four out of nine regional leaders and hundreds of Duma Deputies in the December 1999 election. The next time you hear someone argue that elections in Russia do not matter, ask one of these electoral losers if they agree.'[39]

As I have noted throughout this book, the personality of a president is important to how he governs and his relationship with the legislature. Putin is much more of a negotiator with the Duma than Yel'tsin. I mentioned in the previous section how Putin visited the Duma and talked with Duma Deputies to secure the Unity–Communist coalition over committee appointments. After Deputies from the other parties walked out in protest at the majority voting power the two parties gained as a result of the union, Putin met with individual factions to lessen their anger. Other examples of Putin as a negotiator include his negotiating style on legislation. Yegor Gaidar, co-leader of the Union of Right Forces, who has negotiated with Putin said, 'the president (Putin) preferred to keep balance and flexibility, and it is his style; he likes to be flexible. But, after the fight over the budget and tax court, in which the government and the presidency were close to the liberals and very distant from the Communists, it appeared that Putin just wanted to establish balance, showing he has more possibilities, if necessary, making alliances on the right or on the left.'[40] According to Lilia Shevtsova, Putin openly demonstrates 'that he is at ease with everybody and can form alliances with anybody, including Communists'.[41]

Not only is he able to garner support from Deputies, he also enjoys strong approval ratings with the public. Putin's approval rating of 80 percent in January 2000 fluctuated in the 60–70 percent range throughout 2000.[42] Kas'yanov, his Prime Minister, did not enjoy such popularity. His approval ratings remained in the 40 percent range throughout 2000, according to the same survey.

There were some changes in the structure of executive committees after Putin's election to the presidency. First, in an effort to streamline power and for more centralized control, Putin established fewer executive committees. As for ministries and agencies, he abolished the Ministry for the CIS, Science Ministry, Trade Ministry, Economics Ministry, State Committee for Northern Regions, Environmental Committee, Youth Policy Committee, Federal Service for Civil Aviation, Federal Migration Service, Federal Service for Currency and Export Control, Roads Agency, Cinematography Committee and Land Committee. The two new ministries were the Ministry of Economic Development and Trade and the Ministry of Industry, Science and Technology. In the next section I discuss what effects the changes in the composition and structure of the presidency and parliament had on these institutions' actual powers.

## Actual powers

As outlined earlier in the book, actual powers of the Russian President and Parliament include their use of decrees versus laws, the frequency of cabinet formations and dismissals, the use of vetoes versus veto overrides, and the discussions on the federal budget. The actual powers exercised by the president varied between Yel'tsin's final year in office and Putin's reign. Much of the emphasis of this postscript is on the structural changes because more than anything else a completely new president and parliament are obviously going to affect the powers they exercise. A weak president may use less of his powers than Yel'tsin did, while a pro-Kremlin parliament might act weak and support the president on his policies. In the previous section I discussed a number of these topics, such as Putin's character and the composition of the new Duma. Another entire book could be written on executive–legislative relations between May 1999 and Spring 2001; here it is possible to discuss only briefly the actual use of powers.

### Laws versus decrees

In Putin's first year as President, he and the Duma worked successfully together on many pieces of legislation. This does not mean, of course, that they always agreed, but that democratic mechanisms worked to facilitate negotiations between the branches. According to Thomas Remington, 'if the president and Duma are on the same side of an issue, they will cooperate ... the Tax Code, Criminal Code, judicial reform, and the budget (are) areas where the current president (Putin) and Duma have worked together to produce legislation that represents a compromise between the various political factions in the Duma.'[43] An example from Chapter 4 was the successful negotiations between both branches over the ratification of the START II Treaty, a treaty which Yel'tsin was unsuccessful at negotiating during his entire time in office.

The period between 1999 and February 2001 also saw great improvements in executive–legislative relations regarding the legislative process. For the first time in the history of the Duma, 100 percent of all legislation passed by the Duma was signed into law by the President in the year 2000 as indicated in Table 9.3. During Yel'tsin's presidency, between 58 percent and 64 percent became law. Also, the Duma passed and Putin signed 172 bills into law in 2000. Although this was a drop in the number signed into law by Yel'tsin in 1999, Table 9.3 illustrates that this is more a result of the parliamentary elections in 1999 than a problem with executive–legislative relations. There is a clear trend that before parliamentary elections, the number of bills passed by the Duma and laws signed by the President increase. There is a clear reason for this. Deputies want to ensure that their bills are adopted before a new parliament assumes power which could have a potentially different make-up of parties and may table the former Duma's legislation. In 1995, 228 laws were signed by Yel'tsin and 229 in 1999, both the highest totals of any year. There was also a noticeable decrease in laws and bills in the first year after the new Duma came to power. This is because the Deputies spent the first few months getting organized, such as deciding on committee distributions, internal rules, speaker positions and so on. The 172 laws passed in 2000 under Putin are less of a decline in the number following parliamentary elections than between 1995 and

*Table 9.3* The legislative process in Russia, 1996–2001

| Status of legislation | 1996 | 1997 | 1998 | 1999 | 2000 | Jan. 2001 |
|---|---|---|---|---|---|---|
| **Laws** | | | | | | |
| Total Number of Laws Passed by the Duma and Signed by the President | 145 | 163 | 193 | 229 | 172 | 2 |
| of these laws, the number of constitutional laws | 1 | 3 | 0 | 1 | 3 | 0 |
| of these laws, the number which were ratified treaties | 51 | 53 | 55 | 45 | 54 | 0 |
| **Legislation in the Duma** | | | | | | |
| Legislation Introduced to the Duma | 451 | 782 | 1000 | 1280 | 993 | 66 |
| Legislation Passed by the Duma in the 1st Reading | 388 | 451 | 475 | 417 | 434 | 51 |
| Legislation Passed by the Duma in the Final Reading | 252 | 253 | 301 | 359 | 172 | 15 |
| **Vetoes** | | | | | | |
| Total Number of Vetoes | 89 | 109 | 121 | 134 | 25 | 0 |
| of these vetoes, the legislation vetoed only by the Council of the Federation | 41 | 40 | 56 | 49 | 12 | 0 |
| of these vetoes, the legislation vetoed only by the President | 34 | 58 | 46 | 64 | 11 | 0 |
| of these vetoes, the legislation vetoed by both President and CF | 14 | 11 | 19 | 21 | 2 | 0 |
| **Success rate** | | | | | | |
| % of legislation passed by the Duma which becomes law | 58 | 64 | 64 | 64 | 100 | n/a |

*Source*: Data provided by the Records Department of the Russian State Duma, February 2001. Author granted permission to use these data.

1996, where only 145 became law. Moreover, the Duma grew more selective in the laws it approved in 2000, as only 172 of the 993 bills introduced were approved. Although one could argue that more basic laws were needed in 1995 than in 2000 to set up the rules which govern the country, there has been an important downward shift in the percentage of bills that are introduced versus those that are passed by the Duma. This is a positive sign for democracy as it means that the Duma is using its power to draft effective laws and the content of the bills are discussed more in the Duma before being passed to the CF and President. With the President approving all of the Duma's bills in 2000, though not necessarily the first time round as discussed in the next section on vetoes, the Duma is becoming more the forum where the particulars of legislation are hashed out and the President merely okays it. The steady decline in the percentage of legislation passed by the Duma from the number of bills introduced to the Duma from 1996 to 2001 is as follows: in 1996, the Duma approved 56 percent of all bills introduced, 32.4 percent in 1997, 32 percent in 1998, 28 percent in 1999, and 17 percent in 2000, as calculated from Table 9.3.

Decree power is an important tool used by the president to make policy without the Duma. As I explained in Chapter 4, Yel'tsin's use of his decree power became virtually meaningless towards the end of his rule. His excessive use of his decree power meant that many of the decrees were not implemented or were ignored. In fact, many did not have funding and could not be implemented. Thomas Remington found that 'the great majority of decrees in 1998 and 1999 concerned executive reorganization and many simply rescinded earlier decrees that contradicted subsequent laws and decrees ... The expansion of policy areas regulated by legislation has restricted the president's ability to fill gaps in existing law through the use of decrees.'[44] Extensive data on Putin's decree power were not available to the author at the time of writing this postscript, though a study of Putin's use of decrees will clearly be very important. Remington advances a similar argument to mine (in Chapter 4) that 'contrary to popular impression, the great majority of laws passed by parliament are signed into law; the president does not rule by decree but actively works with parliament to ensure passage of the legislation he wants and needs to have passed, and he devotes substantial resources to this effort'.[45]

### Vetoes and veto overrides

The President's and Parliament's use of veto and veto override power, respectively, significantly differed between Putin and Yel'tsin's presidencies. Eugene Huskey notes that 'the ultimate weapon in the legislative arsenal is the veto override'.[46] But, in 2000, the Duma did not have many vetoes to override. Both the President and Council of the Federation issued only 25 vetoes in total for the year. On all accounts, whether for each body separately or both combined, there were fewer vetoes issued than in any other year, as indicated by Table 9.3. The President and Council of the Federation jointly vetoed only two of the same pieces of legislation in 2000, whereas, under Yel'tsin the number ranged from 11 in 1997 to 21 in 1999. This illustrates how the CF was more pro-Yel'tsin, in this regard, especially in 1998 and 1999, as both CF Members and Yel'tsin agreed to vote against more of the same Duma bills than at any other time. With Putin and the CF agreeing on only two vetoes, it seems as if the CF is more anti-Kremlin than under Yel'tsin. Of course, it is beneficial to democracy to have additional checks on the executive and Duma's power.

The number of vetoes issued by the President and CF independently also declined between 1999 and 2001. In 1999, Yel'tsin vetoed 64 bills approved by the Duma, while Putin vetoed only 11. One could argue that Putin granted the new Deputies a 'honeymoon' period where he chose to cooperate to improve relations, but such a period would not have lasted over a year, nor does this explain the significant drop in vetoes from the CF. CF Members issued only 12 vetoes in 2000 as compared to 49 in 1999. My previous explanation in the section on laws that the Duma is becoming the main forum where legislation is debated, refined and decided seems to hold true with this decline in vetoes. Paul Chaisty and Jeffrey Gleisner concur that 'the Duma has acquired a level of influence within the political system that exceeds its constitutional powers. The political consolidation of the Duma in the shape of assertive factions has created a self-confident legislature. It is increasingly difficult for the government to rule without the consent of the Duma.'[47]

### Cabinet formation and dismissal

The period between May 1999 and May 2000 saw three new prime ministers. Unlike any previous time, all three prime ministers were approved in the first round of voting. Because I have already discussed Primakov's dismissal and the impeachment proceedings in May 1999 in Chapter 6, I will focus here more on Putin's and Kas'yanov's prime ministerial appointments.

After Yel'tsin dismissed Primakov on 12 May 1999, the Duma responded by challenging Yel'tsin's constitutional power. The impeachment process that ensued and the Duma's rounds of voting for a new prime minister threatened a legislative impasse. Primakov was Prime Minister for only eight months and he maintained more of a coalition government than previous prime ministers, including even Communist Party Ministers. Primakov was a compromise prime minister, as explained in Chapter 6. The Kremlin announced that Primakov was dismissed for failing to rescue the economy. Primakov is generally credited with improving executive–legislative relations and helping to halt the economic decline. But, economic stability did not result in a stronger economy. The real reason for Primakov's dismissal appeared to be its use as Yel'tsin's negative response both to the Duma's impeachment hearings and to Primakov's increasing efforts to gather support for the upcoming presidential elections. Yel'tsin feared that Primakov would replace him as president in the elections the following year, so in May 1999 he began to work more to ensure he had an appropriate replacement whom he supported and who would not prosecute him. With Primakov leaning more towards the Communists in many negotiations, Yel'tsin feared Primakov's presidency might advance the Communist Party. Still, what seemed to be a loss for the Duma of having Stepashin as Prime Minister turned more positive when he was replaced after only three months.

Although Yel'tsin threatened to disband the Duma if it did not confirm his choice of Sergey Stepashin as Prime Minister, it seemed to be a threat which he would not carry through. According to Remington, 'while the president may benefit from threatening the Duma with dissolution, the political cost of such an action and the prospect of facing a new Duma perhaps more hostile than the old usually prevent such a drastic measure from being taken ... The Duma has enacted several laws to legally complicate its dissolution, if the president were to try to do so.'[48] The political costs of disbanding the Duma in May 1999 were very high for both the Deputies and Yel'tsin. This was at a time when Yel'tsin has been very ill just days before and the economy was declining as a result of Primakov's dismissal. Stepashin's appointment was a way for Yel'tsin to reassert power on the surface while he was ill and weak.[49] Although there was widespread belief that had the Duma been disbanded and new elections held, the Communist Party and other oppositionist parties would have fared particularly well (and perhaps better than in the December 1995 election), Deputies did not want to risk their jobs. Even though the party might do well, there was a risk that they as individuals might not get re-elected.

Although Stepashin could not obtain the same support in the Duma which Primakov enjoyed, Stepashin did explain in his speech to the Duma that he intended to form a government of professionals, regardless of party affiliation.[50] Given the political turmoil of May 1999, Stepashin was approved on 19 May rather swiftly. Sixty-six percent of Deputies voted for him, 298 in total, while 55 voted against him, 14 abstained and 83 did not vote, as shown in Table 9.4. Our Home is Russia, Russia's Regions and the Liberal-Democratic Party solidly supported Stepashin's nomination, and most Deputies from the Agrarian and People's Party blocs voted for him. 'Yabloko members continued their practice of voting independently: 24 cast their ballots in favor of Stepashin and 12 against. Before the vote Yabloko leader Grigory Yavlinskiy announced that the group cannot give Stepashin its full support since he played a direct role

*Table 9.4* Voting behavior of Duma Deputies on the nominations of Prime Ministers in Russia, 1999–2001

| Candidate for Prime Minister | Voting behavior of Duma Deputies | | | | |
|---|---|---|---|---|---|
| | Yes | No | Abstain | Did not vote | % for |
| *Approved in First Round:* | | | | | |
| Sergey Stepashin: 19 May 1999 | 298 | 55 | 14 | 83 | 66 |
| Vladimir Putin: 16 August 1999 | 233 | 84 | 17 | 116 | 52 |
| Mikhail Kas'yanov: 17 May 2000 | 325 | 55 | 15 | 55 | 72 |

Source: *Gosudarstvennaya Duma: Stenogramma zasedaniy* (Federal'nogo Sobraniya Rossiyskoy Federatsii, Moscow, *Izvestiya*, 19 May and 16 August 1999 and 17 May 2000).

in the war in Chechnya.'[51] Still, Deputies did not want to prolong the political strife and Stepashin was approved. Of course, they received concessions for their support. Immediately before and soon after Stepashin was approved I heard rumors from Deputies that they did not think he would last more than a few months (another possible reason why he was approved). To the delight of many Deputies, Stepashin did not have an opportunity to fully form a government and affect policy as he was, indeed, dismissed within three months.

Following Stepashin's dismissal in August 1999, Yel'tsin nominated Vladimir Putin for Prime Minister. The Kremlin's reasoning was again that Stepashin had not done much to improve the economy, but insiders claim that Stepashin was not well liked by the oligarchs. On 16 August 1999, Duma Deputies approved Vladimir Putin as Prime Minister. Putin received only 52 percent support from Deputies, because Deputies did not know much about him but they did not want a prolonged battle with the executive, realizing that parliamentary elections were four months away anyway. It was more important for democracy that the Duma elections take place on schedule and not be postponed than who should be prime minister for four months. Most Deputies from the Liberal-Democratic Party, Our Home is Russia, and Russia's Regions supported Putin, but among the Communists, 32 voted for him, 52 against, 4 abstained, and 41 did not vote.[52] Both Yabloko and the Communist Party leaders told their Deputies that they could vote as they wished. Putin became the fifth prime minister in 17 months in Russia.

Putin was, however, the last Prime Minister of the Yel'tsin era. As noted earlier, Putin became acting President when Yel'tsin resigned, at which time Putin made Mikhail Kas'yanov Finance Minister. Less than two weeks later on 11 January 2000, Putin replaced Nikolai Aksyonenko and Viktor Khristenko as first Deputy Prime Minister and put Kas'yanov in their place. Kas'yanov was Putin's first deputy Prime Minister and de facto Prime Minister until the March 2000 elections. He is more of an oligarch than an early Yel'tsin-era reformer, such as Gaidar, though he is not tied to any one 'oligarch' group. Kas'yanov is an economist and is representative of the mainstream Yel'tsin economic reform program. He negotiated the USSR's debt in the Paris Club, so he was internationally known before becoming Putin's first deputy PM.

Shortly after Putin was elected President he nominated Kas'yanov as his Prime Minister. Duma Deputies voted on his confirmation on 17 May 2000. He received an overwhelming 72 percent support from Deputies, with 325 voting for him, 55 against, 15 abstaining, and 55 not voting. He even received backing from some Communists. The Communists and Yabloko told their Deputies to vote how they wished and not necessarily according to party lines. 'Even the Communists, who approved former President Boris Yel'tsin's prime ministerial candidates only after heated political wrangling, praised Kas'yanov after meeting him.'[53] No faction explicitly told Deputies not to vote for Kas'yanov.[54] Kas'yanov does not enjoy the same popularity as Putin, as noted above, but some Deputies confirmed him more out of respect for Putin. Nikolai Kharitonov, leader of the Agrarian Party, said that 'the result was not a reflection of the Deputies' personal respect for Kas'yanov. The Deputies respected Putin's choice and want to demonstrate their confidence in the new Russian President.'[55] With such a high approval rating with Deputies and such strong support for Putin, the former tensions between the executive and legislature over prime ministerial confirmations seem to have eased and are improving. Also, the frequency of cabinet dismissals has dropped from five in 17 months to only the one necessary one resulting from the presidential elections, as the Constitution mandates, in 14 months.

### The 2000 and 2001 Federal Budgets

The passage of the 2000 and 2001 Federal Budgets were also signs of improved executive–legislative relations. According to Eugene Huskey, 'on certain issues, most notably the budget and legal reform, the executive cannot govern without some measure of parliamentary consent. Although drafted by the Government, the annual Law on the Budget must pass the legislature. The protracted annual negotiations over budgetary allocations give the Deputies opportunities to wrest concessions from the executive in exchange for passage.'[56]

The 2000 Federal Budget was passed just before the 1999 Duma elections. It was in the interest both of Deputies and of Yel'tsin that the budget be approved before a new group of Deputies, who could be even more hostile to Yel'tsin, was elected. Most of the negotiations and concessions for the budget's passage go on behind closed doors and are not made public, but it seems that there was less need for concessions as both bodies had a mutual interest in adopting a budget quickly. The 2000 Budget turned out to be realistic and fully capable of being implemented. Kas'yanov said in his address to the State Duma before his confirmation as Prime Minister in May 2000 that with the 2000 Budget, 'the formerly acute problem of fiscal balance can now be regarded as resolved, and the government no longer needs to resort to massive borrowing to make the necessary budget spending. As a result of energetic measures, the (2000) federal budget's commitments are being met in full.'[57]

The 2001 Federal Budget is an even better sign of improved executive–legislative relations as there were not the same time constraints and impeding elections as for the 2000 Budget. The 2001 Budget was the first balanced budget in post-Soviet history. The Duma approved the budget earlier than most of the previous budget, on the first day of December 2000. 'The rapid adoption of the budget was ensured by an informal coalition of liberal factions voting according to their convictions, parties that originally had pro-Kremlin agendas, and parties that turned pro-Kremlin after Putin came to power.'[58]

## Conclusions: progress toward democracy?

I disagree with those, such as Stephen Cohen, who argue that democracy, *in the political sphere*, does not exist in Russia. Cohen argues that 'Russia today has elements of democracy, but it does not have a democratic system. Among the essentials missing are a constitution providing for a meaningful separation and balance of powers, [and] real national political parties other than the Communists.'[59] In this book, I have argued that there is a separation of powers between the executive and legislative branches. Also, I question what Cohen means by 'real' as I have shown that there are five effective parties which organize coalitions, challenge the government, and influence policy-making in Russia. I maintain that what is missing is not a separation of powers and political parties in Russia, but rather extensive analysis and understanding of the powers and parties which do exist. It is the present lack of study on the State Duma which causes such misconceptions. We may fear a strong leader, such as Putin, and not realize that parliament is growing stronger at the same time. As I demonstrate in Chapter 2, they are not mutually exclusive. Both the president and parliament can be strong and powerful or both can be very weak. They do not necessarily take power away from each other as one grows stronger. Prime Minister Kas'yanov expressed his continuing desire for cooperative efforts with the Duma during his speech to Deputies on 17 May 2000:

> the meetings and consultations which I held with the State Duma factions have shown graphically that we can rely on the intellectual and professional potential of the Deputy corps. Of course, we shall not be able to do without disputes and compromise solutions but I hope that our mutual understanding will be complete as regards the basic questions relating to the development of the Russian Federation as a leading modern power which occupies a worthy place in the international community.[60]

Michael McFaul explains that 'we misinterpreted weak leaders for a weak political regime as a whole ... the ability of changes at the top to shake up the whole system was underestimated, and too much attention has been focused on alternative power structures, such as oligarchs and regional leaders ... We underestimated the importance of the opposition of institutions like the Duma during the Yel'tsin years.'[61] This book is an attempt to further our understanding of the Duma and its relations with the executive branch and with the Council of the Federation. It is hoped that many other studies will continue to explore these important themes.

# Notes

## 1  Introduction: Theoretical Models of Neo-Institutionalism and the Problem of the Russian Case

1 The transliteration system used in this book is from Archie Brown, Michael Kaser and Gerald Smith (eds), *The Cambridge Encyclopedia of Russia and the Former Soviet Union* (Cambridge: Cambridge University Press, 1994), vi. The Russian soft sign, -ь has been transliterated in all cases, including in Russian names and titles of publications. Proper names beginning with -E are written as -Ye (e.g. Yel'tsin) and those names ending in -й are transliterated as -y. American spelling is used instead of British where spelling differences within the English language occur.

2 Article 121,5 of the 1978 Soviet Constitution stated that the President could not dissolve Parliament (*Konstitutsiya Rossiyskoy Federatsii Rossii* (Izdanie verkhovnogo Soveta Rossiyskoy Federatsii, Moscow: *Izvestiya*, 1992), 57).

3 *Sbornik Federal'nykh Konstitutsionnykh Zakonov i Federal'nykh Zakonov* (Moscow: *Izvestiya*, 1993), no. 1400.

4 Chapter 2 discusses the drafting of the 1993 Constitution further but it is important to note that it was drafted by a team of presidential advisors.

5 In this study the primary focus when referring to the Russian legislature or Parliament will be on the State Duma (lower chamber) because in the 1993 Constitution, and in practice, the Council of the Federation (upper chamber) functions on a part-time basis, only meeting for one or two days a month on average (see Chapter 3), while the State Duma is the full-time parliamentary body. The Council of the Federation's powers in the policy process are still discussed when they are relevant.

6 There are many academics who think that Parliament in Russia is 'weak', while the President is 'strong', and this idea was especially common after the 1993 Constitution and elections. In *Journal of Democracy* 5, 2 (April 1994) some academics, such as Peter Reddaway, John Dunlop and Michael McFaul, published articles to this effect, which formed part of a symposium, see pages 3–42. See also Edward Walker, 'Politics of Blame and Presidential Powers in Russia's New Constitution', *East European Constitutional Review* 2/3, 4/1 (Fall 1993/Winter 1994): 117. Walker thinks that constitutionally Russia has a presidential system due to 'the fact that the president will control the composition of Government'.

7 David Olson and Philip Norton, *The New Parliaments of Central and Eastern Europe* (London: Frank Cass, 1996), 2, state that 'few attempts have been made to consider the role of legislatures in regime transition'. Robert Orttung and Scott Parrish, 'From Confrontation to Cooperation in Russia', *Transition* 2, 25 (13 December 1996): 16–20, briefly discuss the Russian President's and Parliament's power and executive–legislative relations in this article but do not talk about any issues in depth. Similar to this study, they argue that the Duma's power is gradually increasing, though they believe that Russia is still a presidential system.

The literature on legislative power in post-Soviet Russia is limited to in-depth studies of the Russian Parliament from the collapse of the Soviet Union to 1993. Besides the journal articles footnoted in this chapter, an in-depth study of the Russian Parliament from 1994 to 1999 has not been published. Thomas Remington in *Parliaments in Transition: The New Legislative Politics in the Former USSR and Eastern Europe* (Oxford: Westview Press, 1994), Stephen Whitefield (ed.) in *The New Institutional Architecture of Eastern Europe* (New York: St. Martin's Press, 1993), and Jeffrey Hahn (ed.) in *Democratization in Russia: The Developments of Legislative Institutions* (London: M.E. Sharpe, 1996) use an institutional framework to analyze the post-Soviet legislatures in Russia and Eastern Europe, but as Remington's book was published in 1994 and Whitefield's in 1993, and Hahn's book is based on a conference held in October 1993, their analysis only extends to late 1993, that is, before the State Duma came into existence.

Thomas Remington and Steven Smith are the only authors to have written substantially on the Duma elected in 1995, but even these are not in-depth, book-length studies. See Thomas Remington and Steven Smith, 'Communism's Collapse and the Development of Parliamentary Institutions in Russia' (paper presented at the Seminar on the Collapse of Communism and Social Theory, Woodrow Wilson Center, April 1995); Remington and Smith, 'The Development of Parliamentary Parties in Russia', *Legislative Studies Quarterly* 20, 4 (1995): 457–90; Remington and Smith, 'The Early Legislative Process in the Russian Federal Assembly', in David Olson and Philip Norton, *The New Parliaments of Central and Eastern Europe* (London: Frank Cass, 1996); Remington, Smith and Haspel, Moshe, 'Decrees, Laws, and Inter-Branch Relations in the Russian Federation' (paper presented to the AAASS Conference, Seattle, Washington, 20–23 November 1997).

More recently, I. V. Grankin published *Parlament Rossii* (Moscow: Konsaltbankir, 1999) in Russian but the approach and emphasis are different from this book.

8  See Matthew Shugart and John Carey, *Presidents and Assemblies: Constitutional Design and Electoral Dynamics* (Cambridge: Cambridge University Press), ch. 8. See also Alfred Stepan and Cindy Skach, 'Constitutional Frameworks and Democratic Consolidation: Parliamentarism versus Presidentialism', *World Politics* (October 1993): 1–22.

9  I define structural powers by committee strength, electoral cycles, the electoral system, and the length of sessions. An in-depth analysis of these powers is given in Chapter 3.

10  The Third State Duma, which existed from 1907 to 1912, was the first Parliament to survive for its full term without being prematurely dissolved. It did not meet frequently, though, and even went for a year at a time without holding a single session. Terence Emmons, *The Formation of Political Parties and the First National Elections in Russia* (Cambridge: Harvard University Press, 1983), 15. See also Geoffrey Hosking, *The Russian Constitutional Experiment: Government and Duma, 1907–1914* (Cambridge: Cambridge University Press, 1973).

11  Orttung and Parrish, p. 20, and Shugart and Carey, ch. 11. Shugart and Carey determine the effects of the timing of elections and number of parties on a president's and parliament's power.

12  See Orttung and Parrish, p. 20, for their analysis on how the internal structure of the Duma is improving.

13  The neo-institutionalist framework has been used in several in-depth studies of the post-Soviet legislature during and immediately after the 1993 conflict (see footnote 7 for examples) and in journal articles (see footnote 6).

14  James March and Johan Olsen, 'The New Institutionalism: Organizational Factors in Political Life', *American Political Science Review* 78, 3 (1984): 735.

15  Archie Brown in *Soviet Politics and Political Science* (London: Macmillan Press, 1974 – now Palgrave Macmillan), 73–4, shows that some aspects of 'neo'-institutionalism, as defined by March and Olsen, are not entirely new but were to be found in previous institutional analysis.

16  Shugart and Carey, 1. For an in-depth study of neo-institutionalism, see B. Guy Peters, *Institutional Theory in Political Science: The New Institutionalism* (London: Pinter, 1999).

17  March and Olsen, 738–9.

18  See n. 15 above and Brown, 52–3. Merle Fainsod, as cited by Archie Brown in *Soviet Politics and Political Science*, 74, drew attention to the independent power of political institutions in 1940, proving that this is not an entirely new idea (Merle Fainsod, 'Some Reflections on the Nature of the Regulatory Process', *Public Policy* 1 (1940): 299).

19  James March and Johan Olsen, *Rediscovering Institutions: The Organizational Basis of Politics* (New York: The Free Press, 1989), 2.

20  A more detailed debate about the three types of new institutionalism (historical, rational choice, and sociological) and what each school of thought argues can be found in Peter Hall and Rosemary Taylor, 'Political Science and the Three New Institutionalism', *Political Studies* 44, 5 (December 1996): 936–57. See also March and Olsen, 'The New Institutionalism', 734–48. See also B. Guy Peters, *Institutional Theory* (1999). On historical institutionalism, see Sven Steinmo, Kathleen Thelen and Frank Longstreth, *Structuring Politics: Historical Institutionalism in Comparative Analysis* (Cambridge: Cambridge University Press, 1992), ch. 1.

21  Shugart and Carey, *Presidents and Assemblies*, 150–60.

22  Ibid.

23  Ibid., 15. See also Matthew Shugart, 'Executive–Legislative Relations in Post-Communist Europe', *Transition* 2, 25 (6 December 1996): 6–11.

24  Archie Brown, 'Political Leadership in Post-Communist Russia', in Amin Saikal and William Maley, *Russia in Search of its Future* (Cambridge: Cambridge University Press, 1995), 43, argues that 'while the new Russian Constitution owes something to that of the Fifth French Republic and comes into the category of "semi-presidential government" rather than that of pure presidentialism, it would appear, at least, to represent movement away from parliamentarism (especially as compared with the discarded drafts of the Constitutional Commission)'.

25  Shugart and Carey, 157.

26  Shugart and Carey, 156–7. It is important to note that these data do not include post-communist regimes, as their study was published in 1992.

27  Matthew Shugart in 'Executive–Legislative Relations in Post-Communist Europe', *Transition* 2, 25 (6 December 1996): 6–11, Fig. 3. See also Fig. 8.2 in Shugart and Carey, 160, which uses the same factors but does not apply them to post-communist countries.

28  Maurice Duverger, 'A New Political System Model: Semi-Presidential Government', *European Journal of Political Research* 8, 2 (June 1980): 166.
29  Duverger, 167.
30  Ibid., 179.
31  Arend Lijphart (ed.), *Parliamentary versus Presidential Government* (Oxford: Oxford University Press, 1995), 6. Thomas Remington also labels the political system in Russia as presidential in *Parliaments in Transition*, 13.
32  Douglas Verney, *The Analysis of Political Systems* (London: Routledge, 1979), chs 2–3.
33  Stephen Holmes, 'Superpresidentialism and its Problems', *East European Constitutional Review* 2, 4 (Fall 1993/Winter 1994): 123–6.
34  Holmes, 123.
35  Juan Linz, 'Presidential or Parliamentary Democracy: Does It Make a Difference?' in Juan Linz and Arturo Valenzuela (eds), *The Failure of Presidential Democracy: Comparative Perspectives I* (Baltimore: Johns Hopkins University Press), 3–87; Stepan and Skach, 1–22.
36  Linz, 6, 48.
37  Stepan and Skach, 2.
38  Viktor Chernomyrdin was approved, however, by the State Duma's predecessor in December 1992.
39  Duverger, 179.
40  See ch. 5 of the 1993 Russian Constitution in *Konstitutsiya Rossiyskoy Federatsii, 1993* (Moscow: RAU Press, 1993).

## 2  Constitutional Powers of the Russian Presidency and Parliament: the 1993 Russian Constitution

1  Maurice Duverger. 'A New Political System Model: Semi-Presidential Government', *European Journal of Political Research* 8, 2 (June 1980).
2  Matthew Shugart and John Carey, *Presidents and Assemblies: Constitutional Design and Electoral Dynamics* (Cambridge: Cambridge University Press, 1992), 150, Table 8.1. They also use electoral dynamics to determine regime type. These are explored in the next chapter.
3  Shugart and Carey, 149.
4  Ibid., Table 8.2, 155.
5  See Shugart and Carey, 156, Fig. 8.1.
6  For a more extensive analysis of the model see the working paper, 'Comparing the Constitutions of the CIS and Eastern Europe', by Tiffany Troxel and Cindy Skach.
7  Gisbert Franz (ed.), *Constitutions of the Countries of the World* (New York: Oceana Publications, Inc.), Article 62 of the Constitution of Brazil.
8  Franz, *Constitutions of the Countries of the World*, Article 85 of the 27 November 1996 Constitution of Belarus; Article 99 of the 21 November 1991 Constitution of Romania; Article 90 of the 1993 Constitution of the Russian Federation.
9  Ibid., Article 99 of the November 1991 Romanian Constitution.
10  Ibid., Article 85 of the 1997 Belarus Constitution and Article 90 of the 1993 Russian Constitution.

11  Ibid., the 1969 Constitution of Chile and the Constitution of Uruguay.
12  Eugene Huskey, *Executive Power and Soviet Politics: The Rise and Decline of the Soviet State* (Armonk, NY: M.E. Sharpe, 1992), 84.
13  *Constitutions of the World*, Article 122 of the 2 April 1997 Constitution of Poland. Article 122 states that 'the President may refer the bill, with reasons given, to the House of Representatives (Sejm) for its reconsideration. If the said bill is passed again by the House of Representatives (Sejm) by a three-fifths majority vote in the presence of at least half of the statutory number of Deputies, then the President of the Republic shall sign it within seven days and shall order its promulgation in the *Journal of Laws of the Republic of Poland*.'
14  *Constitutions of the World*, Article 19 and 32/C of the December 1996 Hungarian Constitution.
15  Ibid., Article 74 of the 27 November 1996 Belarus Constitution and Article 19 and 30A of the December 1996 Hungarian Constitution.
16  Ibid., Section 5.72 of the February 1994 Constitution of Latvia.
17  Ibid., Article 73 of the January 1992 Macedonian Constitution.
18  The Constitution of the Fifth French Republic of 4 October 1958, Articles 11 and 89, translated in S.E. Finer, Vernon Bogdanor and Bernard Rudden, *Comparing Constitutions* (Oxford: Oxford University Press, 1996), 218.
19  Ibid., 217.
20  The Constitution of the Fifth French Republic, Article 16, translated in Finer, Bogdanor and Rudden, *Comparing Constitutions*, 218.
21  A full classification of 25 countries using the Troxel and Skach model can be found in the working paper, cited above, where the model is presented.
22  Presidential Decree 1400, 'On Gradual Constitutional Reform in the Russian Federation', *Izvestiya* (22 September 1993): 1.
23  *Rossiyskiye vesti* (21 October 1993): 1.
24  Ibid. The procedure and basis for the national vote was decided in a presidential decree on 15 October 1993.
25  *Rossiyskiye vesti* (25 December 1993): 1.
26  For a short discussion of the problems with the 1993 Russian Constitutional vote, including the doubts about whether more than half of the electorate in reality voted, see Robert Sharlet, 'Transitional Constitutionalism: Politics and Law in the Second Republic', *Wisconsin International Law Journal* 14, 3 (1996): 495–521. It is worth noting that the Center for the Study of Public Policy/Paul Lazarsfeld Society (New Russia Barometer III, 1994) questioned the Russian electorate as to who they thought should be more important in the Russian Federation, the president or parliament, or should they have equal powers. The result was that 39 percent thought the president and parliament should be equal, 25 percent voted that the president should be more important, and 22 percent believed parliament should be, while 13 percent were not sure.
27  Thomas Remington, 'Representative Power and the Russian State', in Stephen White, Alex Pravda and Zvi Gitelman, *Developments in Russian and Post-Soviet Politics* (London: Macmillan Press – now Palgrave Macmillan, 1994), 65.
28  Anatoliy Sobchak, former Mayor of St Petersburg, 'The New Russian Constitution: Law as the Basis for Building a Democratic Society', talk given at the University of Michigan, Ann Arbor, 28 February 1995. This was also confirmed by Irina Kotelevskaya, another member of Yel'tsin's committee for drafting the Constitution, a former Member of the Supreme Soviet of the

Soviet Union (1991–93), and Chief of the Secretariat of the First Deputy Chairman of the State Duma. Interview with the author at the State Duma, Moscow, 20 March 1998.

29  Interview with Boris Yel'tsin, *Izvestiya* (2 December 1995).

30  *Konstitutsiya (1993) Rossiyskoy Federatsii* (Moscow: RAU Press, 1993), ch. 4, Article 80.

31  Ch. 6, Article 115.

32  Ch. 7, Article 128.

33  Ch. 4, Article 83.

34  Article 86.

35  Articles 87 and 88.

36  See Ch. 4 of this study for further analysis of federal constitutional laws.

37  Article 93.

38  Article 92.

39  Ch. 5, Article 109 and ch. 6, Articles 111 and 117.

40  Ch. 5, Article 109.

41  Ch. 4, Article 84. Federal Constitutional Law, 'On Referendums in the Russian Federation', published in *Sbornik Federal'nykh Konstitutsionnykh Zakonov i Federal'nykh Zakonov* (10 October 1995), no. 2.

42  Article 90. See, for example, Stephen Holmes, 'Superpresidentialism and its Problems', *East European Constitutional Review* 2, 4 (Fall 1993/Winter 1994): 123–6.

43  The Constitution of the Russian Federation, Section 2, Concluding and Transitional Provisions, no. 9. See also Table 3.11 in Ch. 3 of this study.

44  Ch. 5, Article 101.

45  Article 104.

46  Ch. 6, Article 111.

47  Article 117.

48  See Table 3.11 in Ch. 3 on the frequency of State Duma and Council of the Federation sessions.

49  The Constitution of the Russian Federation, ch. 5, Article 105.

50  Article 107.

51  Article 102.

52  The 1977 Soviet Constitution, ch. 9, Article 174. For an analysis and text of the 1977 Constitution see Robert Sharlet, *The New Soviet Constitution of 1977: Analysis and Text* (Brunswick, Ohio: King's Court Communications, Inc., 1978).

53  The 1993 Constitution of the Russian Federation, ch. 9, Article 134.

54  Ch. 9, Article 136 and ch. 5, Article 108.

55  Ch. 5, Article 108.

56  Ruling of the Constitutional Court, 'On the Case of the Interpretation of Article 136 of the Constitution of the Russian Federation', *Sbornik Federal'nykh Konstitutsionnykh Zakonov i Federal'nykh Zakonov* (31 October 1995), no. 12.

57  The 1993 Constitution of the Russian Federation, ch. 9, Article 136.

58  *Rossiyskaya gazeta* (9 November 1995). See ruling of the Constitutional Court in n. 54.

59  Ch. 9, Article 135. A law on the Constitutional Assembly, which would have to be formed for such full-scale revisions in the Constitution, has yet to be passed.

60 Vil'yam Smirnov, interview by the author, the Institute of State and Law, Moscow, 5 September 1997.
61 Robert Sharlet, 'The Politics of Constitutional Amendments in Russia', *Post-Soviet Affairs* 13, 3 (July–September 1997): 197. Sharlet provides the most comprehensive study to date on attempts to amend the 1993 Russian Constitution.

## 3 Powers Inherent in the Structural Design of the Russian Presidency and Parliament

1 David Olson and Philip Norton, *The New Parliaments of Central and Eastern Europe* (London: Frank Cass, 1996), 9.
2 Arend Lijphart, *Parliamentary versus Presidential Government* (Oxford: Oxford University Press, 1995), 6.
3 Ibid.
4 Juan Linz, 'Presidential or Parliamentary Democracy: Does It Make a Difference?', in Juan Linz and Arturo Valenzuela (eds), *The Failure of Presidential Democracy: Comparative Perspectives I* (Baltimore: Johns Hopkins University Press), 6.
5 Maurice Duverger, 'A New Political System Model: Semi-Presidential Government', *European Journal of Political Research* 8, 2 (June 1980): 166.
6 Olson and Norton, ch. 1 and Shugart and Carey, chs 9 to 12.
7 Olson and Norton, 13. Jon Pammett in 'Elections and Democracy in Russia', *Communist and Post-Communist Studies* 32 (1999): 45–60, examines the importance of structural factors, such as competitive elections and political parties, for democratic stability in Russia.
8 Olson and Norton, 6.
9 Ibid., 9.
10 Arend Lijphart, *Democracies: Patterns of Majoritarian and Consensus Government in 21 Countries* (New Haven: Yale University Press, 1984), 128. Lijphart states that the main factors are socioeconomic, religious, cultural and ethnic, support for regimes, foreign policy, postmaterialism, and urban and rural issues.
11 Rein Taagepera and Matthew Shugart, *Seats and Votes: The Effects and Determinants of Electoral Systems* (New Haven: Yale University Press, 1989), 234.
12 Maurice Duverger, *Political Parties: Their Organization and Activity in the Modern State* (New York: Wiley, 1954). See also Maurice Duverger, *Les Partis politiques* (Paris: Le Seuil, 1951). Robert Moser, in 'The Impact of the Electoral System on Post-Communist Party Development: The Case of the 1993 Parliamentary Election', *Electoral Studies* 14, 4 (1995): 377–98 found that Duverger's law, when applied to the Russian Parliament after the 1993 Constitution, had the effect of favoring some political parties over others. This is because of the contradiction Moser highlights in the electoral rules of the Russian political system: the Russian Parliament is elected in a combined plurality and PR election. For a thorough discussion of Duverger's law, including the criticisms and responses, see Giovanni Sartori, *Comparative Constitutional Engineering: An Inquiry into Structures, Incentives and Outcomes* (New York: New York University Press, 1994), 29–52.

13  Matthew Shugart and John Carey, *Presidents and Assemblies: Constitutional Design and Electoral Dynamics* (Cambridge: Cambridge University Press, 1992), 207.

14  Shugart and Carey, 221 and 229.

15  Viktor Sheynis, Interview with the author, 19 September 1997, State Duma, Moscow.

16  *Sobranie Zakonodatel'stva Rossiyskoy Federatsii* (Moscow: Izvestiya, October 1993). For a more detailed analysis of the 1993 and 1995 electoral systems in Russia, see Thomas Remington, 'Political Goals, Uncertainty, Institutional Context, and the Choice of an Electoral System: The Russian Parliamentary Election Law', working paper, 1–53, 1998. See also Moser, 'The Impact of the Electoral System on Post-Communist Party Development', *Electoral Studies* (1995): 377–98.

17  *Konstitutsiya (1993) Rossiyskoy Federatsii* (Moscow: RAU Press, 1993), ch. 4, Article 81 and ch. 5, Article 96.

18  'O poryadke formirovaniya Soveta Federatsii Federal'nogo Sobraniya Rossiyskoy Federatsii', *Vedomosti Federal'nogo Sobraniya Rossiyskoy Federatsii*, 35 (Federal'nogo Sobraniya Rossiyskoy Federatsii, Moscow: Izvestiya, 21 December 1995), no. 1657.

19  For a detailed discussion of the procedure for electing State Duma Deputies and Council of the Federation Members, see A. P. Lyubimov, *Parlamentskoe pravo Rossii* (St Petersburg: Kodex-info, 1997), 7–13.

20  Robert Moser, 'The Impact of Parliamentary Electoral Systems in Russia', *Post-Soviet Affairs* 13, 3 (July–September 1997): 284–302. See also Robert Moser, *Electoral Systems, Political Parties, and Representation in Russia* (Pittsburgh: University of Pittsburgh Press, 2000).

21  Sheynis, Interview with the author, 19 September 1997, State Duma, Moscow. Sheynis discusses the effect of the 5 percent barrier on individual parties in detail in 'Proyden li istoricheskiy rubezh?' *Polis* 1, 37 (1997): 84–96.

22  See also n. 12 about Moser's objection that Russia does not fit Duverger's model very well.

23  For further discussion of the consolidation of the political parties in Russia, see Robert Moser, 'The Electoral Effects of Presidentialism in Post-Soviet Russia', in John Lowenhardt, *Party Politics in Post-Communist Russia* (London: Frank Cass, 1998), 54–75.

24  Markku Laakso and Rein Taagepera, 'Effective Number of Parties: A Measure with Application to West Europe', *Comparative Political Studies* 12, 1 (1979): 3–27.

25  Ibid.

26  Alfred Stepan and Cindy Skach, 'Constitutional Framework and Democratic Consolidation: Parliamentarism versus Presidentialism', *World Politics* 46, 1 (October 1993): 8, Table 1.

27  See Stephen Whitefield and Geoffrey Evans, 'The Emerging Structure of Partisan Divisions in Post-Soviet Russia', and William Reisinger, Arthur Miller and Vicki Hesli, 'Ideological Divisions and Party-Building Prospects in Post-Soviet Russia', in Matthew Wyman, Stephen White and Sarah Oates (eds), *Elections and Voters in Post-Communist Russia* (Cheltenham, 1998).

28  Taagepera and Shugart, 1989. See also Gallagher's Least Square Index to measure disproportionality in Michael Gallagher, 'Proportionality, Disproportionality and Electoral Systems', *Electoral Studies* 10 (1991): 33–51.

For further discussion of this measure see Arend Lijphart, *Electoral Systems and Party Systems* (Oxford: Oxford University Press, 1994), 57–62.

29 Moser, 'The Electoral Effects of Presidentialism in Post-Soviet Russia', 1998, 60, uses the Least-Square Index to find disproportionality in Russia, the results being as follows: 4.94 for 1993 PR, 20.56 for 1995 PR, 4.27 for 1993 Plurality, 11.09 for 1995 Plurality, and 64.72 for Round 1 of the 1996 Presidential election and 46.17 for Round 2. There is a difference in the scale for the results using this index, but the conclusions are similar to what I found using Taagepera and Shugart's measure of disproportionality. Stephen White, Richard Rose and Ian McAllister, in *How Russia Votes* (Chatham: Chatham House Publishers, Inc., 1997), Fig. 11.1, 228, found similar results to Table 3.3 for disproportionality in Russia.

30 Maurice Duverger, 'Duverger's Law Thirty Years Later', in Bernard Grofman and Arend Lijphart, *Electoral Laws and Their Political Consequences* (New York: Agathon Press, 1986).

31 See Shugart and Carey, ch. 9 on how electoral dynamics affect the efficiency of parliament.

32 For a detailed analysis of changes in voter preferences between elections to the Duma, Council of the Federation, and Presidency, see Michael McFaul and Nikolai Petrov, 'Russian Electoral Politics after Transition: Regional and National Assessments', *Post-Soviet Geography and Economics* 38, 9 (1997): 507–49.

33 Adam Przeworski and John Sprague, *Paper Stones: A History of Electoral Socialism* (Chicago: University of Chicago Press, 1986).

34 Aleksandr Ponomarev, State Duma Deputy of the Communist Party of the Russian Federation, Interview by the author at the State Duma, Moscow, 1 April 1998.

35 There is some conjecture as to the validity of these results. See Elizabeth Owen, 'Vote Called Fair in General, Biased in Parts', *Moscow Times* (6 July 1996): 4.

36 Duverger, *Political Parties* (1954).

37 Shugart and Carey, 258.

38 Ibid., 221.

39 Ibid.

40 See further analysis of the President's and Council of the Federation's vetoes and veto overrides by the Duma in ch. 5.

41 Olson and Norton, 11. For further discussion on the ability of parliaments to act more autonomously from the executive because of committees, see John Lees and Malcolm Shaw, *Committees in Legislatures: A Comparative Analysis* (Durham: Duke University Press, 1979) and David Olson and Michael Mezey, 'Parliaments and Public Policy', in Olson and Mezey (eds), *Legislatures in the Policy Process: The Dilemmas of Economic Policy* (Cambridge: Cambridge University Press, 1991), 14–15.

42 For specific information about the rules, regulations and structure of Duma committees, see *Reglament Gosudarstvennoy Dumy Federal'nogo Sobraniya Rossiyskoy Federatsii* (Moscow: Gosudarstvennaya Duma, Izvestiya, 1998) 24–6.

43 Oleg Medvedev, 'Duma Elects Its Leadership', *Kommersant Daily* (19 January 1994): 3.

44   Olson and Norton, 11.
45   See *Kommersant Daily* (18 January 1994): 3 and (19 January 1994): 3.
46   Olson and Norton, 11.
47   Thomas Remington and Steven Smith, 'The Early Legislative Process in the Russian Federal Assembly', in Olson and Norton, 178.
48   Boris Kuznetsov, Interview with the author, State Duma, Moscow, 8 April 1998.
49   Vladimir Averchev, Interview by the author at the State Duma, Moscow, 19 September 1997.
50   Aleksey Avtonomov, Interview with the author, Fund for the Development of Parliamentarism in Russia, Moscow, 17 April 1998.
51   Olson and Norton, 11.
52   *Konstitutsiya (1993) Rossiyskoy Federatsii*, ch. 9, Section 2.
53   Viktor Sergeyev, Interview by the author at MGIMO, Moscow, 24 March 1999.
54   Gennadiy Zyuganov, Interview by the author, Wadham College, Oxford, 31 October 1997. For more details about the composition and function of the Supreme Council, see Gleb Cherkasov, *Segodnya* (22 November 1996): 1.
55   'Roundtable Talks Postponed', *OMRI Daily Digest* 1, 177 (11 December 1997): 1.
56   Vladimir Lukin, Interview by the author at the State Duma, Moscow, 26 March 1999.
57   Olson and Norton, 12.
58   Archie Brown, *The Gorbachev Factor* (Oxford: Oxford University Press, 1996), 179–80.
59   Confirmed by Valeriy Fadeev, State Duma consultant and expert for the Duma Committee on International Affairs, Interview with the author, State Duma, Moscow, 26 September 1997. Mary McAuley notes in *Russia's Politics of Uncertainty* (Cambridge: Cambridge University Press, 1997) that Duma Deputies are not always in their home constituencies during this time. While they are usually away from the Duma during this period, they may be away on conferences, vacation, or attending to other matters, instead of their constituencies.
60   *Konstitutsiya (1993) Rossiyskoy Federatsii*, ch. 5, Article 104.1.

# 4   Actual Legislative Powers of the Russian President and Parliament: Parliamentary Laws versus Presidential Decrees

1   See n. 17 in Ch. 1 of this study.
2   On why and to what degree legislators are motivated by re-election possibilities see, for example, David Mayhew, *Congress: The Electoral Connection* (New Haven: Yale University Press, 1974).
3   Legislators' consideration of to what extent they want to oppose or support the executive and reasons for such a decision are advanced in such studies as Sharyn O'Halloran, *Politics, Process, and American Trade Policy* (Ann Arbor: University of Michigan Press, 1995).
4   See, for example, David Epstein and Sharyn O'Halloran, *Delegating Powers: A Transaction Cost Politics Approach to Policy Making under Separate Powers* (Cambridge: Cambridge University Press, 1999).

5 For further analysis of these preferences, see John Carey and Matthew Shugart (eds), *Executive Decree Authority: Calling Out the Tanks, or Filling Out the Forms?* (Cambridge: Cambridge University Press, 1998). See also Judith Chase, 'Russian Executive Policy-Making: Delegation in the Duma', (paper presented at the 1997 Meeting of the APSA, 28–31 August 1997).

6 *Vedomosti Federal'nogo Sobraniya Rossiyskoy Federatsii* (Federal'nogo Sobraniya Rossiyskoy Federatsii, Moscow: Izvestiya, 1994).

7 See *Sbornik Federal'nykh Konstitutsionnykh Zakonov i Federal'nykh Zakonov* 1 (Moscow: Izvestiya, 1994).

8 Many of the non-normative decrees were unpublished from 1994 to 1998 because they concerned issues of state security. Scott Parrish found that quite a few were on the Chechen War ('Presidential Decree Power in the Second Russian Republic, 1993–1996 and Beyond', Paper presented at the 1996 Meeting of the APSA, August 1996). Moreover, Thomas Remington, Steven Smith and Moshe Haspel found that 'like classified executive branch directions in the United States, [these unpublished decrees] do not concern more general policy matters, including a number of decisions relating to the organization of the military itself ... Presidential decrees concerned with economic, social, and political issues are not classified, since the President's ability to achieve policy and political success with them depends on public awareness of them' ('Decrees, Laws, and Inter-Branch Relations in the Russian Federation', Paper presented at the 1997 Meeting of the AAASS, 20–23 November 1997).

9 Viktor Luchin, pamplet entitled ' "Rule by Decree" in Russia', reprinted in *Kommersant Daily* (26 February 1997): 1. See also Scott Parrish, 'Presidential Decree Authority in Russia, 1991–1995', in John Carey and Matthew Shugart, *Executive Decree Authority* (Cambridge: Cambridge University Press, 1998), 83.

10 *Sbornik Federal'nykh Konstitutsionnykh Zakonov i Federal'nykh Zakonov*. The titles of the decrees in the August 1996 issue of *Sbornik* clearly show that many of the pre-election decrees were revised or discarded by these later decrees.

11 Ibid. See the January to September 1994 issues.

12 Remington, Smith and Haspel, 'Decrees, Laws, and Inter-Branch Relations in the Russian Federation', Table 4, 25.

13 Gennadiy Seleznyov, *Vsya vlast'* – *Zakonu!* (*Zakonodatel'stvo i Traditsii Ukaznogo Prava v Rossii*) (Moscow: Segodnya Gruppa, 1997), 128, Table 1.

14 Parrish, 'Presidential Decree Authority in Russia', 84–92.

15 Yuriy Golotyuk, 'The Deputies Gave an Unfriendly Welcome to William Perry', *Segodnya*, no. 192 (18 October 1996): 2.

16 Ibid.

17 'Senior Yel'tsin Aide Calls Ratification of START II "Unrealistic," ' *BBC Summary of World Broadcasts* 1, SU 2810 (7 January 1997): 5.

18 *Rossiyskaya gazeta* (4 January 1993): 1.

19 Igor Rodionov, as quoted in *Segodnya* (17 October 1996): 1.

20 Nikolay Stolyarov, Deputy from the Duma's Committee on International Affairs, Interview with the author at the State Duma, Moscow, 6 April 1998.

21 Sergey Rogov, 'Russia–U.S.A.', *Nezavisimaya gazeta* (26 March 1997): 4.

22 Parrish, 'Presidential Decree Authority in Russia', 83.

## 5   Vetoing and Overriding Vetoes on Legislation in Russia

1   'Svedeniya o zakonakh, prinyatykh Gosudarstvennoy Dumoy, napravlen-
    nykh v Sovet Federatsii, podpisannykh ili otklonennykh Prezidentom
    Rossiyskoy Federatsii' (Internal Document, Moscow: Record Office of the
    State Duma, 1996 to 1998).
2   Table 2.1 in Ch. 2 and *Konstitutsiya (1993) Rossiyskoy Federatsii* (Moscow: RAU
    Press, 1993), Article 107. For a comparative analysis of a president's veto pow-
    ers in Russia, France and the United States, see Ara Balikian, 'The New Russian
    Federation Constitution: A Legal Framework Adopted and Implemented in
    a Post-Soviet Era', *Suffolk Transnational Law Review* 18, 237 (1995): 250–3.
3   According to the 1993 Russian Constitution, the Council of the Federation
    must consider legislation relating to the federal budget; federal taxes and
    charges; financial, foreign currency, credit and customs regulation and money
    issues; the ratification and denunciation of international treaties of Russia; the
    status and protection of the state border of Russia; and, war and peace (Ibid.,
    Article 106). Even for the bills which the Council of the Federation is not con-
    stitutionally required to examine, a two-thirds vote in both houses is still nec-
    essary to override the President's veto on all legislation.
4   For an in-depth examination of the veto and veto override powers of the
    President and Parliament in the 1993 Constitution, see M. V. Baglay,
    *Konstitutsionnoe pravo Rossiyskoy Federatsii* (Moscow: NORMA–INFRAM, 1998),
    520–34. On presidential vetoes, see also 'Pravo prezidentskogo veto', in Lev
    Okun'kov, *Prezident Rossiyskoy Federatsii: Konstitutsiya i politicheskaya praktika*
    (Moscow: INFRAM–NORMA Group, 1996), 72–5. On the Duma's constitutional
    power to override vetoes, see Aleksandr Shokhin, *Vzaimodeystvie vlastey v zakon-
    odatel'nom protsesse* (Moscow: Nash Dom–L'Age d'Homme, 1997), 42–6, 65–6.
5   Ibid., Article 105.
6   See Eyal Winter ('Voting and Vetoing', *American Political Science Review* 90,
    4 (December 1996): 813–21) for a detailed study on the effects of time
    constraints on veto powers. Winter found that the 'excessive power of veto
    members can be reduced if delay is costly or if an exogenous deadline for the
    negotiations is imposed ... [If the deadline for vetoing] is exogenously fixed,
    the bargaining power of veto members decreases' (820).
7   The law 'On the Formation of the Council of the Federation' changed the
    procedure for composing the upper chamber from presidential appointees to
    elected representatives from Russia's 89 regions (*Vedomosti Federal'nogo
    Sobraniya Rossiyskoy Federatsii* (Federal'nogo Sobraniya Rossiyskoy Federatsii,
    Moscow: Izvestiya, 1995)). For further discussion of this law and the prob-
    lems in adopting it, see Stephen White, Richard Rose and Ian McAllister, *How
    Russia Votes* (Chatham, NJ: Chatham House Publishers, Inc., 1997), 194–5.
8   'Yel'tsin Criticizes the Duma', *OMRI Daily Digest* 1, 125 (25 September 1997): 1.
9   As confirmed by Anatoliy Eliseev, Head of the Records Office of the State
    Duma, 6 April 1998 and 26 March 1999.
10   Thomas Remington and Steven Smith, 'The Early Legislative Process in the
    Russian Federal Assembly', in David Olson and Philip Norton, *The New
    Parliaments of Central and Eastern Europe* (London: Frank Cass, 1996), 186.
    Remington and Smith do not state how many vetoes were issued by the
    Council or the number of vetoes overridden by Deputies.

11  Pavel Borisov, *Segodnya* (15 August 1995): 2.

12  Aleksey Kirpichnikov, *Segodnya* (13 October 1994): 2.

13  Pavel Borisov, *Segodnya* (15 August 1995): 2.

14  *Gosudarstvennaya Duma: Stenogramma zasedaniy* (Federal'nogo Sobraniya Rossiyskoy Federatsii, Moscow: Izvestiya, 21 April, 11 May, 9 June, 27 October, 17 November and 5 December 1995).

15  Yel'tsin threatened to issue a decree on the procedure for parliamentary elections if the Duma did not pass these bills (Anna Ostapchuk and Yevgeniy Krasnikov, *Nezavisimaya gazeta* (24 May 1995): 1, and Yelena Tregubova, *Segodnya* (15 August 1995): 2).

16  See Ch. 6 for further analysis.

17  *Vedomosti Federal'nogo Sobraniya Rossiyskoy Federatsii* (Federal'nogo Sobraniya Rossiyskoy Federatsii, Moscow: Izvestiya, December 1995), law no. 192.

18  Aleksey Kirpichnikov, *Segodnya* (8 December 1995): 1.

19  *Rossiiskaya gazeta* (28 December 1993): 1.

20  White, Rose and McAllister, *How Russia Votes* (1997), 190.

21  Ibid., 192.

22  Viktor Sheynis, Interview by the author at the State Duma, Moscow, 3 April 1998.

23  *Gosudarstvennaya Duma: Stenogramma zasedaniy* (Federal'nogo Sobraniya Rossiyskoy Federatsii, Moscow: Izvestiya, 11 May 1995).

24  Boris Yel'tsin, as quoted in *Nezavisimaya gazeta* (17 May 1995): 1.

25  Anna Ostapchuk and Yevgeniy Krasnikov, *Nezavisimaya gazeta* (24 May 1995): 1.

26  Viktor Sheynis, Interview with the author at the State Duma, Moscow, 3 April 1998.

27  Yevgeniy Yuryev, *Kommersant Daily* (10 June 1995): 3.

28  *Nezavisimaya gazeta* (29 November 1995): 5.

29  See the policy areas of legislation which the Council of the Federation must approve in fn. 3 of this chapter.

30  A detailed analysis on the appointment and dismissal of Sergey Kiriyenko as Prime Minister follows in the next chapter.

31  Aleksey Avtonomov, Interview by the author at the Foundation for the Development of Parliamentarism in Russia, Moscow, 17 April 1998.

# 6 Actual Non-Legislative Powers of the Russian President and Parliament: Cabinet Formation and Dismissal

1  Federal Constitutional Law, no. 2, 'On the Government of the Russian Federation', *Sbornik Federal'nykh Konstitutsionnykh Zakonov i Federal'nykh Zakonov* (Moscow: Izvestiya, 31 December 1997), Articles 4 and 13. For an analysis of this law, see MV. Baglay, *Konstitutsionnoe pravo Rossiyskoy Federatsii* (Moscow: NORMA–INFRAM, 1998), 571–5.

2  *Konstitutsiya (1993) Rossiyskoy Federatsii* (Moscow: RAU Press, 1993), Articles 111 and 117.

3  Ibid., Article 117.

4  Ibid., Article 111.

5  Ibid., Article 111 of the Russian Constitution does not state whether the President can nominate the same person more than once for Prime Minister. This was challenged when the President resubmitted Kiriyenko for Prime Minister in April 1998, but it was decided that there was nothing in the Constitution which prevented him from doing so.

6  In May 1999, because of contradictions and omissions in the Constitution, the problem was addressed regarding what the constitutional outcome would be when impeachment proceedings had commenced and the Duma rejected the President's nomination for Prime Minister three times. (See Articles 109 and 111 of the 1993 Russian Constitution.) As the Constitution does not state how this issue should be decided, whether the President's nominated candidate would become Prime Minister or remain acting Prime Minister and whether the Duma would still be dissolved, and the Constitutional Court never ruled on this, people began to conjecture what the outcome would be in May 1999 when the Duma seemed likely to vote for impeaching the President and Yel'tsin had dismissed Primakov's Government. The Duma fell 17 votes short of the 300 required to proceed with impeachment so this discrepancy was not resolved (*Gosudarstvennaya Duma: Stenogramma zasedaniy* Federal'nogo Sobraniya Rossiyskoy Federatsii, Moscow: Izvestiya, 15 May 1999). Russia's acting Justice Minister Pavel Krasheninnikov stated on 14 May 1999 that President Boris Yel'tsin can constitutionally disband the Duma even after impeachment proceedings have started because Article 109, which explains that the Duma cannot be dissolved once the impeachment process begins, does not override Article 111, requiring the President to dismiss the Duma if it does not confirm his choice of Prime Minister a third time (*Nezavisimaya gazeta* (14 May 1999): 1). According to the Constitution, however, this is not correct. Article 109 states that 'the State Duma may be dissolved by the President of the Russian Federation in the circumstances provided for in Articles 111 and 117 of the Constitution of the Russian Federation... The State Duma may not be dissolved (in the circumstances provided for in Articles 111 and 117) from the moment it lays a charge against the President of the Russian Federation until the adoption of the appropriate decision by the Council of the Federation' (*Konstitutsiya (1993) Rossiyskoy Federatsii* Moscow: RAU Press, 1993).

7  Federal Constitutional Law, no. 2, 'On the Government of the Russian Federation', *Sbornik Federal'nykh Konstitutsionnykh Zakonov i Federal'nykh Zakonov* (Moscow: Izvestiya, 31 December 1997). For more details about the debates on this law and the President's repeated refusals to sign it, see Yevgeniy Yuryev, *Segodnya* (12 April 1997): 3 and Gleb Cherkasov and Vladimir Shpak, *Kommersant Daily* (29 November 1997): 1.

8  Viktor Chernomyrdin received 60.7 percent of the vote in the Congress of People's Deputies on 14 December 1992 so Yegor Gaidar was forced to resign as Prime Minister (Gleb Cherkasov, *Segodnya* (13 August 1996): 1).

9  See Tables 6.2 to 6.4 in this chapter.

10  Article 111(2) of the 1993 Russian Constitution mandates that the President must submit a nomination for Prime Minister to the Duma within two weeks of a presidential election (*Konstitutsiya (1993) Rossiyskoy Federatsii* Moscow: RAU Press, 1993).

11  Vladimir Nikitin, Interview with the author at the State Duma, Moscow, 6 April 1998. The collapse of the ruble on 11 October 1994, which Nikitin refers to, is known as 'Black Tuesday'.

12  Vladimir Lukin, Interview by the author at the State Duma, Moscow, 26 March 1999.

13  Yekaterina Lakhova, as quoted in Thomas de Waal and Leonid Bershidskiy, 'Government Survives No-Confidence Vote', *Moscow Times* (28 October 1994): 1.

14  Ibid.

15  Vladimir Zhirinovskiy withdrew a motion to raise a confidence vote in the Government on 7 April 1997 after Deputies who endorsed the decision to hold such a vote revoked their support. This is not considered in this chapter because Deputies did not use it to threaten the executive and retracted the motion before it was even debated.

16  Yevgeniy Yuryev, *Kommersant Daily* (22 June 1995): 3.

17  G.D.G. Murrell, *Russia's Transition to Democracy: An Internal Political History* (Brighton: Sussex Academic Press, 1997), 232.

18  Yevgeny Yuryev, *Kommersant Daily* (22 June 1995): 1, 3.

19  Grigory Yavlinskiy, as quoted in Aleksey Kirpichnikov, *Segodnya* (22 June 1995): 2.

20  Gleb Cherkasov and Dmitry Volkov, *Segodnya* (29 June 1995): 1.

21  Boris Yel'tsin as quoted by his Press Service, printed in *Rossiyskaya gazeta* (23 June 1995): 1.

22  Viktor Chernomyrdin countered this second vote by requesting a confidence motion in the Government, 'which if not passed would have led to either the Duma or the Government falling within a week. Threatened with imminent dissolution, a second vote of no-confidence on 1 July failed to pass, and thereupon Chernomyrdin withdrew his confidence motion' (Richard Sakwa, *Russian Politics and Society* (London: Routledge, 1996), 153).

23  Ivan Rybkin, as quoted in *Kommersant Daily* (24 June 1995): 3.

24  Yevgeniy Yuryev, *Kommersant Daily* (28 June 1995): 3.

25  See Table 6.3.

26  Aleksey Avtonomov, Interview by the author at the Foundation for the Development of Parliamentarism in Russia, Moscow, 29 March 1999.

27  See Fig. 9.2 in Stephen White, Richard Rose and Ian McAllister, *How Russia Votes* (Chatham, NJ: Chatham House Publishers, Inc., 1997), 186, which shows the percentage of Deputies in parties voting no-confidence on 1 July 1995. White, Rose and McAllister also argue that there was a 'high degree of cohesiveness in voting for or against the Government' on this motion (186).

28  Azat Khamaev, Interview by the author at the State Duma, Moscow, 1 April 1998.

29  Vil'yam Smirnov, Interview by the author at the Institute of State and Law, Moscow, 5 September 1997.

30  See Table 6.4. Thomas Remington found that 'parliamentary parties have achieved cross-party agreement on a number of legislative matters ... among the (7) most important cases of cooperation among parties are the following: the Duma confirmation of Viktor Chernomyrdin as Prime Minister in August 1996 ... (and) the defeat of the motions of no-confidence in the Government on two separate occasions in 1994 and 1995' ('Political Conflict and Institutional Design: Paths of Party Development in Russia', *Journal of Communist Studies and Transition Politics* 14, 1–2 (March/June 1998): 206–7).

31  Dmitry Zaks, 'Warning Ups Stakes in Budget Standoff', *Moscow Times* (15 October 1997): 1.
32  Gleb Cherkasov, *Kommersant Daily* (16 October 1997): 1.
33  Boris Yel'tsin, radio address on 17 October 1997 transcribed in *Rossiyskiye vesti* (18 October 1997): 3.
34  Nikolay Ryzhkov, as quoted in Christian Lowe, 'Yel'tsin Delays Tax Code in Duma Truce', *Moscow Times* (22 October 1997): 2.
35  See fn. 7 in this chapter.
36  Nikolay Podlipskiy, *Kommersant Daily* (22 October 1997): 1.
37  Resolution of the State Duma, 'On the Social and Economic Policy of the Russian Federation Government', *Sbornik Federal'nykh Konstitutsionnykh Zakonov i Federal'nykh Zakonov* (Moscow: Izvestiya, November 1994).
38  Aleksey Kirpichnikov, *Segodnya* (5 November 1994): 2.
39  Boris Fyodorov, as quoted in *Segodnya* (5 November 1994): 1.
40  Egor Gaidar, as quoted in *Izvestiya* (5 November 1994): 2.
41  Vasily Kononenko, *Izvestiya* (5 November 1994): 2.
42  Sergey Parkhomenko, *Segodnya* (5 November 1994): 1.
43  Deputies voted no-confidence in Viktor Yerin, Minister of Internal Affairs, for a second time on 10 March 1995 (*Segodnya* (11 March 1995): 1) and Yel'tsin removed him in June 1995 as a concession to Deputies.
44  Chubais regained his position in the Government on 7 March 1997, when he was appointed First Deputy Prime Minister (Presidential Decree, 'On A. Chubais', *Sbornik Federal'nykh Konstitutsionnykh Zakonov i Federal'nykh Zakonov* (Moscow: Izvestiya, March 1997).
45  Gleb Cherkasov and Daniil Osmolovskiy, *Kommersant Daily* (20 November 1997): 1.
46  Daniil Osmolovskiy, *Kommersant Daily* (21 November 1997): 1.
47  Ibid.
48  Elena Shestopal explained that 'Chubais and Nemtsov are perceived in very negative colors by Deputies and in order to deal with the Duma they usually use some pressure and domination. They do not have good relations with the Duma' (Interview with the author at Moscow State University, Moscow, 9 September 1997).
49  Azat Khamaev, Interview by the author at the State Duma, Moscow, 1 April 1998. This was confirmed by Elena Shestopal who stated that 'people who become Deputies are to a large extent very interested in continuing their political careers and the Government can always promise them something' (Interview by the author at Moscow State University, Moscow, 9 September 1997).
50  Vladimir Averchev, Interview by the author at the State Duma, Moscow, 19 September 1997.
51  Federal Constitutional Law, no. 2, 'On the Government of the Russian Federation', *Sbornik Federal'nykh Konstitutsionnykh Zakonov i Federal'nykh Zakonov* (Moscow: Izvestiya, 31 December 1997).
52  Boris Yel'tsin, televised address on 23 March 1998, as transcribed in *Trud* (24 March 1998): 1.
53  Lyudmila Telen, *Moskovskiye novosti*, no. 11 (22–29 March 1998): 2.
54  Yel'tsin appointed Chernomyrdin as a special Russian envoy to Kosovo in Spring 1999 during the war in Kosovo.

55 An undisclosed Government official, as quoted in Sergey Parkhomenko, *Itogi*, no. 12 (31 March 1998): 14–17.

56 Lilia Shevtsova, Interview by the author at the Carnegie Center, Moscow, 23 March 1998 and Lilia Shevtsova, *Moskovskiye novosti*, no. 12 (29 March–5 April 1998): 10.

57 Headlines, such as 'Sergey Who?'(*Moscow News*, no. 11 (26 March–1 April 1998): 1), on the day after Kiriyenko's nomination demonstrated that he was relatively unknown and an unlikely candidate for Prime Minister.

58 According to Article 92 of the 1993 Constitution, 'in all instances where the President of the Russian Federation is unable to perform his duties, they shall be temporarily carried out by the Chair of the Government (Prime Minister)' *Konstitutsiya (1993) Rossiyskoy Federatsii* (Moscow: RAU Press, 1993).

59 This view was confirmed prior to the Duma's first vote on Kiriyenko by Deputy Igor' Mal'kov, Interview with the author at the State Duma, Moscow, 3 April 1998 and Azat Khamaev, Interview by the author at the State Duma, Moscow, 1 April 1998.

60 *Konstitutsiya (1993) Rossiyskoy Federatsii*, Article 111(3).

61 Gennadiy Seleznyov, in *OMRI Daily Digest* 2, 75 (20 April 1998): 1.

62 Laura Belin, 'Zyuganov Says New Elections "Could Be Useful" ', *OMRI Daily Digest*, no. 75 (20 April 1998): 1.

63 Boris Yel'tsin, nationwide radio address, 10 April 1998.

64 Azat Khamaev, Interview by the author at the State Duma, Moscow, 1 April 1998. Boris Kuznetsov also stated this in an interview with the author at the State Duma, Moscow, 8 April 1998.

65 *Konstitutsiya (1993) Rossiyskoy Federatsii*, Article 111(3).

66 Alastair Macdonald, 'Premier Delay Shows Constitution Wrangling', *Moscow Times* (4 April 1998): 2.

67 Sergey Kiriyenko, comment to reporters on 10 April 1998, at which the author was present, immediately following the first vote on his approval as Prime Minister in the State Duma.

68 Gennadiy Seleznyov's comments on his meeting with Boris Yel'tsin on 14 April 1998, as printed in *Izvestiya* (15 April 1998): 1.

69 Boris Yel'tsin, as quoted by Georgy Bovt, *Segodnya* (14 April 1998): 1, 3.

70 As explained by Gleb Cherkasov, Sergey Aksyonov and Marina Rassafonova in *Kommersant Daily* (23 April 1998): 1, because of contradictions in the electoral law, the President could legally modify the law by presidential decree.

71 Gennadiy Seleznyov confirmed (in *Izvestiya* (15 April 1998): 1) that the Duma's fate as an institution was more important than whether Kiriyenko was Prime Minister.

72 Ibid., 3.

73 See Vyacheslav Nikonov, *Izvestiya* (12 May 1998): 2.

74 Konstantin Levin, *Kommersant Daily* (5 May 1998): 1.

75 Pyotr Akopov, *Nezavisimaya gazeta* (1 July 1998): 1, 4.

76 Natalya Timakova, *Kommersant Daily* (15 July 1998): 1.

77 Tat'yana Koshkaryova and Rustam Narzikulov, *Nezavisimaya gazeta* (14 August 1998): 1, 3.

78 Aleksey Avtonomov, Interview by the author at the Foundation for the Development of Parliamentarism in Russia, Moscow, 29 March 1999.

79  See quotes from most of the Duma's elite in *Segodnya* (22 August 1998): 1, in which they ask for Kiriyenko to be dismissed and warn that they will vote no-confidence in the Government in two days.
80  Boris Yel'tsin, televised address on 24 August 1998, transcribed in *Kommersant Daily* (25 August 1998): 1.
81  Gennadiy Zyuganov, statement released on 26 August 1998, printed in *Izvestiya* (27 August 1998): 1.
82  Yelena Dikun and Sergey Gavrilov, *Obshchaya gazeta*, no. 35 (3–9 September 1998): 7.
83  Igor Kirillov, *Kommersant Daily* (2 September 1998): 1.
84  Ibid.
85  Irina Granik, *Kommersant Daily* (1 September 1998): 1.
86  Svetlana Ilyina, *Nezavisimaya gazeta* (8 September 1998): 1, 3.
87  Boris Slavin, *Pravda* (14 October 1997): 2.

## 7   Budgetary Powers: the Power Struggle between the Executive and Legislature

1  *Konstitutsiya (1993) Rossiyskoy Federatsii* (Moscow: RAU Press, 1993), ch. 6, Article 114 (1a). For analysis of the Government, Duma, and Council of the Federation's constitutional powers during budgetary proceedings, see pages 452–5, 488–96, 576–7, respectively, in M. V. Baglay, *Konstitutsionnoe pravo Rossiyskoy Federatsii* (Moscow: NORMA–INFRAM, 1998).
2  Ibid., ch. 5, Article 106.
3  Ibid., ch. 5, Article 105.
4  Ibid., ch. 5, Article 107(2).
5  Ibid., ch. 5, Article 105.
6  Ibid., ch. 6, Article 114(1a) and ch. 5, Article 101(5).
7  Ibid., ch. 6, Article 114(1a).
8  Ibid., ch. 5, Article 101(5).
9  See, for example, the resolution 'On the Procedures for Implementing the Federal Budget during the First Quarter of 1998', *Sbornik Federal'nykh Konstitutsionnykh Zakonov i Federal'nykh Zakonov* (Moscow: Izvestiya, 15 December 1997).
10  Aleksandr Zhukov, Interview with the author at the State Duma, Moscow, 18 September 1997.
11  Archie Brown, 'The Russian Crisis: Beginning of the End or End of the Beginning?' *Post-Soviet Affairs*, 15, 1 (1999): 63.
12  Yevgeniy Primakov as quoted in Leonid Mlechin, *Yevgeniy Primakov: Istoriya Odnoy Kar'eri* (Moscow: Tsentropoligraf, 1999), 406.
13  Aleksey Golovkov, Interview with the author at the State Duma, Moscow, 6 April 1998.
14  Aleksandr Zhukov, Interview with the author at the State Duma, Moscow, 18 September 1997. See also interviews with Deputies of the Budget Committee for further discussion of the role of the special commissions in the budgetary process in *Byudzhet-97* (Moscow: Business Press, 1996 and 1997).
15  Chrystia Freeland, 'Yel'tsin Gives Ministers New Warning', *Financial Times* (24 February 1998): 2.

16 *Gosudarstvennaya Duma: Stenogramma zasedaniy* (Federal'nogo Sobraniya Rossiyskoy Federatsii, Moscow: Izvestiya, 27 October 1994).
17 Sergey Nikiforov, Interview with the author at the State Duma, Moscow, 6 April 1998. See also Konstantin Levin, 'State Duma Threatens Primakov', *Kommersant Daily* (13 March 1999): 3. Oleg Preksin, Government official in the Ministry of Economy, confirmed that 'the federal budget is one of the major obstacles for receiving foreign loans' ('Foreign Direct Investment and Russia's Regions', talk given at St Antony's College, Oxford, 5 March 1998).
18 Konstanin Levin, *Kommersant Daily* (22 July 1998): 1. For explanations of the causes of the August 1998 economic crisis, see Anders Aslund, 'Russia's Current Economic Dilemma: A Comment', *Post-Soviet Affairs* 15 (1999): 83–6, and Jacques Sapir, 'Russia's Crash of August 1998: Diagnosis and Prescription', *Post-Soviet Affairs* 15 (1999): 1–36.
19 Irina Granik, *Kommersant Daily* (16 July 1998): 1.
20 Besides the President's annual message to the Federal Assembly, Yel'tsin has also visited the Duma to lobby support for federal budgets (e.g. on 6 December 1997 for the 1998 Budget). Prime Ministers have tried this tactic too, for example, with Viktor Chernomyrdin speaking in the Duma on 6 December 1997 in support of the 1998 Budget and Primakov on 25 December 1998 for the 1999 Budget's readings. Further analysis of closed meetings and concessions will follow in the next section.
21 For a detailed discussion of the 1996 Budget proceedings, see M. N. Sidorov, 'Economicheskaya Politika i Pokazateli Federal'nogo Byudzheta, 1996', *Ekonomka Predprinimatel'stvo Okruzhayushchaya Sreda* 2, 7 (1996): 3–13. On the 1995 Budget and for comparisons between the Russian budgets and budgets in other countries, see Mikhail Dmitriev, *Byudzhetnaya Politika v Sovremennoy Rossii* (Moscow: Moskovskiy Tsentr Karnegi, 1997).
22 Arkadiy Dvorkovitch, Interview with the author at the Ministry of Finance, Moscow, 26 March 1999.
23 *Gosudarstvennaya Duma: Stenogramma zasedaniy* (Federal'nogo Sobraniya Rossiyskoy Federatsii, Moscow: *Izvestiya*, 11 May, 8 and 24 June 1994).
24 Arkadiy Dvorkovitch, Interview by the author at the Ministry of Finance, Moscow, 26 March 1999. See also Ivan Rodin, *Nezavisimaya gazeta* (21 July 1994): 1.
25 *Gosudarstvennaya Duma: Stenogramma zasedaniy* (11 May, 8 and 24 June 1994).
26 *Gosudarstvennya Duma: Stenogramma zasedaniy* (23 December 1994, and 25 January, 24 February and 15 March 1995).
27 Ibid.
28 Sergey Shtogrin, Member of the Duma's Budget Committee, Interview by the author at the State Duma, Moscow, 8 April 1998.
29 *Gosudarstvennya Duma: Stenogramma zasedaniy* (15 November and 6 December 1995).
30 Arkadiy Dvorkovitch, Interview by the author at the Ministry of Finance, Moscow, 26 March 1999.
31 Aleksandr Ponomarev, Interview with the author at the State Duma, Moscow, 1 April 1998.
32 See Chapter 3 for further analysis.

33  *Gosudarstvennya Duma: Stenogramma zasedaniy* (24 December, 1998, 19 January, 29 January, 5 February 1999).
34  *Gosudarstvennya Duma: Stenogramma zasedaniy* (on the 1997 Budget: 15, 20, 28 December 1996, 24 January 1997; on the 1998 Budget: 5, 25 December 1997, 5 February and 4 March 1998).
35  Aleksey Golovkov, Interview with the author at the State Duma, Moscow, 6 April 1998. See also interviews with Deputies of the Budget Committee about the power of the Duma in budget negotiations in *Byudzhet-97* (Moscow: Business Press, 1996 and 1997).
36  Aleksandr Shokhin, 'Economic Transition in Russia', Talk given at St Antony's College, Oxford, 8 December 1997.
37  'Russian Economy: Trends and Perspectives' (Moscow: Institute for the Economy in Transition, February 1998), 3.
38  Leonid Bershidskiy, '1995 Budget Passes Key Hurdle in State Duma', *Moscow Times* (27 February 1995).
39  Arkadiy Dvorkovitch, Interview by the author at the Ministry of Finance, Moscow, 26 March 1999.
40  Svetlana Lolayeva, *Segodnya* (16 November 1995): 1.
41  Gennadiy Zyuganov in *Segodnya* (16 December 1996): 1.
42  David McHugh, 'Long Overdue Budget Clears the Duma', *Moscow Times* (5 March 1998).
43  Yevgeniy Govorov and Aleksandr Malyutin, *Kommersant Daily* (19 December 1997): 1.
44  Irina Granik, *Kommersant Daily* (25 December 1998): 1.
45  Arkadiy Dvorkovitch, Interview by the author at the Ministry of Finance, Moscow, 26 March 1999.
46  Aleksandr Zhukov, Interview with the author at the State Duma, Moscow, 18 September 1997.
47  Oleg Bocharov, Interview with the author at the Moscow City Duma, Moscow, 25 March 1999.
48  Valeriy Fadeev, Interview by the author at the State Duma, Moscow, 20 March 1998.
49  Aleksandr Bekker, *Segodnya* (26 August 1997): 1.
50  Irina Granik, *Kommersant Daily* (25 December 1998): 1.
51  *Sovet Federatsii: Stenogramma zasedaniy* (Federal'nogo Sobraniya Rossiyskoy Federatsii, Moscow: Izvestiya, 24 June 1994, 17 March, 19 December 1995, 12 February 1997, 12 March 1998, 17 February 1999).
52  Vladimir Shumeyko as quoted in *Segodnya* (13 January 1994): 1.
53  Gennadiy Seleznyov, *Kommersant Daily* (2 October 1997): 2.
54  *Sovet Federatsii: Stenogramma zasedaniy* (Federal'nogo Sobraniya Rossiyskoy Federatsii, Moscow: Izvestiya, 12 February 1997).
55  Ibid. (1994 to 1999) and *Gosudarstvennaya Duma: Stenogramma zasedaniy* (Federal'nogo Sobraniya Rossiyskoy Federatsii, 1994 to 1999).
56  Boris Yel'tsin, radio address transcribed in *Rossiyskiye vesti* (1 March 1997): 4.
57  Gennadiy Seleznyov, *Kommersant Daily* (2 October 1997): 2.
58  Aleksandr Zhukov, Interview by the author at the State Duma, Moscow, 18 September 1997.
59  Boris Yel'tsin, Message to the Council of the Federation (Moscow: State Duma's Library, 5 May 1997).

60 Vladislav Kuzmichov, *Nezavisimaya gazeta* (28 March 1998): 1.
61 Aleksandr Shokhin, 'Economic Transition in Russia', Talk given at St Antony's College, Oxford, 8 December 1997.
62 Boris Yel'tsin as quoted in Chrystia Freeland, 'Yel'tsin Gives Ministers New Warning', *Financial Times* (24 February 1998): 2.
63 Vladimir Nikitin, Interview with the author at the State Duma, Moscow, 6 April 1998.
64 Boris Yel'tsin, radio address transcribed in *Rossiyskiye vesti* (1 March 1997): 4.
65 Aleksandr Bekker, *Segodnya* (27 May 1997): 6. The law 'On Production-Sharing Agreements' was delayed for four years but its passage through Parliament was one of Primakov's greatest achievements as Prime Minister.
66 Viktor Chernomyrdin in Svetlana Lolayeva, 'Viktor Chernomyrdin Expects Teamwork from the New Cabinet: The Importance of the Government Apparatus Will Substantially Increase', *Segodnya* (23 August 1996): 2.
67 Ibid.
68 Sergey Sklyarov, *Ekspert*, no. 32 (26 August 1996): 6.
69 Peter Rutland, 'Government Has New Draft Budget', *OMRI Daily Digest*, no. 208 (25 October 1996).
70 Natalia Gurushina, 'Battle Over Budget Begins', *OMRI Daily Digest*, no. 235 (6 December 1996).
71 Ibid. The views of party and faction leaders in the Duma towards the 1997 Budget are discussed in 'Gosudarstvennaya Duma: Analiticheskoe Upravlenie' (Informatsionno-analiticheskiy Byulleten, no. 10, Moscow: State Duma, 2 October to 20 December 1996), 23–33.
72 Irina Savvateyeva, *Izvestiya* (3 December 1996): 2.
73 Sergey Belyayev, quoted in *ITAR-TASS News Agency* (World Service) (Moscow, 5 December 1996).
74 Peter Rutland, 'Duma Approves Budget', *OMRI Daily Digest*, no. 246 (30 December 1996).
75 Gennadiy Seleznyov, State Duma Speaker, quoted in *ITAR-TASS News Agency* (Moscow, 28 December 1996).
76 Natalia Gurushina, 'Yasin Slams the Budget', *OMRI Daily Digest*, no. 20 (29 January 1997).
77 Law 'On Procedures for Considering the Budget', *Vedomosti Federal'nogo Sobraniya Rossiyskoy Federatsii* (Federal'nogo Sobraniya Rossiyskoy Federatsii, Moscow: Izvestiya, 1996).
78 Boris Yel'tsin, radio address transcribed in *Rossiyskiye vesti* (1 March 1997): 4.
79 Oksana Dmitriyeva, *Segodnya* (16 October 1996): 5.
80 Thomas Remington, 'Democratization and the New Political Order in Russia', in Karen Dawisha and Bruce Parrott, *Democratic Changes and Authoritarian Reactions in Russia, Ukraine, Belarus, and Moldova* (Cambridge: Cambridge University Press, 1997), 113.
81 *Sbornik Federal'nykh Konstitutsionnykh Zakonov i Federal'nykh Zakonov* (Moscow: Izvestiya, November 1997).
82 Mikhail Zadornov's statement in Laura Belin, 'Government to Ignore Budget Provision', *OMRI* (4 March 1998).
83 Robert Orttung and Scott Parrish, 'From Confrontation to Cooperation in Russia', *Transition* 2, 25 (13 December 1996): 19.

84 Boris Yel'tsin, Message to the Council of the Federation (Moscow: State Duma's Library, 5 May 1997).
85 Svetlana Lolayeva, *Segodnya* (19 April 1996): 2.
86 Ibid.
87 Igor' Mal'kov, Interview with the author at the State Duma, Moscow, 3 April 1998.
88 Aleksandr Kozyrev, Interview with the author at the State Duma, Moscow, 26 September 1997.
89 Aleksey Andreev, Interview by the author at the State Duma, Moscow, 20 March 1998.
90 A separate provision for this must be included in the budget law before it becomes law.
91 *Vedomosti Federal'nogo Sobraniya Rossiyskoy Federatsii* (Federal'nogo Sobraniya Rossiyskoy Federatsii, Moscow: Izvestiya, Federal Law no. 9 of 1 July 1994).
92 Ibid. Federal Laws no. 39, 150, 212 of 1995.
93 Ibid. On the 1996 Budget, Federal Law no. 228 of 31 December 1995, Federal Laws no. 82, 117, 120, 128, 146, 156 of 20 June; 19, 21, 23, August, 28 November, 17 December 1996, Federal Laws no. 3, 66 of 8 January 26 February and 20 March 1997; On the 1997 Budget, Federal Law no. 29, 98, 154 of 26 February, 14 July, 26 December and Federal Law No. 12 of 9 January 1998.
94 Arkadiy Dvorkovitch, Interview by the author at the Ministry of Finance, Moscow, 26 March 1999.
95 Vyacheslav Kuznetsov, Interview with the author at the State Duma, Moscow, 8 April 1998.
96 *OECD Economic Surveys: The Russian Federation 1995* (Paris: OECD, 1995), 44–5.
97 Boris I. Makarenko, Interview by the author at the Center for Political Technologies, Moscow, 21 April 1998.

## 8  Conclusions: Parliamentary Power and the Democratic Transition and Consolidation Process in Russia

1 Juan Linz and Alfred Stepan, *Problems of Democratic Transition and Consolidation: Southern Europe, South America, and Post-Communist Europe* (London: The Johns Hopkins University Press, 1996), 1, 7. There are several other approaches for determining the prospects for democracy in Russia. Archie Brown, for example, applied Robert Dahl's eight requirements for democracy (from *Polyarchy: Participation and Opposition* (New Haven: Yale University Press, 1971)) to Russia in 'Russia and Democratization', *Problems of Post-Communism* 46, 5 (September/October 1999): 3–13. See also Harry Eckstein, Frederic Fleron, Erik Hoffmann and William Reisinger, *Can Democracy Take Root in Post-Soviet Russia?* (Oxford: Rowman & Littlefield Publishers, Inc., 1998).

   On the debate about the adaptability of the concepts of democratic transition and consolidation to non-Western settings see, for example, Guillermo O'Donnell, who argues that democratic consolidation cannot be adapted to non-European countries in 'Illusions about Consolidation', *Journal of Democracy* 7, 2 (April 1996): 34–51. Richard Gunther, P. Nikiforos Diamandouros and Hans-Jurgen Puhle offer a critique of O'Donnell's article in 'O'Donnell's "Illusions": A Rejoinder', *Journal of Democracy* 7, 4 (October 1996). See also Larry Diamond, Juan Linz, and Seymour Lipset, *Politics in Developing Countries: Comparing Experiences with Democracy* (London: Lynne Rienner Publishers, 1995), and Scott Mainwaring, Guillermo O'Donnell and J. Samuel Valenzuela (eds), *Issues in Democratic Consolidation: The New South American Democracies in Comparative Perspective* (Notre Dame, Indiana: University of Notre Dame Press, 1992).

2   Ibid., 8.

3   See Nicolai Petro, *The Rebirth of Russian Democracy: An Interpretation of Political Culture* (Cambridge, Massachusetts: Harvard University Press, 1995).

4   Peter Reddaway, 'Instability and Fragmentation', *Journal of Democracy* 5, 2 (April 1994): 13. This article is one of several which formed part of a symposium in this issue of the *Journal of Democracy* and similar views to Reddaway's are echoed by the other authors. I, however, believe that this is because the issue of the journal was published soon after the 1993 conflict. In the uncertainties and climate of the time their pessimistic views (see pp. 13, 19, 27 especially) are understandable, although I do not agree with them. Of these authors, Reddaway still remains as pessimistic as ever, as shown by his comments in an article co-authored with Dmitri Glinski, 'The Yeltsin Era in the Light of Russian History: Reform or Reaction?', *Demokratizatsiya* 6 (1998): 518–34 and in his co-authored book with Glinski, *The Tragedy of Russia's Reforms: Market Bolsherism against Democracy* (Washington, DC: United States Institute of Peace Press, 2001). An even bleaker view is held by Stephen Cohen in 'Russian Studies without Russia', *Post-Soviet Affairs* 15 (1999): 37–55; and Cohen, *Failed Crusade: America and the Tragedy of Post-Communist Russia* (New York: W.W. Norton, 2000).

5   Thomas Remington (ed), *Parliaments in Transition: The New Legislative Politics in the Former USSR and Eastern Europe* (Oxford: Westview Press, 1994), 21, 23. See also Evgeni Tanchev, 'Parliamentarism Rationalized', *East European Constitutional Review* 2, 1 (Winter 1993): 33–5.

6   See Alfred Stepan and Cindy Skach, 'Constitutional Frameworks and Democratic Consolidation: Parliamentarism versus Presidentialism', *World Politics* 46, 1 (October 1993): 1–22. Adam Przeworski and Mike Alvarez, 'Parliamentarism and Presidentialism: Which Works? Which Lasts? (Lublin: Polish Sociological Association Congress, 27–30 June 1994). Edward Walker, in 'Politics of Blame and Presidential Powers in Russia's New Constitution', *East European Constitutional Review* 2/3, 4/1 (Fall 1993/Winter 1994): 119, thinks that because power in Russia is concentrated in the presidency it will also mean a decline in support for the president and democracy, and thus, democratic consolidation will be more problematic.

7   Juan Linz, 'Presidential or Parliamentary Democracy: Does it Make a Difference?' in Juan Linz and Arturo Valenzuela (eds), *The Failure of Presidential Democracy: Comparative Perspectives I and II* (Balitmore: The Johns Hopkins University Press, 1994), 3–87.

8   See Donald Horowitz, 'Comparing Democratic Systems', *Journal of Democracy* 1 (1990): 73–9. See also Matthew Shugart and John Carey, *Presidents and Assemblies: Constitutional Design and Electoral Dynamics* (Cambridge,

Cambridge University Press, 1995). Gerald Easter applies these findings to Russia to determine how presidentialism affects democracy in the NIS ('Preference for Presidentialism: Postcommunist Regime Change in Russia and the NIS', *World Politics* 49, 2 (1997): 184–211).

9   Scott Mainwaring, 'Presidentialism, Multipartism, and Democracy: The Difficult Combination', *Comparative Political Studies* 26, 2 (July 1993): 198–228.

10  Stephen Holmes, 'Superpresidentialism and its Problems', *East European Constitutional Review* 2, 4 (Fall 1993/Winter 1994): 123–6. See Philip Roeder, 'Varieties of Post-Soviet Authoritarian Regimes', *Comparative Politics* (1995), on how semi-presidential systems can become authoritarian and superpresidential systems in CIS countries. See also Ray Taras (ed), *Post-Communist Presidents* (Cambridge: Cambridge University Press, 1997).

11  Shugart and Carey, 157.

12  Linz and Stepan, 398.

13  See, for example, John Lloyd, *Rebirth of a Nation: An Anatomy of Russia* (London: Michael Joseph, 1998), 34.

14  David Lane, *Russia in Transition: Politics, Privatization, and Inequality* (London: Longman, 1995). For others who have held this view see, for example, n. 6 in Ch. 1 of this study.

15  See Giovanni Sartori, 'Neither Presidentialism nor Parliamentarism', in Linz and Valenzuela (eds), *The Failure of Presidential Democracy*, 106–88, for an analysis of why semi-presidential or semi-parliamentary are more conducive to democratic consolidation than presidential or parliamentary systems. According to Sartori, 'semipresidentialism can improve presidentialism and, similarly, (that) semiparliamentary systems are better than plain parliamentary ones', 110. On the adaptability of the semi-presidential system of the French Fifth Republic to non-Western countries, see Alfred Stepan and Ezra Suleiman, 'The French Fifth Republic: A Model for Import? Reflections on Poland and Brazil', in H.E. Chehabi and Alfred Stepan (eds), *Politics, Society and Democracy: Comparative Studies* (Boulder: Westview Press, 1995): 393–414.

16  Guillermo O'Donnell, 'Delegative Democracy', *Journal of Democracy* 5, 1 (January 1994): 55–69.

17  See O'Donnell, 59–62.

18  Ibid., 67.

19  John Lowenhardt, *The Reincarnation of Russia: Struggling with the Legacy of Communism, 1990–1994* (Harlow: Longman House, 1995), 25. Regina Smyth also states that a parliament 'may well be an essential element of a Russian democracy. The development of a stable legislature within a system of checks and balances on the other branches of government could be a strong force in the consolidation of democracy by channeling conflict and fostering compromise' in Douglas Blum, *Russia's Future: Consolidation or Disintegration?* (Oxford: Westview Press, 1994), 41.

## 9   Postscript: Parliamentary Power in Russia from May 1999 to January 2001

1   Michael McFaul, '"The Thermidor Period"' (135 Days Conference, Carnegie Center Moscow, transcript published by the Carnegie Center, 19 September 2000).

2 Since the main part of the book was written, several books have been published arguing that democracy does not exist in Russia. The political system has been characterized as 'a hybrid – a mixture of arbitrariness, kleptocracy, and democracy' by Archie Brown in 'From Democratization to "Guided Democracy" ', *Journal of Democracy* 12, 4 (October 2001): 37. Also in Archie Brown, 'Evaluating Russia's Democratization', in Archie Brown, *Contemporary Russian Politics: A Reader* (Oxford: Oxford University Press, 2001), 564. Others, such as Alexander Lukin, suggest that Russia has 'electoral clanism … where elections are not a means of selecting public officials according to law … rather they are merely the means of settling disputes among posttotalitarian clans that generally operate outside the law or in a situation of legal confusion' (Lukin, 'Electoral Democracy or Clanism?' in Brown, *Contemporary Russian Politics*, 544). Rather than dispute the validity of such claims, this book examines one factor in most commonly regarded definitions of democracy, that of the formation of political institutions. I do not argue that Russia is a democracy (because to do so I would have to consider civil society, economics, and so on), but that in the one aspect I study, democratic tendencies are apparent.

3 See n. 10 in Ch. 1 regarding Dumas in Russia prior to the Soviet Union.

4 *IFES Election Guide* (Moscow: International Foundation for Election Systems, December 1999).

5 Nikolai Petrov, 'Parliamentary Elections in Russia: Disposition of Forces and Rules of the Game', *Carnegie Center Briefings* (Moscow: Carnegie Center, October 1999), 1.

6 Brown, 'From Democratization to "Guided Democracy" ', 39.

7 M. Steven Fish, 'Putin's Path', *Journal of Democracy* 12, 4 (October 2001): 77.

8 Adam Przeworski and John Sprague, *Paper Stones: A History of Electoral Socialism* (Chicago: University of Chicago Press, 1986).

9 See Table 3.4 in Ch. 3.

10 Richard Rose, 'How Floating Parties Frustrate Democratic Accountability: A Supply-Side View of Russia's Elections', in Brown, *Contemporary Russian Politics*, 217.

11 Fish, 'Putin's Path', 77.

12 See n. 24 in Ch. 3.

13 See n. 28 in Ch. 3.

14 See n. 30 in Ch. 3.

15 Sergey Stepashin, as stated in his talk attended by the author, 'Russia's Presidential Elections and the Battle against Corruption', John F. Kennedy School of Government, Harvard University, 14 March 2000.

16 Valeriy Airapetov, quote from his talk, 'Is Democracy Doomed in Russia? Views from Yabloko and the Union of Right Forces', John F. Kennedy School of Government, Harvard University (21 September 2000).

17 Boris Mints, quote from his talk, 'Can the Alliance of Russia's Democrats Last?', Harvard University (20 June 2000).

18 Yegor Gaidar, as quoted during his talk, 'The Political and Economic Situation in Russia' (Carnegie Endowment, Washington, DC, 29 January 2001).

19 Yulia Malysheva, quote from her talk attended by the author, 'Is Democracy Doomed in Russia? Views from Yabloko and the Union of Right Forces', John F. Kennedy School of Government, Harvard University (21 September 2000).

20   Irina Kuzmina, quote from her talk attended by the author, 'Is Democracy Doomed in Russia? Views from Yabloko and the Union of Right Forces', John F. Kennedy School of Government, Harvard University (21 September 2000).
21   Data on committee changes provided by the Records Department of the State Duma, January 2001.
22   Nikolai Petrov, 'Parliamentary Elections in Russia: Disposition of Forces and Rules of the Game', *Carnegie Center Briefings* (Moscow: Carnegie Center, October 1999), 3.
23   Roy Medvedev, *Post-Soviet Russia: A Journey through the Yeltsin Era* (New York: Columbia University Press, 2000), 359.
24   Vladimir Gelman, 'The Bear (Unity) Rules the Forest', *Russian Election Watch*, no. 7 (Harvard University, 4 February 2000): 12.
25   Steven Smith and Thomas Remington maintain that the effects of the Communist and Unity Party alliance were not lasting. The parties were at odds over the important land reform law and some of the Communists' committee posts were later changed (Steven Smith and Thomas Remington, *The Politics of Institutional Choice: The Formation of the Russian State Duma* (Princeton: Princeton University Press, 2001), 152).
26   Regina Smyth, as quoted during her talk, 'Evolution of Political Parties and the Party System in Comparative Perspective', at the conference 'Russia Votes: A Preview of Russia's Duma Election' (Harvard University, 29 November 1999).
27   Alexander Surikov, as quoted in *Russia Watch*, no. 2 (August 2000): 3.
28   Michael McFaul, as stated during his talk, ' "The Thermidor Period" ' (135 Days Conference, Carnegie Endowment, Moscow Office, 19 September 2000).
29   Tiffany Troxel, 'Former Russian Prime Minister Talks about Corruption', *BCSIA Publications* (Cambridge, MA: Harvard University, March 2000). The quote from Sergey Stepashin was from an interview with the author on 14 March 2000 in Cambridge, Massachusetts.
30   Yeltsin took power illegally in December 1991, though he was legally elected President of the RSFSR in June 1991. One could dispute how democratic the 2001 Presidential Election was given Yeltsin's sudden resignation and proclaimed choice of Putin as a successor, but he was democratically elected and his main competitors (Zyuganov, Yavlinskiy, and Zhirinovskiy) were all previously presidential candidates and were well-known party leaders.
31   Yavlinskiy thinks 'the results of the [2001] elections were just as shamelessly manipulated to favor the "party of power" ' (Grigory Yavlinskiy, 'Going Backwards', *Journal of Democracy* 12, 4 (October 2001): 80). He believes that Putin received closer to 45 percent of the vote in the first round. Even though the *Moscow Times* shortly after the 2001 Presidential Election checked election results in a number of regions, the data were not comprehensive and did not include all 89 republics. At present, there is no clear evidence that while there may have been some corruption the election results could have been vastly different and resulted in a run-off.
32   For additional writing on Putin's character and how it compares with Yeltsin's see Archie Brown and Lilia Shevtsova (eds), *Gorbachev, Yeltsin, and Putin: Political Leadership in Russia's Transition* (Washington, DC: Carnegie Endowment, 2001).

33  *Financial Times* (27 March 2000).
34  Sergey Stepashin, as quoted in *Nezavisimaya Gazeta* (14 January 2000).
35  Vladimir Putin, 'State of the Nation Address', *Gosudarstvennaya Duma: Stenogramma zasedaniy* (Moscow: Izvestiya, 8 July 2000).
36  Vladimir Putin, 'State of the Nation Address', *Gosudarstvennaya Duma: Stenogramma zasedaniy* (Moscow: Izvestiya, 8 July 2000).
37  Zoltan Barany and Robert Moser (eds), *Russian Politics: Challenges of Democratization* (Cambridge: Cambridge University Press, 2001), 65.
38  Martha Olcott and Marina Ottaway, 'The Challenge of Semi-Authoritarianism' (working paper, published by the Carnegie Center Moscow, 2000).
39  Michael McFaul, 'Russia's 2000 Presidential Elections: Implications for Russian Democracy and U.S.–Russian Relations', Testimony before the US Senate Committee on Foreign Relations (transcript published by the Carnegie Endowment, Washington, DC, 12 April 2000), 2.
40  Yegor Gaidar, as quoted during his talk, 'The Political and Economic Situation in Russia' (Carnegie Endowment, Washington, DC, 29 January 2001).
41  Lilia Shevtsova, as stated during her talk, ' "Yel'tsin's Terminator" or "Disciplined Yel'tsinism?" ' (135 Days Conference, Carnegie Endowment, Moscow Office, 19 September 2000).
42  All-Russian Center for the Study of Public Opinion, survey of 1600 respondents (January to November 2000).
43  Thomas Remington, 'Is There a Separation of Powers in Russia?', *Carnegie Center Report* 3, 1 (January 2001): 2.
44  Thomas Remington, *The Russian Parliament: Institutional Evolution in a Transitional Regime, 1989–1999* (New Haven: Yale University Press, 2001), 221–2.
45  Ibid., 229–30.
46  Eugene Huskey, *Presidential Power in Russia* (Armonk, NY: M.E. Sharpe, 1999), 169.
47  Paul Chaisty and Jeffrey Gleisner, 'The Consolidation of Russian Parliamentarism: The State Duma, 1993–8' in Neil Robinson (ed), *Institutions and Political Change in Russia* (Basingstoke: Macmillan Press, 2000 – now Palgrave Macmillan), 66–7.
48  Thomas Remington, 'Is There a Separation of Powers in Russia?', *Meeting Report of the Carnegie Endowment* 3, 1 (9 January 2001): 1.
49  The evening before Stepashin's confirmation Yel'tsin was reported as being ill. He cancelled a meeting with Prime Minister Jose Marie Aznar. 'Stepashin Urges Reforms on the Eve of Russian PM Vote', *CNN Report* (18 May 1999): 1.
50  Sergey Stepashin, 'Address to the Duma', *Gosudarstvennaya Duma: Stenogramma zasedaniy* (Moscow: Izvestiya, 19 May 2000).
51  'Stepashin Sails through Confirmation Process', *RFE/RL Newsline* (19 May 1999): 1.
52  'Duma Confirms Putin', *RFE/RL Newsline* (17 August 1999).
53  'Kas'yanov Approved as Russian Prime Minister', *CNN Report* (17 May 2000).
54  'Two Putin Nominees Breeze by Legislators', *RFE/RL Newsline* (17 May 2000).
55  Nikolai Kharitonov, as quoted in Leonid Sborov, 'Kas'yanov Approved Despite Lack of Policy', *Rossiyskaya Gazeta* (17 May 2000).

56   Eugene Huskey, *Presidential Power in Russia* (Armonk, NY: M. E. Sharpe, 1999), 168.
57   Mikhail Kas'yanov as stated during his Address to the State Duma, *Gosudarstvennaya Duma: Stenogramma zasedaniy* (Moscow: Izvestiya, 17 May 2000).
58   David Rekhviashvili, 'Duma Strives for First Balanced Budget in Russia's Post-Soviet History', *Russia Watch*, no. 4 (December 2000): 2.
59   Stephen Cohen, *Failed Crusade: America and the Tragedy of Post-Communist Russia* (New York: W. W. Norton, 2000).
60   Mikhail Kas'yanov, 'Address to the State Duma', *Duma: Stenogramma zasedaniy* (17 May 2000).
61   Michael McFaul, as stated during his talk, '"The Thermidor Period"' (135 Days Conference, Carnegie Endowment, Moscow Office, 19 September 2000).

# Bibliography

Aslund, Anders, 'Russia's Current Economic Dilemma: A Comment', *Post-Soviet Affairs* 15 (1999): 83–6.

Avtonomov, A. S., L. N. Zavadskaya, A. A. Zakharov, A. P. Lyubimov and E. M. Orlova, *Zakonodatel'nyy Protsess v Rossii: Grazhdane i Vlast'* (Programma Podderzhki Obshchestvennykh Initsiativ, Tsentr za Demokratiyu, Mezhdunarodnyy Respublikanskiy Institut, i Fond Razvitiya Parlamentarizma v Rossii, Moscow, AIA-Print, 1996).

Baglay, M. V., *Konstitutsionnoe pravo Rossiyskoy Federatsii* (Moscow, NORMA–INFRAM, 1998).

Balikian, Ara, 'The New Russian Federation Constitution: A Legal Framework Adopted and Implemented in a Post-Soviet Era', *Suffolk Transnational Law Review* 18, no. 237 (1995): 237–67.

Baranova, L. G., O. V. Vrublevskaya, T. E. Kosareva and L. A. Yurinova, *Byudzhetnyy Protsess v Rossiyskoy Federatsii* (Moscow, Perspektiva, INFRAM, 1998).

Barany, Zoltan and Robert Moser (eds), *Russian Politics: Challenges of Democratization* (Cambridge, Cambridge University Press, 2001).

Barry, Donald, *Toward the 'Rule of Law' in Russia? Political and Legal Reform in the Transition Period* (London, M. E. Sharpe, 1992).

Baylis, Thomas, 'Presidents versus Prime Ministers: Shaping Executive Authority in Eastern Europe', *World Politics* 48 (April 1996): 297–323.

Biryukov, Nikolai and V. M. Sergeev, *Russia's Road to Democracy: Parliament, Communism and Traditional Culture* (Aldershot, Edward Elgar, 1993).

Blondel, Jean and Maurizio Cotta, *Party and Government: An Inquiry into the Relationship between Governments and Supporting Parties in Liberal Democracies* (1996).

Blum, Douglas (ed.), *Russia's Future: Consolidation or Disintegration?* (Oxford, Westview Press, 1994).

Brown, Archie (ed.), *Contemporary Russian Politics: A Reader* (Oxford, Oxford University Press, 2001).

——, 'From Democratization to "Guided Democracy" ', *Journal of Democracy* 12, no. 4 (October 2001): 35–41.

——, *The Gorbachev Factor* (Oxford, Oxford University Press, 1996).

——, *New Thinking in Soviet Politics* (Oxford, Macmillan Press, 1992 – now Palgrave Macmillan).

——, 'Political Leadership in Post-Communist Russia', in Amin Saikal and William Maley, *Russia in Search of its Future* (Cambridge, Cambridge University Press, 1995): 28–45.

——, 'Russia and Democratization', *Problems of Post-Communism* 46, no. 5 (September/October 1999): 3–13.

——, 'The Russian Crisis: Beginning of the End or End of the Beginning?', *Post-Soviet Affairs* 15, no. 1 (1999): 56–73.

——, *Soviet Politics and Political Science* (London, Macmillan Press, 1974 – now Palgrave Macmillan).

Brown, Archie, Michael Kaser and Gerald Smith (eds), *The Cambridge Encyclopedia of Russia and the Former Soviet Union* (Cambridge, Cambridge University Press, 1994).

—— and Lilia Shevtsova (eds), *Gorbachev, Yeltsin and Putin: Political Leadership in Russia's Transition* (Washington, DC, Carnegie Endowment for International Peace, 2001).

*Byudzhet-97* (Moscow, Business Press, 1996 and 1997).

Carey, John and Matthew Shugart (eds), *Executive Decree Authority: Calling Out the Tanks, or Filling Out the Forms?* (Cambridge, Cambridge University Press, 1998).

Chaisty, Paul and Jeffrey Gleisner, 'The Consolidation of Russian Parliamentarism: The State Duma, 1993–8', in Neil Robinson (ed.), *Institutions and Political Change in Russia* (Basingstoke, Macmillan Press, 2000 – now Palgrave Macmillan).

Chase, Judith, 'Russian Executive Policy-Making: Delegation in the Duma', (paper presented at the 1997 APSA, 28–31 August 1997).

Cohen, Stephen, *Failed Crusade: America and the Tragedy of Post-Communist Russia* (New York, W. W. Norton and Co., 2000).

——, 'Russian Studies without Russia', *Post-Soviet Affairs* 15 (1999): 37–55.

Colton, Timothy and Robert Tucker, *Patterns in Post-Soviet Leadership* (Oxford, Westview Press, 1995).

'Constitution Watch: Russia', *East European Constitutional Review* (various editions from 1995 to 1998).

Croft, Steven, 'In Defense of Arms Control', *Political Studies* 44, 5 (December 1996): 888–905.

Dahl, Robert, *Polyarchy: Participation and Opposition* (New Haven, Yale University Press, 1971).

Dalton, Russell, Scott Flanagan, James Alt and Paul Beck, *Electoral Changes in Advanced Industrial Democracies: Realignment or Dealignment?* (Princeton, Princeton University Press, 1984).

Dawisha, Karen and Bruce Parrott, *Democratic Changes and Authoritarian Reactions in Russia, Ukraine, Belarus and Moldova* (Cambridge, Cambridge University Press, 1997).

Diamond, Larry, Juan Linz and Seymour Lipset, *Politics in Developing Countries: Comparing Experiences with Democracy* (London, Lynne Rienner Publishers, 1995).

Di Palma, Giuseppe, *To Craft Democracies: An Essay in Political Transition* (Berkeley, University of California Press, 1990).

Dmitriev, Mikhail, *Byudzhetnaya Politika v Sovremennoy Rossii* (Moscow, Moskovskiy Tsentr Karnegi, 1997).

Duverger, Maurice, *Les Partis politiques* (Paris, Le Seuil, 1951).

——, 'A New Political System Model: Semi-Presidential Government', *European Journal of Political Research* 8, no. 2 (June 1980): 165–88.

——, *Political Parties: Their Organization and Activity in the Modern State* (New York, Wiley, 1954).

Dvorkin, Vladimir, 'Yadernoe Sderzhivanie i Dogovor SNV-2', *Yadernoe Rasprostranenie* (Moscow, Moskovskiy Tsentr Karnegi, May 1997): 6–15.

Easter, Gerald, 'Preference for Presidentialism: Postcommunist Regime Change in Russia and the NIS', *World Politics* 49, no. 2 (1997): 184–211.

Easton, David, *The Analysis of Political Structure* (London, Routledge, 1990).

Eckstein, Harry, Frederic Fleron, Erik Hoffmann and William Reisinger, *Can Democracy Take Root in Post-Soviet Russia?* (Oxford, Rowman & Littlefield, 1998).

Emmons, Terence, *The Formation of Political Parties and the First National Elections in Russia* (Cambridge, Harvard University Press, 1983).

Epstein, David and Sharyn O'Halloran, *Delegating Powers: A Transaction Cost Politics Approach to Policy Making under Separate Powers* (Cambridge: Cambridge University Press), 1999.

Evans, Peter, Dietrich Rueschmeyer and Theda Skocpol (eds), *Bringing the State Back In* (Oxford, Oxford University Press, 1985).

Fainsod, Merle, 'Some Reflections on the Nature of the Regulatory Process', *Public Policy* 1 (1940).

*Federal'noe Sobranie: Sovet Federatsii i Gosudarstvennaya Duma (Federal Assembly: Council of the Federation and the State Duma)* (Moscow, Fond Razvitiya Parlamentarizma v Rossii, 1995).

Finer, S. E., Vernon Bogdanor and Bernard Rudden, *Comparing Constitutions* (Oxford, Oxford University Press, 1996).

Fish, M. Steven, *Democracy from Scratch: Opposition and Regime in the New Russian Revolution* (Princeton, Princeton University Press, 1995).

——, 'Putin's Path', *Journal of Democracy* 12, no. 4 (October 2001): 71–8.

Fond 'Obshchestvennoe Mnenie', 'Rossiyane ne Doveryayut Tem, Kogo Svobodno Vybirayut', *Vlast'*, no. 8 (August 1997): 19.

Franz, Gisbert (ed.), *Constitutions of the Countries of the World* (New York, Oceana Publications), editions from 1989 to 1998.

Frye, Timothy, 'A Politics of Institutional Choice: Post-Communist Presidencies', *Comparative Political Studies* (October 1997): 523–52.

Gallagher, Michael, 'Proportionality, Disproportionality and Electoral Systems', *Electoral Studies* 10 (1991): 33–51.

*Gosudarstvennaya Duma: Stenogramma zasedaniy* (Federal'nogo Sobraniya Rossiiskoy Federatsii, Moscow, Izvestiya, 1994 to 1999).

Grankin, I. V., *Parlament Rossii* (Moscow, Konsaltbankir, 1999).

Grofman, Bernard and Arend Lijphart, *Electoral Laws and Their Political Consequences* (New York, Agathon Press, 1986).

Gunther, Richard, P. Nikiforos Diamandouros and Hans-Jurgen Puhle 'O'Donnell's "Illusions": A Rejoinder', *Journal of Democracy* 7, no. 4 (October 1996).

Hahn, Jeffrey (ed.), *Democratization in Russia: The Developments of Legislative Institutions* (London, M. E. Sharpe, 1996).

Hall, Peter and Rosemary Taylor, 'Political Science and the Three New Institutionalisms', *Political Studies* 44, no. 5 (December 1996): 936–57.

Holmes, Stephen, 'Superpresidentialism and its Problems', *East European Constitutional Review* 2, no. 4 (Fall 1993/Winter 1994): 123–6.

—— and Christian Lucky, 'Storm Over Compatibility', *East European Constitutional Review* 2/3, no. 4/1 (Fall 1993/Winter 1994): 120–3.

Horowitz, Donald, 'Debate: Presidents vs. Parliaments: Comparing Democratic Systems', *Journal of Democracy* 1 (Fall 1990): 73–83.

Hosking, Geoffrey, *The Russian Constitutional Experiment: Government and Duma, 1907–1914* (Cambridge, Cambridge University Press, 1973).

Huber, Robert and Donald Kelley, *Perestroika-Era Politics: The New Soviet Legislature and Gorbachev's Political Reforms* (London, M. E. Sharpe, 1991).

Huskey, Eugene, *Executive Power and Soviet Politics: The Rise and Decline of the Soviet State* (Armonk, NY, M. E. Sharpe, 1992).

Huskey, Eugene, *Presidential Power in Russia* (Armonk, NY: M. E. Sharpe, 1999).

*IFES Election Guide* (Moscow, International Foundation for Election Systems, December 1999).

Isakov, V. B. and A. S. Avtonomov, *Parlamentskoe Pravo Rossii: Osnovnye Istochniki* (St Petersburg, Kodeks, 1997).

Johnson, Janet and Richard Josyln, *Political Science Research Methods* (Washington, DC, Congressional Quarterly, Inc., 1995).

Kas'yanov, Mikhail, 'Address to the State Duma', *Gosudarstvennaya Duma: Stenogramma Zasedaniy* (Moscow, Izvestiya, 17 May 2000).

Khromov, Gennadiy, 'Real'ny li Sokrashcheniya Amerikanskoy Strategicheskoy Triady po Dogovoru SNV-2?' *Yadernoe Rasprostranenie* (Moscow, Moskovskiy Tsentr Karnegi, May 1997): 16–18.

*Konstitutsiya (1978) Rossiyskoy Federatsii – Rossii* (Izdanie verkhovnogo Soveta Rossiyskoy Federatsii, Moscow, Izvestiya, 1992).

*Konstitutsiya (1993) Rossiyskoy Federatsii* (Moscow, RAU Press, 1993).

Koroleva, V. Yu., 'Gosudarstvennaya Duma: Tekhnologiya Ekonomicheskogo Lobbirovaniya Khozyaystvuyushchikh Sub'ektov,' *Predstavitel'naya Vlast'* 2, 3 (1997): 69–76.

Laakso, Markku and Taagepera, Rein, 'Effective Number of Parties: A Measure with Application to West Europe', *Comparative Political Studies* 12, no. 1 (1979): 3–27.

Lane, David (ed.), *Russia in Transition: Politics, Privatization, and Inequality* (London, Longman, 1995).

Lapaeva, V. V., 'Effektivnost' Zakona i Metody ee Izucheniya', *Effektivnost' Zakona* (Moscow, Institut Zakonodatel'stva i Spavnitel'nogo Pravovedeniya pri Pravitel'stve Rossiyskoy Federatsii, 1997): 28–43.

Lapidus, Gail (ed.), *The New Russia: Troubled Transformation* (Boulder, Westview Press, 1995).

Laver, Michael and Kenneth Shepsle, *Making and Breaking Governments: Cabinets and Legislatures in Parliamentary Democracies* (Cambridge, Cambridge University Press, 1995).

Lees, John and Malcolm Shaw, *Committees in Legislatures: A Comparative Analysis* (Durham, Duke University Press, 1979).

Lijphart, Arend, 'Constitutional Choices for New Democracies', *Journal of Democracy* 2 (1991).

——, 'Democracies: Forms: Performance, and Constitutional Engineering', *European Journal of Political Research* 25 (1994): 1–17.

——, *Democracies: Patterns of Majoritarian Consensus Government in 21 Countries* (New Haven, Yale University Press, 1984).

——, *Electoral Systems and Party Systems* (Oxford, Oxford University Press, 1994).

——, *Parliamentary Versus Presidential Government* (Oxford, Oxford University Press, 1995).

Linz, Juan, 'The Perils of Presidentialism', *Journal of Democracy* 1, no. 1 (1990): 51–70.

—— and Alfred Stepan, *Problems of Democratic Transition and Consolidation: Southern Europe, South America, and Post-Communist Europe* (London, The Johns Hopkins University Press, 1996).

——, 'Toward Consolidated Democracies', *Journal of Democracy* 7, no. 2 (April 1996): 14–33.

—— and Valenzuela, Arturo (eds), *The Failure of Presidential Democracy: Comparative Perspectives I and II* (Baltimore, Johns Hopkins University Press, 1994).

Lloyd, John, *Rebirth of a Nation: An Anatomy of Russia* (London, Longman, 1995).

Lowenhardt, John, *Party Politics in Post-Communist Russia* (London, Frank Cass, 1998).

——, *The Reincarnation of Russia: Struggling with the Legacy of Communism, 1990–1994* (Harlow, Longman House, 1995).

Ludwikowski, Rett, *Constitution-making in the Region of Former Soviet Dominance* (Durham, NC, Duke University Press, 1996).

Lukin, Alexander, 'Electoral Democracy or Electoral Clanism? Russian Democratization and Theories of Transition', in Archie Brown (ed.), *Contemporary Russian Politics: A Reader* (Oxford, Oxford University Press, 2001), 530–45.

Lysenko, Vladimir, 'Toward Presidential Rule', *Journal of Democracy* 5, no. 2 (April 1994): 9–13.

Lyubimov, A. P., *Parlamentskoe pravo Rossii* (St Petersburg, Kodex-info, 1997).

Mainwaring, Scott, 'Presidentialism, Multipartism, and Democracy: The Difficult Combination', *Comparative Political Studies* 26, no. 2 (July 1993): 198–228.

——, Guillermo O'Donnell, J. Samuel Valenzuela (eds), *Issues in Democratic Consolidation: The New South American Democracies in Comparative Perspective* (Notre Dame, Indiana, University of Notre Dame Press, 1992).

Makarenko, Boris, 'Prezentatsiya v "Politii": Tsentr Politicheskikh Tekhnologiy o Rossiyskikh Realiyakh', *Politiya* (Fall 1997): 5–19.

——, 'Russian Political System: Halfway to Elections?' (Research Project on Political Development in Russia, Moscow, DIHR/USAID, April 1998).

Malcolm, Neil, Alex Pravda, Roy Allison and Margot Light, *Internal Factors in Russian Foreign Policy* (Oxford, Oxford University Press, 1996).

March, James and Johan Olsen, 'The New Institutionalism: Organizational Factors in Political Life', *American Political Science Review* 78, no. 3 (1984): 734–49.

——, *Rediscovering Institutions: The Organizational Basis of Politics* (New York, Free Press, 1989).

Mayhew, David, *Congress: The Electoral Connection* (New Haven, Yale University Press, 1974).

McAuley, Mary, *Russia's Politics of Uncertainty* (Cambridge, Cambridge University Press, 1997).

McFaul, Michael, 'Explaining the Vote', *Journal of Democracy* 5, no. 2 (April 1994): 4–9.

——, *Post-Communist Politics: Democratic Prospects in Russia and Eastern Europe* (Washington, DC, The Center for Strategic and International Studies, 1993).

——, *Russia between Elections: What the December 1995 Results Really Mean* (Washington, DC, Carnegie Endowment for International Peace, 1996).

——, 'Russia's 2000 Presidential Elections: Implications for Russian Democracy and U.S.–Russian Relations', Testimony before the US Senate Committee on Foreign Relations (transcript published by the Carnegie Endowment, Washington, DC, 12 April 2000).

——, *Russia's Unfinished Revolution: Political Change from Gorbachev to Putin* (Ithaca, Cornell University Press, 2001).

—— and Nikolai Petrov, 'Russian Electoral Politics after Transition: Regional and National Assessments', *Post-Soviet Geography and Economics* 38, no. 9 (November 1997): 507–49.

Medvedev, Roy, *Post-Soviet Russia: A Journey through the Yeltsin Era* (New York, Columbia University Press, 2000).

Mikhailovskaya, Inga, 'Russian Voting Behavior as a Mirror of Social-Political Change', *East European Constitutional Review* 5, no. 2/3 (Spring/Summer 1996): 57–63.

Mitrokhin, S. S., I. F. Faseev and R. K. Nadeev, *Kommentariy k Federal'nomu Zakonu: Ob Obespechenii Konstitutsionnykh Prav Grazhdan Rossiyskoy Federatsii Izbirat' i Byt' Izbrannymi v Organy Mestnogo Samoypravleniya* (Moscow, Gosudarstvennaya Duma, 1997).

Mityukov, M. A., 'Resheniya Konstitutsionnogo Suda Rossiyskoy Federatsii kak Istochnik Parlamentskogo Prava', *Effektivnost' Zakona* (Moscow, Institut Zakonodatel'stva i Sravnitel'nogo Pravovedeniya pri Pravitel'stve Rossiyskoy Federatsii, 1997): 135–49.

Mlechin, Leonid, *Yevgeniy Primakov: Istoriya Odnoy Kar'eri* (Moscow, Tsentropoligraf, 1999).

Moser, Robert, *Unexpected Outcomes: Electoral Systems, Political Parties and Representation in Russia* (Pittsburgh, University of Pittsburgh Press, 2000).

——, 'The Impact of the Electoral System on Post-Communist Party Development: The Case of the 1993 Russian Parliamentary Election', *Electoral Studies* 14, no. 4 (1995): 377–398.

——, 'The Impact of Parliamentary Electoral Systems in Russia', *Post-Soviet Affairs* 13, no. 3 (July–September 1997): 284–302.

Murrell, G. D. G., *Russia's Transition to Democracy: An Internal Political History* (Brighton, Sussex Academic Press, 1997).

Norton, Philip, 'The Legislative Powers of Parliament', in C. Flinterman, A. Heringa and L. Waddington (eds), *The Evolving Role of Parliaments in Europe* (Antwerp, MAKLU, 1994).

O'Donnell, Guillermo, 'Delegative Democracy', *Journal of Democracy* 5, no. 1 (January 1994): 55–69.

——, 'Illusions about Consolidation', *Journal of Democracy* 7, no. 2 (April 1996): 34–51.

*OECD Economic Surveys: The Russian Federation 1995* (Paris, OECD, 1995).

O'Halloran, Sharyn, *Politics, Process, and American Trade Policy* (Ann Arbor, University of Michigan Press, 1995).

Okun'kov, Lev, *Prezident Rossiyskoy Federatsii: Konstitutsiya i politicheskaya praktika* (Moscow, NORMA–INFRAM Group, 1996).

Olcott, Martha and Marina Ottaway, 'The Challenge of Semi-Authoritarianism', (Moscow, Carnegie Center, 2000).

Olson, David, *Democratic Legislative Institutions* (London, M. E. Sharpe, 1994).

—— and Michael Mezey, *Legislatures in the Policy Process: The Dilemmas of Economic Policy* (Cambridge, Cambridge University Press, 1991).

—— and Philip Norton, *The New Parliaments of Central and Eastern Europe* (London, Frank Cass, 1996).

Orttung, Robert, 'A Balancing Act', *Transition* 2, no. 25 (13 December 1996): 5.

——, 'Battling Over Electoral Laws', *Transition* (25 August 1995): 32–6.

—— and Scott Parrish, 'From Confrontation to Cooperation in Russia', *Transition* 2, no. 25 (13 December 1996): 16–20.

*Ot El'tsina k … É El'tsinu: Prezidentskaya Gonka-96* (Rossiyskiy Nezavisimyy Institut Sotsial'nykh i Natsional'nykh Problem, Moscow, TERRA, 1997).

Pammett, Jon, 'Elections and Democracy in Russia', *Communist and Post-Communist Studies* 32 (1999): 45–60.

*Parlamentariszm v Rossii: Federal'noe Sobranie, 1993–1995* (Moscow, Fond Razvitiya Parlamentarizma v Rossii, 1996).

*Parlamentariszm v Rossii: Opyt i Perspektivy, 1994* (Moscow, Fond Razvitiya Parlamentarizma v Rossii, 1994).

Parrish, Scott, 'Presidential Decree Power in the Second Russian Republic, 1993–6 and Beyond' (Paper presented at the APSA Meeting in San Franscisco, August 1996).

Peters, B. Guy, *Institutional Theory in Political Science: The New Institutionalism* (London, Pinter, 1999).

Petro, Nicolai, *The Rebirth of Russian Democracy: An Interpretation of Political Culture,* (Cambridge, Harvard University Press, 1995).

Petrov, Nikolai, 'Parliamentary Elections in Russia: Disposition of Forces and Rules of the Game', *Carnegie Center Briefings* (Moscow, Carnegie Center, October 1999).

Powell, Walter, *The New Institutionalism in Organizational Analysis* (1991).

Przeworski, Adam (ed.), *Sustainable Democracy* (Cambridge, Cambridge University Press, 1995).

—— and Mike Alvarez, 'Parliamentarism and Presidentialism: Which Works? Which Lasts?' (Lublin, Polish Sociological Association Congress, 27–30 June 1994).

——, Jose Cheibub and Fernando Limongi, 'What Makes Democracies Endure?', *Journal of Democracy* 7, no. 1 (January 1996): 39–55.

—— and John Sprague, *Paper Stones: A History of Electoral Socialism* (Chicago, University of Chicago Press, 1986).

Putin, Vladimir, 'State of the Nation Address', *Gosudarstvennaya Duma: Stenogramma Zasedaniy* (Moscow, Izvestiya, 8 July 2000).

Rae, Douglas, *The Political Consequences of Electoral Laws* (New Haven, Yale University Press, 1971).

Reddaway, Peter, 'Instability and Fragmentation', *Journal of Democracy* 5, no. 2 (April 1994): 13–19.

—— and Dmitri Glinski, 'The Yeltsin Era in the Light of Russian History: Reform or Reactions?' *Demokratizatsiya* 6 (1998): 518–34.

—— and Glinski *The Tragedy of Russia's Reforms: Market Bolshevism against Democracy* (Washington, DC: United States Institute of Peace Press, 2001).

*Reglament Gosudarstvennoy Dumy Federal'nogo Sobraniya Rossiyskoy Federatsii* (Moscow, Gosudarstvennaya Duma, 1998).

Remington, Thomas, 'Is There a Separation of Powers in Russia?', *Meeting Report of the Carnegie Endowment* 3, 1 (9 January 2001).

——, *Parliaments in Transition: The New Legislative Politics in the Former USSR and Eastern Europe* (Oxford, Westview Press, 1994).

——, 'Political Conflict and Institutional Design: Paths of Party Development in Russia', *Journal of Communist Studies and Transition Politics* 14, no. 1–2 (March/June 1998): 201–23.

——, *Politics in Russia* (New York, Longman, 1999).

——, *The Russian Parliament: Institutional Evolution in a Transitional Regime, 1989–1999* (New Haven, Yale University Press, 2001).

—— and Steven Smith, 'Communism's Collapse and the Development of Parliamentary Institutions in Russia' (paper presented at the Seminar on the

Collapse of Communism and Social Theory, Woodrow Wilson Center, April 1995).

Remington, Thomas, 'The Development of Parliamentary Parties in Russia', *Legislative Studies Quarterly* 20, no. 4 (1995): 457–90.

——, 'The Early Legislative Process in the Russian Federal Assembly', in David Olson and Philip Norton, *The New Parliaments of Central and Eastern Europe* (London, Frank Cass, 1996): 161–92.

——, 'Political Goals, Uncertainty, Institutional Context, and the Choice of an Electoral System: The Russian Parliamentary Election Law', *American Journal of Political Science* 40 (1996): 1253–79.

——, 'Theories of Legislative Institutions and the Organization of the Russian Duma' (paper presented at the 1996 Annual Meeting of the American Political Science Association, San Francisco, 28 August–1 September 1996, reprinted in the *American Journal of Political Science*, April 1998).

—— and Moshe Haspel, 'Decrees, Laws, and Inter-Branch Relations in the Russian Federation' (Paper presented to the AAASS Conference, Seattle, Washington, 20–23 November 1997).

—— 'Electoral Institutions and Party Cohesion in the Russian Duma', *Journal of Politics* (May 1998).

Roeder, Philip, 'Varieties of Post-Soviet Authoritarian Regimes', *Comparative Politics* (1995).

Rose, Richard, *What is Europe?* (New York: Longman, 1996).

—— and Christian Haerpfer, *New Russian Barometer III: The Results* (Glasgow, University of Strathclyde Studies in Public Policy, 1994), no. 228.

*Rossiya: Desyat' Voprosov o Samom Vazhnom* (Moscow, Moskovskiy Tsentr Karnegi, 1997).

'Russian Economy: Trends and Perspectives' (Moscow, Institute for the Economy in Transition, February 1998).

Saikal, Amin and William Maley (eds), *Russia in Search of its Future* (Cambridge, Cambridge University Press, 1995).

Sakwa, Richard, *Russian Politics and Society* 1st and 2nd edns (London, Routledge, 1993 and 1996).

——, 'Subjectivity, Politics and Order in Russian Political Evolution', *Slavic Review* 54, no. 4 (Winter 1995): 943–64.

Sapir, Jacques, 'Russia's Crash of August 1998: Diagnosis and Prescription', *Post-Soviet Affairs* 15 (1999): 1–36.

Sartori, Giovanni, *Comparative Constitutional Engineering: An Inquiry into Structures, Incentives and Outcomes* (New York, New York University Press, 1994).

——, 'The Influence of Electoral Systems: Faulty Laws or Faulty Method?', in Bernard Grofman and Arend Lijphart (eds), *Electoral Laws and Their Political Consequences* (New York, Agathon, 1986).

——, 'Neither Presidentialism not Parliamentarism', in Juan Linz and Arturo Valenzuela, *The Failure of Presidential Democracy: Comparative Perspectives I and II* (Baltimore, Johns Hopkins University Press, 1994), 106–18.

*Sbornik Federal'nykh Konstitutsionnykh Zakonov i Federal'nykh Zakonov* (Moscow, Izvestiya, 1994–99).

Seleznyov, Gennadiy, *Vsya vlast' – Zakonu! (Zakonodatel'stvo i Traditsii Ukaznogo Prava v Rossii)* (Moscow, 'Segodnya' Gruppa, 1997).

Sergeyev, Victor and Nikolai Biryukov, *Russia's Road to Democracy: Parliament, Communism and Traditional Democracy* (Cheltenham, Edward Elgar, 1993).

Sharlet, Robert, 'The Making of a President, Russian-Style', *Post-Soviet Prospects* 4, no. 9 (September 1996): 1–4.

——, *The New Soviet Constitution of 1977: Analysis and Text* (Brunswick, OH, King's Court Communications, Inc., 1978).

——, 'The Politics of Constitutional Amendments in Russia', *Post-Soviet Affairs* 13, no. 3 (July–September 1997).

——, 'Reinventing the Russian State: Problems of Constitution Implementation', *John Marshall Law Review* 28, no. 4 (1995): 775–86.

——, 'Transitional Constitutionalism: Politics and Law in the Second Republic', *Wisconsin International Law Journal* 14, no. 3 (1996): 495–521.

Shevtsova, Lilia, *Yeltsin's Russia: Myths and Reality* (Washington, DC, Carnegie Endowment for International Peace, 1999).

Sheynis, Viktor, 'Proyden li istoricheskiy rubezh?', *Polis* 1, no. 37 (1997): 84–96.

Shokhin, Aleksandr, *Vzaimodeystvie vlastey v zakonodatel'nom protsesse* (Moscow, Nash Dom–L'Age d'Homme, 1997).

Shugart, Matthew, 'Building the Institutional Framework: Electoral Systems, Party Systems, and Presidents' (working paper 2.26, Berkeley, Center for German and European Studies, University of California, 1994).

——, 'The Electoral Cycle and Institutional Sources of Divided Presidential Government', *American Political Science Review* 89, no. 2 (June 1995): 327–43.

——, 'Executive–Legislative Relations in Post-Communist Europe', *Transition* 2, no. 25 (6 December 1996): 6–11.

——, 'Of Presidents and Parliaments', *East European Constitutional Review* 2, no. 1 (Winter 1993): 30–2.

—— and John Carey, *Presidents and Assemblies: Constitutional Design and Electoral Dynamics* (Cambridge, Cambridge University Press, 1992 and 1995).

Sidorov, M. N., 'Ekonomicheskaya Politika i Pokazateli Federal'nogo Byudzheta, 1996', *Ekonomika Predprinimatel'stvo Okruzhayushchaya Sreda* 2, no. 7 (1996): 3–13.

Smith, Steven, and Thomas Remington, *The Politics of Institutional Choice: The Formation of the Russian State Duma* (Princeton, Princeton University Press, 2001).

Smyth, Regina, 'The Russian Parliament and Political Consolidation', in Douglas Blum, *Russia's Future: Consolidation or Disintegration?* (Boulder, Westview Press, 1994), 31–45.

*Sobranie Zakonodatel'stva Rossiyskoy Federatsii* (Moscow, Izvestiya, 1994–98).

Solnick, Steven, 'Federal Bargaining in Russia', *East European Constitutional Review* 4, no. 4 (Fall 1995): 52–8.

*Sovet Federatsii: Stenogramma Zasedaniy* (Federal'nogo Sobraniya Rossiyskoy Federatsii, Moscow, Izvestiya, 1994–98).

'Statement of Official 2000 Russian Presidential Election Results' (Moscow, Central Electoral Commission, 6 April 2000).

'Statement of Results: Decision No. 65/764–3' (Moscow, Central Electoral Commission, 29 December 1999).

Steinmo, Sven, Kathleen Thelen and Frank Longstreth, *Structuring Politics: Historical Institutionalism in Comparative Analysis* (Cambridge, Cambridge University Press, 1992).

Stepan, Alfred and Cindy Skach, 'Constitutional Frameworks and Democratic Consolidation: Parliamentarism versus Presidentialism', *World Politics* 46, no. 1 (October 1993): 1–22.

—— and Ezra Suleiman, 'The French Fifth Republic: A Model for Import? Reflections on Poland and Brazil', in H. E. Chehabi and Alfred Stepan (eds), *Politics, Society and Democracy: Comparative Studies* (Boulder, Westview Press, 1995), 393–414.

Stepashin, Sergey, 'Address to the Duma', *Gosudarstvennaya Duma: Stenogramma Zasedaniy* (Moscow, Izvestiya, 19 May 2000).

Taagepera, Rein and Matthew Shugart, *Seats and Votes: The Effects and Determinants of Electoral Systems* (New Haven, Yale University Press, 1989).

Tanchev, Evgeni, 'Parliamentarism Rationalized', *East European Constitutional Review* 2, no. 1 (Winter 1993): 33–5.

Taras, Ray (ed.), *Post-Communist Presidents* (Cambridge, Cambridge University Press, 1997).

Troxel, Tiffany, 'Former Russian Prime Minister Talks About Corruption', *BCSIA Publications* (Cambridge, MA: Harvard University, March 2000).

—— and Cindy Skach, 'Comparing the Constitutions of the CIS and Eastern Europe' (working paper), 2000.

*Vedomosti Federal'nogo Sobraniya Rossiyskoy Federatsii* (Federal'nogo Sobraniya Rossiyskoy Federatsii, Moscow, Izvestiya, 1994–98).

Verney, Douglas, *The Analysis of Political Systems* (London, Routledge, 1979), chs 2–3.

Walker, Edward, 'Politics of Blame and Presidential Powers in Russia's New Constitution', *East European Constitutional Review* 2/3, no. 4, 1 (Fall 1993/Winter 1994): 116–19.

Weimer, David (ed.), *Institutional Design* (Norwell, MA, Kluwer Academic Publishers, 1995).

Weingast, Barry, 'The Political Foundations of Democracy and the Rule of Law', *American Political Science Review* 91, no. 2 (June 1997): 245–63.

White, Stephen, 'Parties and Voters in the 1995 Russian Duma Elections', *Europe-Asia Studies* 49, no. 5 (July 1997): 767–98.

——, *Russia's New Politics: The Management of a Postcommunist Society* (Cambridge, Cambridge University Press, 2000).

——, Alex Pravda and Zvi Gitelman, *Developments in Russian and Post-Soviet Politics* I and IV (London, Macmillan Press, 1994 and 1997 – now Palgrave Macmillan).

——, Richard Rose and Ian McAllister, *How Russia Votes* (Chatham, NJ, Chatham House Publishers, Inc., 1997).

Whitefield, Stephen (ed.), *The New Institutional Architecture of Eastern Europe* (New York, St. Martin's Press – now Palgrave Macmillan, 1993).

—— and Geoffrey Evans, 'Support for Democracy and Political Opposition in Russia, 1993–1995', *Post-Soviet Affairs* 12, no. 3 (July–September 1996): 218–42.

Winter, Eyal, 'Voting and Vetoing', *American Political Science Review* 90, no. 4 (December 1996): 813–21.

Wyman, Matthew, Stephen White and Sarah Oates (eds), *Elections and Voters in Post-Communist Russia* (Cheltenham, Edward Elgar, 1998).

Yavlinskiy, Grigory, 'Going Backwards', *Journal of Democracy* 12, no. 4 (October 2001): 79–86.

Yin, Robert, *Case Study Research: Design and Methods* (London, Sage Publications, Applied Social Research Methods Series 5, 1994).

Zlobin, Nikolay, 'Interview with Oleg Mironov', *Demokratizatsiya* 5, no. 2 (1997): 281–90.

## Personal/internal letters and documents

'Gosudarstvennaya Duma: Analiticheskoe Upravlenie' (Internal Document, Informatsionno-analiticheskiy Byulleten, Moscow, State Duma, various bulletins from 1994 to 1998).

Reshul'skiy, S. (Letter to Gennadiy Seleznyov, Chairman of the State Duma, Moscow, State Duma Library, 13 September 1997).

'Svedeniya o zakonakh, prinyatykh Gosudarstvennoy Dumoy, napravlennykh v Sovet Federatsii, podpisannykh ili otklonennykh Prezidentom Rossiyskoy Federatsii' (Internal Document, Moscow, Record's Office of the State Duma, 1996 to 1998).

Yel'tsin, Boris, Message to the Council of the Federation (Moscow, State Duma's Library, 5 May and 24 September 1997).

——, Letter on the Law on the Formation of the Council of the Federation (Moscow, State Duma's Library, 11 November 1995), no. 1625.

——, 'Poslanie Prezidenta Rossiyskoy Federatsii Federal'nomu Sobraniyu' (Internal Document Containing Official Transcripts of President Yel'tsin's Speeches to the Federal Assembly and a Brief on Yel'tsin's Opinions on Power, Economics and Reforms, Moscow, Izvestiya, 1998).

## Periodicals and newspapers/news services

*BBC Summary of World Broadcasts*
*Business Press: Informatsionnoe Agentstvo*
*CNN Report*
*Ekspert*
*Financial Times*
*ITAR-TASS News Agency*
*Itogi*
*Izvestiya*
*Kommersant and Kommersant Daily*
*Moskovskiye novosti* and *Moscow News*
*Moscow Times*
*Nezavisimaya gazeta*
*Obshchaya gazeta*
*OMRI Daily Digest*
*Pravda*
*Prezident, Parlament, Pravitel'stvo*
*Radio Russia*
*RFE/RL Newsline*
*Rossiyskiye vesti*
*Rossiyskaya gazeta*
*Russian Election Watch*

*Russia Watch*
*Russkiy telegraf*
*Segodnya*
*Trud*


## Public speeches attended by the author (following which, the author questioned the speaker)

Airapetov, Valeriy, 'Is Democracy Doomed in Russia? Views from Yabloko and the Union of Right Forces', Kennedy School, Harvard University, 21 September 2000.

Gaidar, Yegor, 'The Political and Economic Situation in Russia' Carnegie Endowment, Washington, DC, 29 January 2001.

Kuzmina, Irina, 'Is Democracy Doomed in Russia? Views from Yabloko and the Union of Right Forces', Kennedy School of Government, Harvard University, 21 September 2000.

Lvov, Dmitry, member of the Government's Council of Experts under former Prime Minister Yevgeniy Primakov, Academician of the Russian Academy of Sciences, St Antony's College, Oxford University, 3 December 1998.

Malysheva, Yulia, 'Is Democracy Doomed in Russia? Views from Yabloko and the Union of Right Forces,' Kennedy School of Government, Harvard University, 21 September 2000.

McFaul, Michael, ' "The Thermidor Period" ' 135 Days Conference, Moscow, Carnegie Endowment, 19 September 2000.

Mints, Boris, 'Can the Alliance of Russia's Democrats Last?', Harvard University, 20 June 2000.

Nemtsov, Boris, former First Deputy Prime Minister of Russia, leader of the 'Just Cause' party, former Governor of Nizhniy Novgorod Oblast, St Antony's College, Oxford University, 3 June 1999.

Preksin, Oleg, Government official in the Ministry of the Economy, 'Foreign Direct Investment and Russia's Regions', talk given at St Antony's College, Oxford University, 5 March 1998.

Shevtsova, Lilia, ' "Yel'tsin's Terminator" or "Disciplined Yel'tsinism?" ' 135 Days Conference, Carnegie Endowment, Moscow Office, 19 September 2000.

Shokhin, Aleksandr, Leader of Our Home is Russia, Former First Deputy Chairman of the Duma, Former First Deputy Prime Minister, St Antony's College, Oxford University, 8 December 1997.

Smyth, Regina, 'Evolution of Political Parties and the Party System in Comparative Perspective', at the conference 'Russia Votes: A Preview of Russia's Duma Election', Harvard University, 29 November 1999.

Sobchak, Anatoliy, former Mayor of St Petersburg, 'The New Russian Constitution: Law as the Basis for Building a Democratic Society', talk given at the University of Michigan, Ann Arbor, 28 February 1995.

Stepashin, Sergey, 'Russia's Presidential Elections and the Battle against Corruption', Kennedy School of Government, Harvard University, 14 March 2000.

Yavlinskiy, Grigoriy, Leader of Yabloko Party, Oxford Union, England, 28 November 1997.

Zyuganov, Gennadiy, Leader of the Communist Party of the Russian Federation, Schools, Oxford University, 31 October 1997.

# List of interviews
(place, name, profession – at the time of the interview, political party, date)

### 1. Moscow, September 1997
*Duma Deputies*

**Vladimir Averchev**, Member of the Committee on International Affairs, Deputy of the 'Yabloko' Party, Interview at the State Duma, Moscow, 19 September 1997.

**Vyacheslav Igrunov**, Vice-Chairman of the 'Yabloko' Party, Vice-Chairman of the Committee for the Commonwealth of Independent States Affairs and Relations with Compatriots, Head of the Institute of Humanities and Political Research, Interview at the State Duma, Moscow, 12 September 1997.

**Aleksandr Kozyrev**, Vice-Chairman of the Committee on International Affairs, Deputy of the Liberal-Democratic Party of Russia, Interview at the State Duma, Moscow, 26 September 1997.

**Aleksandr Ponomarev**, Member of the Committee on International Affairs, Deputy of the Communist Party of the Russian Federation, Interview at the State Duma, Moscow, 19 September 1997.

**Sergey Popov**, Member of the Committee on Legislation and Judicial-Legal Reform, Deputy of the 'Yabloko' Party, Interview at the State Duma, Moscow, 15 September 1997.

**Yuliy Rybakov**, Member of the Committee on Legislation and Judicial-Legal Reform, Independent Deputy, Interview at the State Duma, Moscow, 19 September 1997.

**Viktor Sheynis**, Member of the Committee on Legislation and Judicial-Legal Reform, one of the authors of the 1995 Electoral Law, Deputy of the 'Yabloko' Party, Interview at the State Duma, Moscow, 19 September 1997.

**Aleksandr Zhukov**, Chairman of the State Duma Committee on the Budget, Taxes, Banks, and Finance, Deputy of 'Russia's Regions' Faction, Interview at the State Duma, Moscow, 18 September 1997.

*Academics and Advisors*

**Oleg Leonov**, Advisor to the State Duma Committee on the Budget, Taxes, Banks and Finance, Interview at the State Duma, Moscow, 25 September 1997.

**Dr Aleksandr Obolonskiy**, Doctor of Law, Head Research Fellow at the Institute of State and Law of the Russian Academy of Sciences, Interview at the Institute of State and Law, Moscow, 9 September 1997.

**Andrey Piontkovskiy**, Academic, Interview at the Institute for Strategic Studies, Moscow, 22 September 1997.

**Professor Elena Shestopal**, Professor at the Sociological Department at Moscow State University, Interview at Moscow State University, Moscow, 9 September 1997.

**Dr Vil'yam Smirnov**, Doctor of Law, First Vice-President of the Russian Political Science Association, Head of the Department for Political Science Studies at the Institute of State and Law of the Russian Academy of Sciences, Interview at the Institute of State and Law, Moscow, 5 and 9 September 1997.

**Dmitriy Trenin**, Deputy Director of the Carnegie Moscow Center, Interview at the Carnegie Center, Moscow, 24 September 1997.

## 2. Oxford, October to December 1997
*Duma Deputies and Members of the Government*

**Aleksandr Shokhin**, Leader of Our Home is Russia, Former First Deputy Chairman of the Duma, Former First Deputy Prime Minister, St Antony's College, Oxford, 8 December 1997.

**Grigoriy Yavlinskiy**, Leader of Yabloko Party, Oxford Union Society's Old Library, 28 November 1997.

**Gennadiy Zyuganov**, Leader of the Communist Party of the Russian Federation, Interview at Wadham College, Oxford University, 31 October 1997.

## 3. Moscow, March and April 1998
*Duma Deputies and Members of the Government*

**Aleksey Andreev**, Vice-Chairman of the Committee on International Affairs, Interview at the State Duma, Moscow, 20 March 1998.

**Valeriy Fadeev**, Former Moscow City Duma Deputy, Advisor to the State Duma Committee on International Affairs, Interview at the State Duma, Moscow, 20 March 1998.

**Aleksey Golovkov**, Vice-Chairman of the State Duma Committee on the Budget, Taxes, Banks, and Finance, Former Head of President Boris Yel'tsin's Staff, Interview at the State Duma, Moscow, 6 April 1998.

**Azat Khamaev**, Member of the State Duma Committee on International Affairs, Interview at the State Duma, Moscow, 1 April 1998.

**Sergey Kiriyenko**, Prime Minister of Russia, Responses to reporters' questions in the State Duma at which the author was present and also asked a question, State Duma, 10 April 1998, immediately following the Duma's first vote on the approval of Kiriyenko as Prime Minister.

**Boris Kuznetsov**, Vice-Chairman of the Faction 'Our Home is Russia', Vice-Chairman of the State Duma Committee on the Budget, Taxes, Banks and Finance, Interview at the State Duma, Moscow, 8 April 1998.

**Igor' Mal'kov**, Member of the Committee on International Affairs, Interview at the State Duma, Moscow, 3 April 1998.

**Sergey Nikiforov**, Member of the State Duma Committee on the Budget, Taxes, Banks and Finance, Interview at the State Duma, Moscow, 6 April 1998.

**Vladimir Nikitin**, Chairman of the Foreign and Customs Exchange Regulations, External Debt, Precious Metals and Gems Sub-Committee, Vice-Chairman of the Committee on the Budget, Taxes, Banks, and Finance, Interview at the State Duma, Moscow, 6 April 1998.

**Aleksandr Ponomarev**, Member of the Committee on International Affairs, Deputy of the Communist Party of the Russian Federation, Interview at the State Duma, Moscow, 1 April 1998.

**Viktor Sheynis**, Member of the Committee on Legislation and Judicial-Legal Reform, One of the drafters of the 1995 Electoral Law, Deputy of the 'Yabloko' Party, Interview at the State Duma, Moscow, 3 April 1998.

**Sergey Shtogrin**, Member of the State Duma Committee on the Budget, Taxes, Banks and Finance, Interview at the State Duma, Moscow, 8 April 1998.

**Nikolay Stolyarov**, Major-General, Vice-Chairman of the Committee on International Affairs, Interview at the State Duma, Moscow, 6 April 1998.

**Andrey Zakharov**, Former Duma Deputy, 1993 to 1995, Independent, and First Deputy Director General, Foundation for the Development of Parliamentarism in Russia, Interview at the Foundation for the Development of Parliamentarism in Russia, Moscow, 27 March 1998.

*Academics and Advisors*

**Aleksey Avtonomov**, Director of Legal Department and Legal Advisor to the State Duma, Foundation for the Development of Parliamentarism in Russia, Interview at the Foundation for the Development of Parliamentarism in Russia, Moscow, 17 April 1998.

**Mikhail Il'in**, Professor at the Institute of International Relations in Moscow, President of the Russian Political Science Association, Editor of the journal *Polis (Politicheskie Issledovaniya)*, Interview in Moscow, 10 April 1998.

**Irina Kotelevskaya**, Former Member of the Supreme Soviet of the Soviet Union, 1991 to 1993, Chief of the Secretariat of the First Deputy Chairman of the State Duma, Doctor of Law, Interview at the State Duma, Moscow, 20 March 1998.

**Boris I. Makarenko**, Deputy Chief of the Center for Political Technologies, a Kremlin campaign advisor, Interview at the Center for Political Technologies, Moscow, 21 April 1998.

**Michael McFaul**, Senior Associate, Carnegie Moscow Center, Interview at the Carnegie Center, Moscow, 26 March 1998.

**Christian Nadeau**, Director, International Foundation for Election Systems, Interview at the International Foundation for Election Systems, Moscow, 13 April 1998.

**Nikolay Petrov**, Program Associate, Carnegie Moscow Center, Interview at the Carnegie Center, Moscow, 10 April 1998.

**Andrey Ryabov**, Program Associate, Carnegie Moscow Center, Interview at the Carnegie Center, Moscow, 27 March 1998.

**Lilia Shevtsova**, Senior Associate, Carnegie Moscow Center, Interview at the Carnegie Center, Moscow, 23 March 1998.

**4. Moscow, July to September 1998 and March to April 1999**

*Duma Deputies and Members of the Government*

**Oleg Bocharov**, Deputy of the Moscow City Duma (1994–99) and Chairman of the Commission on Legislation and Security, Russia's Regions Deputy, Interview at the Moscow City Duma, Moscow, 25 March 1999.

**Arkadiy Dvorkovitch**, Head of the Economic Group of the Ministry of Finance and Assistant to the Deputy Minister of Finance Oleg V'yugin, Interview at the Ministry of Finance, Moscow, 26 March 1999.

**Vladimir Lukin**, Chairman of the Committee on International Affairs in the State Duma, Vice-Chairman of the Yabloko Party, Interview at the State Duma, Moscow, 26 March 1999.

*Academics and Advisors*

**Galina Anisimova**, Consultant to the State Duma Committee on Federation Affairs and Regional Policy and the Committee on the Budget, Taxes, Banks and Finance, Interview at the State Duma, Moscow, 26 March 1999.

**Aleksey Avtonomov**, Director of Legal Department and Legal Advisor to the State Duma, Foundation for the Development of Parliamentarism in Russia, Interview at the Foundation for the Development of Parliamentarism in Russia, Moscow, 29 March 1999.

**Anatoliy Eliseev**, Head of the Records Office of the State Duma, State Duma, Moscow, 6 April 1998 and 26 March 1999.

**Aleksey Kuzmin**, Professor and Director of the Institute for Humanities and Political Studies, Yabloko Party's Consultant, Interview at the Institute, Moscow, 25 March 1999.

**Viktor Sergeyev**, Professor and Director of International Politics at MGIMO, Advisor to the State Duma Committee on Science and Education, Interview at MGIMO, Moscow, 24 March 1999.

**5. Cambridge, MA, March 2000**

**Sergey Stepashin**, Former Prime Minister, Interview at the John F. Kennedy School of Government, Cambridge, Massachusetts, 14 March 2000.

# Index